John B. Baldwin

Baltimore

1993

THE ART OF LOVE

University of Pennsylvania Press
MIDDLE AGES SERIES
Edward Peters, Series Editor

A complete listing of the books in this series
appears at the back of this volume

THE
ART
OF
LOVE

Amatory Fiction from Ovid to
the *Romance of the Rose*

———

Peter L. Allen

upp

University of Pennsylvania Press

Philadelphia

Library of Congress Cataloging-in-Publication Data

Allen, Peter L., 1957–
    The art of love: amatory fiction from Ovid to the Romance of the Rose / Peter L. Allen.
        p.   cm. — (Middle Ages series)
    Includes bibliographical references and index.
    ISBN 0-8122-3188-0
    1. Courtly love in literature.   2. Ovid, 43 B.C.–17 or 18 A.D.—Criticism and
interpretation.   3. Jean, de Meun, d. 1305—Criticism and interpretation.   4. Guillaume,
de Lorris, fl. 1230—Criticism and interpretation.   5. André, le chapelain—Criticism and
interpretation.   6. Love poetry, Latin—(Medieval and modern)—History and
criticism.   I. Title.   II. Series.
PN682.L68A45   1992
809'.93354—dc20   92-21610
                                                                              CIP

In memory of my Rose and my Ami:

ROSE ROSES GROSSMAN
(1901–1990)

STEWART CHARLES TELFER
(1955–1990)

Contents

Acknowledgments

This project would never have reached completion without the material and moral support of many people and institutions; I express my gratitude to some of them here.

Parts of this work were written while I was supported by a Harriet Barnard fellowship from my loyal Department of Modern Languages and Literatures of Pomona College, by an Andrew Mellon Post-Doctoral Fellowship at the hospitable Department of French and Italian of the University of Southern California, and by a generous Steele Foundation Fellowship from Pomona College. The libraries of Stanford University, the University of Southern California, UCLA, and the Claremont Colleges—particularly their inter-library loan departments—helped me track down hundreds of common and uncommon references. Pomona College also provided unstinting research funding. For generous permission to reprint material, I thank Gerald Duckworth & Co., Oxford University Press, *Exemplaria: A Journal of Theory in Medieval and Renaissance Studies*, and Champion-Slatkine; for permission to reproduce the cover illustration, I thank the department of photographic services of the Bibliothèque Nationale. For enterprising and patient research assistance, I am grateful to Mike Dahlin, Eric Fang, and especially Michael Sharp.

Friends and colleagues from many places gave generous guidance. These include, but are hardly limited to, Pete Wetherbee, Peter Dembowski, Ralph Johnson, Leslie Cahoon, Paolo Cherchi, Peggy Waller, Mike Henry, SunHee Kim Gertz, Jeff Rider, Carolyn Dinshaw, Howard Bloch, Constance Jordan, Sylvia Huot, Paul Gehl, Joan DeJean, Gerald Bond, Chris Cannon, Barbara Taylor, and Jennifer Taylor, as well as Jerry Singerman and the readers and helpful staff of the University of Pennsylvania Press. For any flaws that remain, I urge my readers to remember that *errare humanum est, parcere diuinum*.

Finally, I would like to express my profound indebtedness to the two people I miss the most: my best of grandmothers, Rose Grossman, and most beloved of friends, Stewart Telfer. Unable to read what I was writing, they nevertheless unfailingly gave me the faith and encouragement I needed. In small return of great gifts, I dedicate this book to them.

Primary Texts

P. Ouidi Nasonis. *Amores, Medicamina faciei femineae, Ars amatoria, Remedia amoris*. Ed. E. J. Kenney. Oxford Classical Texts. Oxford: Clarendon Press, 1961.

Andreas Capellanus on Love. Ed. and trans. P. G. Walsh. Duckworth Classical, Medieval, and Renaissance Editions. London: Gerald Duckworth & Co., Ltd., 1982.

Guillaume de Lorris and Jean de Meun. *Le Roman de la Rose*. Ed. Félix Lecoy. 3 volumes. Les Classiques français du Moyen Age, 92, 95, 98. Paris: Librairie Honoré Champion, 1973–82.

Introduction

If one were to assemble a list of French texts central to the literature of what is commonly called "courtly love," it would no doubt include the works of a number of troubadours and trouvères, the romances of Chrétien de Troyes, the *lais* of Marie de France, a version of the Tristan legend, and two works dealing with the art of love: Andreas Capellanus's *De amore* and the *Roman de la Rose* (the *Romance of the Rose*), begun by Guillaume de Lorris and completed by Jean de Meun. The two latter works, however, do not fit comfortably into the mold of the others: while the lyric poems and courtly romances tend to be ethereal, somewhat magical, and clearly set apart from ordinary life as fiction or at least as fantasy, the *De amore* and the *Roman de la Rose* are more didactic, heavy-handed, and problematic. They teach would-be lovers how to behave in order to have others accomplish their desires, yet they also contain vociferous passages that dissuade their protagonists from the practice of this art, which, they claim, leads not only to earthly destruction but also to eternal damnation. These works, furthermore, are profoundly self-contradictory, misogynistic, and deceitful: the art of love, it would seem, is a troubled one. Yet these two works continue to be tantalizing, both for their own interest and for what they may be able to reveal about a tradition that has been one of the central modern foci in the study of medieval literature.

I argue in the present study that these two texts are, in fact, essential to understanding the love poetry of the Middle Ages, particularly of medieval France, and that they teach not the "art of love" but the ways and means of amatory fiction—to be precise, how love becomes art. The *De amore* and the *Roman de la Rose* show that, in medieval literature, love and fiction are intertwined to such a degree that they can be seen as aspects of one another, and that this intimate linkage derives clearly and unambiguously from the amatory works of Ovid—particularly the *Ars amatoria* (*The Art of Love*) and *Remedia amoris* (*Cures for Love*), published around I A.D. In these two works, Ovid teaches his readers that literary love (as manifested in the Roman elegiac tradition, and specifically in his own elegies, the *Amores*) is a conventional and constructed fiction which poet and reader create together, and which can exist only within the clearly designated bounds of the textual world. The *Ars* shows its readers how to construct this kind of love out of fantasy and illusion, while the *Remedia*, piece by piece, dissolve these illusions and reveal that the fantasy is only a fantasy—one person's solitary creation, rather than a love that can exist between two people. Both the *De amore* and the *Roman de la Rose* offer this twofold lesson, creating an imaginary love and then dismantling it. Andreas's work re-creates Ovid's twofold text in the literary context of the late twelfth century. Like Ovid, Andreas presents an art of love that is based on contemporary literature and confronts it with elements of disillusionment and dissolution. In the twelfth-century literary world, however, the stakes were higher than at Rome (though even at Rome they were high: the *Ars* was one of the reasons Ovid was exiled in A.D. 8). The motifs of trouvère and troubadour lyric and of courtly romance which Andreas borrows are fiercely attacked by the *remedia amoris* of medieval ecclesiastical morality that he includes in the third book of his *De amore*. Andreas's text is more ambiguous and less self-assured than Ovid's, but even so, Andreas's work was an important step toward legitimating medieval fiction.

One hundred years later, Jean de Meun followed in Andreas's footsteps when he continued and completed Guillaume de Lorris's *Roman de la Rose*. Even more complex than the *De amore*, Jean's text fragments the *praeceptor amoris* into a multitude of speaking voices and focuses not just on love but on many other arts as well. Jean engages, too, in a struggle with Ovid and with the author of the first part of the *Rose*, Guillaume de Lorris, both of whom he attempts to supplant. Yet for all the complexity of his text, Jean's rôle as author is always already prefigured by Ovid, as his poem is by the *Ars*. The medieval texts, like the *Ars*, are not only works of literature, but also important works of theory that illuminate the texts around them, manipulating their readers in order to help them discover how they participate in the process of creating fictions.

Despite their differences, these three treatises on the art of love clearly need to be read as a group. They are linked not only by a remarkably strong and solid tradition that placed Ovid's amatory poetry at the center of medieval European education and literature, but also by their common insights into the relationship of love, fantasy, and fiction. Ovid's texts provide not only a point of departure for later authors, but also inspiration and guidance: for the Middle Ages, Ovid's *Amores, Ars amatoria*, and *Remedia amoris are* amatory fiction, and every medieval author who writes in this vein must become to some degree a *Naso nouus*, a new Ovid. The following chapters will explore how the *Ars* teaches its readers and how it served as a model for the medieval tradition. Before we begin our textual analysis, however, we will need to take a little time to examine some of the theoretical issues involved in the relationship of love poetry, literary theory, and the art of love.

Love poetry is in many ways one of the most stable genres in Western literary history. The epic has largely faded away; the drama has changed a great deal from age to age, as a comparison between a Greek play and an American film will quickly show; and the novel, though extremely popular, is a relatively new form. But love poems seem to be a constant. There is a direct kinship between classical lyric and popular ballads on the radio today. Their elements, for example, are the same: the lover's desire, his or her separation from the beloved, the need to express emotion in song. Now as in the past, love poetry is static; it voices feelings that remain forever caught up in their own lyrical expression, rather than advancing a relationship between lover and beloved. Furthermore, poetry of this kind is not only constant in form, but is also consistently emotionally moving: it has an extraordinary power to recall and evoke feelings with which most readers and listeners can identify. This is why love poems are so satisfying: they are concrete representations of thoughts and feelings that need to be put into words. Love poems represent these desires in ways that do not threaten their readers, since the poems articulate emotions without the burden of actual confrontation and possible rejection. Rather than confronting the success or failure they would find in the world of experience, the reader's feelings remain in the safe and isolated realm of fantasy; love poems turn emotions into literary objects, works of art. Let us explore how this transformation occurs.

The simplest form of love poetry is the lyric, which, virtually isolated from time, represents a moment of suspended desire from the perspective of one person, the "lyric I." This "I," who is typically male but otherwise has few marks of identity, is in love with someone (typically, a woman) who is also unidentified; all that can consistently be stated about her is that she is beyond the lover's grasp, or that she is unwilling to accede to his desires.[1] Lyric's focus on the "I" and its emotions, and its exclusion of external referents, make it easy for this poetry to embody any individual reader's feelings. Neither the reader's nor the speaker's individuality matters: the "I" is a mask or point of view that the reader may easily assume.

As important as the lyric "I" are the poem's conventions—familiar stylistic techniques, motifs, and situations, borrowed from pre-existing texts, which evoke the genre's traditional effects. One of the most significant of these features is the fact that lyric love is, almost by definition, monologic and unrequited. If the lover's wishes were granted, there would be no poem. It is the denial of these wishes that produces the text.[2] Like meter, verse forms, and imagery, this conventional encapsulation of changeable desire both provides the reader with a palpable and constant emotional experience—that of amatory and sexual tension—and identifies the poem as a particular type of literature with known rules and a recognized rôle for the reader.[3] By framing itself in conventions,[4] the lyric places itself in a fictional space analogous to that of completely subjective love, whether concealed or expressed but unrequited. In both the real experience of this kind of passion and its literary incarnation, the beloved is external to the lover's longing, stimulating it without participating in the process, being loved as an object (often an unwitting object, in fact), rather than loving in return. In love poetry, as in subjective love, the reader experiences the eroticism of his or her own desire in fantasy form.

In order for literary depictions of love to be successful, the reader must be willing to participate emotionally in the text,[5] to believe—at least while reading—in the persona's love even though the persona is fictional[6] and though his love is denoted by a series of signs which, being conventional, are clearly not "sincere" in any personal sense but are, rather, literary commonplaces.[7] By crossing through the frame and leaving his or her own consciousness behind, the reader thus accepts a conventionalized sincerity[8] and a temporary identification with the persona.

The fictional frame is one of the elements that make it possible for the reader to accept the conventionalized sincerity of love poetry. Inside the frame, the literary experience of love is secure, so readers are rarely encouraged to test the boundaries that set it apart from the world of experience. The *Ars amatoria* and the medieval works that are modeled after it, on the other hand, claim that the love they teach can be taken outside the frame and used to manipulate real people with consequences no more painful than those the reader encounters in the fantasy of the literary text. By affirming that its conventions are, in fact, both the link with and the point of difference between traditional love poetry and the treatises on the art of love, the *Ars* forces its readers to test the limits of fiction again and again. Conventions, then, are one of the keys to how the treatises convey their message and their meaning to their readers.

Semiotic theory suggests that meaning is carried by signs, which, since Plato's time, have traditionally been grouped in two categories, "conventional" and "natural." Natural signs are spontaneously produced by their causes. Because they are not willed, they cannot confuse; to interpret them, one need only understand the association between signifier and signified, and their meaning is clear. Thus, in the common expression "Where there's smoke, there's fire," smoke is a spontaneous and natural sign produced by fire, involuntary and hence unambiguous. The meaning of conventional signs, on the other hand, depends on their relationship with other elements in the system, and so it will vary according to both producer's and interpreter's understandings of how the system works.[9] Thus natural and conventional signs are linked by the relationship between producer and interpreter[10]—a fact that has direct bearing on how the treatises on the art of love are related to the texts whose conventions they borrow.

For the simplest and most spontaneous of natural signs, then, meaning is automatic. As one moves further from this end of the spectrum, however, meaning grows more ambiguous. In speech, for example, ideas pass from the speaker's intention to the listener's understanding through the systems of language, and ambiguities and misunderstandings become possible. In writing, where author and reader are more distant from one another than in a conversation, even more gaps are possible because, as text, the message gains an existence independent of its producer.[11] Further still along this scale is the poetic text, which not only carries a message but also alludes to other texts and so depends even more than simple writing on conventions and the interpreter's broad knowledge of the literary context to establish meaning.[12] The treatises on the art of love, finally, are about as far as they can be from natural signs: rather than signifying spontaneously, they focus attention on the process of making meaning—on language itself—by concentrating on how the reader permits and even causes the poetic system to function. The meaning of these treatises thus depends heavily on the work of the reader, who must choose among the wide range of meanings available in the signs the poet offers and so create a text that reflects his or her interests, capacities, and literary knowledge. The treatises are "open texts," in Maria Corti's phrase[13]—texts in which the reader participates in the process of making meaning. By being given this responsibility, the reader takes on some of the writer's functions and so learns how to construct a literary text him- or herself.[14]

Thus the treatises—unlike the lyric or the courtly romance, which clearly surround their fictions with frames—appear to welcome the reader directly into the textual world and so to make love accessible to him or her. In love poetry proper, love is at once familiar and mystical; in the treatises, love is represented as unfamiliar (the reader is portrayed as being ignorant of love's art) but also teachable: the narrator claims that he can provide instruction in it. (Ovid, in fact, calls his narrator the *praeceptor amoris,* "love's preceptor.") Thus the reader's experience varies in the two genres. In love poetry, the reader is introduced into a carefully enclosed fantasy that is ruled by the God of Love. In the treatises, on the other hand, the preceptor's matter-of-fact, practical advice on amatory inter-actions makes it plain that the reader is living in a much more cynical world—one in which love is not free and spontaneous but is subject to will, desire, and manipulation, techniques in which the preceptor, as he explains, is skilled. Secrets are abolished, and love is there for the reader's taking.

And yet the openness of these works, appealing as it may seem, has concomitant dangers. If there is no frame, the reader is much more at risk. The reader of the treatises does not *pretend* to be like the poetic lover. He or she *is* the lover these texts represent. Since his or her love is therefore real rather than imagined, it lacks the protective cushioning of fantasy. And since the text claims to be true—unlike love poetry, which defines itself as fictional—it runs the risk of being proven false if it does not co-incide with the reader's experience and expectations. These dangers do in fact materialize as the reader proceeds through these expositions of the "art of love." In the process of reading the treatises, the reader is obliged to confront the preceptors' untrustworthiness and the illusory nature of the love they teach, and to question the whole poetic structure that has created this love. In the end, this questioning leads to a new understanding of the textual process, but the path to that understanding is circuitous and uncertain.

One element of this process is the relationship between the reader and the narrator. In traditional love poetry, this relationship scarcely exists. There, the reader enters the fantasy by identifying with the lover (or the beloved) rather than trying to construct a relationship *in propria persona* with these characters. In the didactic texts, on the other hand, the reader is directly addressed by the preceptor in the second person[15] and thus becomes a figured part of the textual structure. By constructing an I-you relationship between himself and the reader, the preceptor recalls the wished-for I-you relationship of lover and beloved in lyric poetry, and even appears to achieve it. Thus the lover-beloved couple of lyric is transmuted into the unexpected pairing of preceptor and reader.

Setting up this close relationship between teacher and student at first makes it easy to become the inscribed reader, to enter into the text, because there is no frame or boundary to cross, no fictional identity to assume. But the more deeply one is involved in this relationship, the more confusing it becomes. The first source of difficulties is the fact that the reader enters into a relationship with the preceptor not in the expectation of becoming intimate with *him*, but in the hope of learning how to become intimate with someone else. So as the reader is drawn closer to the preceptor, he or she is led away—in fact, seduced away—from his or her original goal. Second, though the treatises claim to address any and all readers, they in fact inscribe a specific kind of reader—a naïve, uninformed, trusting figure who is subject to the preceptor's manipulations. The further one enters the text, the more one is constrained to become this character, but without the protection that the conventional frame offers in lyric and romance. Because the text does not acknowledge that it is a fiction, one cannot maintain a separation between the rôles of "real reader" and "implied reader"; one cannot identify only provisionally. The more the preceptors insist on literal reading (as they invariably do), the more difficult it is for readers to be comfortable, to accept their rôle of complaisant "you" to the preceptor's demanding "I."

This discomfort increases until it reaches the point at which the relationship with the narrator disintegrates under the strain, and readers are forced to disengage themselves from the text and to reconsider the entire process of reading. This point is difficult to reach, but I believe that it is the true goal of these treatises on the art of love, which serve as theoretical texts that elucidate the way in which author and reader work together to create the fictions of love poetry. Thus the preceptor works to throw his readers off balance, to disorient them, in order to make them see themselves and the reading process from a new angle. One of the fundamental lessons he teaches is closely connected with a subject we have already discussed, that of conventions. The treatises show their readers not how to *feel* like lovers, but how to *look* like them—how to substitute conventional, artificial signs of love for natural and spontaneous ones. Thus the treatises use conventions in the opposite way from the way love poetry does. In love poems, the reader is asked to pretend that conventional motifs are actually natural signs. In the treatises, on the other hand, conventionality is emphasized—not spontaneity, but the intent to signify; not naturalness, but the imitation of nature; not sincerity, but conscious literariness. Whether the producer of these signs is actually in love is of no interest to the preceptor, whose concern is rather that the interpreter (the beloved) *think* the sign-producer (the student/lover/reader) is in love. The precep-tor takes advantage of the gap between signified and signifier that is char-acteristic of conventional signs: he divides conventions from love, surface from substance. Doing what a lover would do, in this world, is a perfectly adequate substitute for being in love.

This procedure turns love poetry inside out. Love poetry is built on the convention of sincerity; in the treatises, on the other hand, everything is substitution, imitation, or deception—all techniques the reader learns in his or her relationship with the preceptor. Though this apprentice rela-tionship is instructive, it also endangers the reader, who cannot simply play out the fantasy of love poetry but must directly confront a teacher who teaches his students how to seduce those who trust them. In the preceptor's world, the appearance of love is essential, while true emotion is anathema, as these texts make clear. One should not *be* in love but *look* like a lover, in hopes of attracting people to seduce; though fidelity is absent in practice, its appearance is to be cultivated; money and gifts (com-mon topics) are not tokens of love but completely sufficient substitutes for it. The signs of love poetry are removed from their context and altered by the transfer. They become—or are revealed to be—wholly artificial.[16]

This use of signs is closely connected with the relationship between frames and belief in the two genres. By abandoning the frame traditional love poetry uses to signal its fictionality,[17] the treatises demand the reader's belief, but their repeated emphasis on illusion, deception, and seduction makes it almost impossible to judge them anything but false. Thus by denying their own fictive status, the treatises raise the stakes for which the reader must play: to trust the text in all its dishonesty, or to reject it completely.

The problem of belief becomes even more profound when the reader discovers that it is necessary not only to learn how to deceive others (the "readers" of the "love story" he or she will write), but also how to submit to others' deceit. This reciprocal dishonesty causes all kinds of reading problems. A magician's audience, for example, could not believe in his or her act if they were shown the tricks from the illusionist's perspective,[18] and readers of the treatises cannot maintain their familiar images of them-selves, the people they desire, or the preceptors, as the texts unfold. By trusting the treatise, the reader becomes the victim of the preceptor's eager desire for an audience; in trying to learn how to seduce others, the reader discovers that it is he or she who has been seduced, and then abandoned.[19] Only after this disillusionment can the reader begin to understand the true lessons the treatises teach.

In Ovid's works on the art of love, this recognition is built into the text in the gap between the *Ars amatoria* and the *Remedia amoris*. Having been taught by the *Ars* how to create love's illusions, the reader is suddenly confronted by the *Remedia*, a book that represents love and its conventions as dangerous and false. In the *De amore*, this gap is found between Book 2 (entitled "Qualiter amor retineatur" [How to Retain Love]) and Book 3 ("De reprobatione amoris" [The Condemnation of Love]); in the *Roman de la Rose*, it is replicated numerous times, as each allegorical speaker presents a new view of what love is and repudiates that which the preceding speaker has taught. Though every disillusionment seeks to destroy what has gone before, not one of them can: even if the illusions are gone, the reader still knows that he or she entertained them, and cannot help questioning the trusting relationship the preceptor tried to create. If the reader was willing to accept the preceptor's rhetoric in the first part of the text, he or she is likely to reject it here, or vice versa: the reader has been forced into a position that is fundamentally inconsistent with the one first held.

How can one cope with such inconsistency? The simplest strategy is to stop reading, but this choice offers little satisfaction.[20] The next simplest approach, and the one most widely represented in both the medieval and the modern reception of the *De amore* and Jean de Meun's continuation of the *Roman de la Rose*, is to read the entire work, but then to dismiss one of its points of view while championing the other. Such interpretations are to some degree logical, since they mirror the fragmentation of the texts, but they do not account for the multifaceted reading experience the treatises provide. Furthermore, readings which emphasize one aspect of the text over the other ignore the structural unity of the treatises themselves. Ovid's *Ars* and *Remedia* are closely linked to one another by subject, imagery, language, and poetic situations, as are Andreas's three books and the speeches of Jean's various characters. In light of this consistency, it is impossible to believe that one part of the text carries the only significant meaning and that the others are to be discarded.

The treatises on the art of love are not documents that make one real and one specious argument. They are, I believe, unities that present both sides of a discussion and acknowledge—even emphasize—the gap between them. Far from being an accident or a deficiency, the gap and reversal in these texts are their mark of identity and the source of their significance.[21] Gradually, the reader loses his or her willingness to accept anything the texts say as true and recognizes that they teach lessons not about life but about art. The gap in the middle of the text is an opportunity the author provides for the reader to disengage him- or herself from his or her relationship with the preceptor, to slip out of the frame and reflect on how the text functions as a whole. If the reader does not make use of this opportunity but simply accepts, without reflection, one side of the argument or the other, he or she can reach only a partial understanding of the work. If, on the other hand, the reader can recognize that the whole process of creating illusions and then withdrawing from them is a demonstration of the power of fiction, analogous to the acts of reading and writing themselves, then both the text and its gap become significant. As Wolfgang Iser notes, disturbing events in the text or shocking actions by its characters act as a blank to which the reader must respond; even the failure to bridge such gaps gives the reader an opportunity to step back, re-evaluate his or her understanding, and constitute for him- or herself the meaning of the text.[22]

By stepping out of the text and taking responsibility for his or her rôle in the fictional process, the reader learns to read not just passively but actively—learns how, in other words, to create a frame, how to establish the conventions that govern literary love.[23] The process, in schematic form, works as follows. First, the preceptor asks for the reader's trust and teaches him or her how to impose a frame between him- or herself and the object of desire by acting like a lover: the reader is taught to make the love affair a conventional fiction, like love poetry. After a while, however, the reader gradually becomes aware that even the preceptor's professed affection for him or her is only a seductive semblance, not a sincere concern. The reader may then choose to recognize that the whole textual process in which he or she has been participating is a conventional fiction, and must therefore be itself enclosed in a frame. At this point, the experience of reading the treatises becomes a lesson in how to read love poetry, since both genres are seen to be fictions. Viewed in this way, the *Ars amatoria* and its medieval analogues can be seen not as manuals of amatory instruction but as works of literary theory.

The reading process here applied to the treatises on the art of love—that of discovering a work's meaning at the end of the reading process and then retrospectively reinterpreting the text—has been proposed by a number of modern theorists of reading. Iser, for example, notes that some narrators are so unreliable as to cause readers to question the entire reading process; Clayton Koelb invents the category of the "apistic fiction," a fiction "we disbelieve because our disbelief is somehow solicited."[24] Michael Riffaterre points out that the reading process is always retrospective, reaching its full meaning only at the end of the text: "At the rate at which he advances through the text, the reader remembers what he has just read and modifies his conception of it in relation to that which he is decoding. . . . *It is the text as a whole which constitutes the unit of meaning.*"[25] The reader can thus accommodate internal contradictions by developing an understanding of the text as a complete unit.[26] As we have seen, love poetry facilitates this process by using conventions to construct a boundary around the fiction of love. The reader's task in interpreting the treatises is to recognize that these texts, too, are conventional and must be recognized as such; thus he or she must impose a literary frame on them and so participate in the author's job of constructing a fictional world.

This kind of reading is very similar to the process of reading allegory. There, as Maureen Quilligan notes, the reader is the central character, participating actively in the text and gradually discovering him- or herself in the process.[27] Once the reader recognizes the importance of his or her rôle in the text, he or she can see the treatises as guided tours through the experience of reading love poetry—an experience whose difficulties love poetry itself does not and cannot acknowledge. These problems are implicit in every experience of reading. What makes the treatises hard—but also instructive—is that they bring these difficulties to the surface, and thus articulate the importance of the reader's rôle in fiction.[28]

The intersection of the theoretical and the literary in these treatises on the art of love mirrors another intersection they contain. In his book *Essai de poétique médiévale*, Paul Zumthor performs a close semantic analysis of the vocabulary of lyric poems in Old French. He finds that in certain poems the meaning of *aimer* is subordinate to that of *chanter*, and that this compound semantic field intersects with that of *trouver*: to love, to sing, and to write poetry are sometimes overlapping, even interchangeable, actions.[29] If this is the case, then it is no great stretch to see that a book on the art of love can easily be read as a treatise on the art of love poetry: the art of love and the art of writing can be one and the same. Every classical and medieval literary work discusses others; text and interpretation, literature and theory can never be entirely separate.[30]

It is true that the treatises on love discussed in this book do not conform to our usual expectations of classical and medieval critical texts, expectations which require that these texts explicate others from the outside in a clear and relatively forthright way. Such classical and medieval critical documents as Aristotle's *Poetics*, Horace's *Ars poetica*, or Geoffrey of Vinsauf's *Poetria nova* (to name a few of the most familiar ones) are reasonably straightforward, but they do not provide much information on classical and medieval practices of reading and interpretation. The *Ars*, the *De amore*, and the *Rose*, on the other hand, follow not this plan but the more subversive model of the Socratic dialogues or of post-structuralist literary theory: their authors fight with their readers, making them examine and finally destroy their presuppositions in order to find out where they are really going and why—not an easy enterprise, but an illuminating one. In order to show how the illusions of fiction work, the arts of love confuse their readers and immerse them in contradictions, demonstrating that these deceptive procedures are ones the readers have been using all along. Thus the act of making one's way through the treatises reveals how one has already been reading the poetic texts on which the treatises comment— by alternately accepting the illusions and recognizing them as only provisional realities. What these texts do that most love poetry does not is to cause a confrontation between these two beliefs. And it is only at the moment at which the treatises oblige their readers to see the gap between these fictions and another level of thought that the nature of the illusions becomes clear.

This interpretive method teaches the reader how fictional lovers behave and what that rôle demands. It also shows the reader how to bridge the gap between his or her individual identity and the identity of the reader inscribed in the texts, and demonstrates the power of literary conventions and the pleasures of amatory fiction. Such reading is itself a kind of love, as Roland Barthes notes: the reader participates in an erotic relationship with the text,[31] and through this erotic interaction the reader engenders meaning and discovers the power of literature to show how language works.[32] The problematic experience of the treatises thus reveals how classical and medieval love poems create fictional worlds by using frames and conventions to set them apart from nonliterary constraints, and by involving the reader actively in making fiction work as fantasy.

In the following four chapters, we will see how Ovid constructed a model of fiction and how certain medieval readers and writers received and modified it in view of the literary concerns of the times. For Ovid (the subject of Chapter 1), the art of love was a game readers could enjoy as long as they recognized its limits—the boundaries of fiction, created by literary conventions. As time passed and the Roman Empire gave way to the Christian Middle Ages, the most basic elements of Ovid's poetry— such concepts as secular fiction and erotic love—were called into question by the church. Yet because Roman letters were the basis of medieval education and culture, Ovid's works continued to be read, taught, and imitated, as Chapter 2 demonstrates. The amatory works offered medieval writers a model for constructing fictions of their own, a model which may have been particularly welcome because it provided a way to express, in literature, desires that could not be fulfilled in medieval Christian society.[33] The *Ars* and *Remedia* were particularly useful for this purpose, since they carried the authority of their classical origin and since, by giving the responsibility for determining their meaning so clearly to their readers, they could not be easily categorized either as moral or immoral in themselves.

The final two chapters examine in detail the Ovidian works of two such writers: Andreas Capellanus and Jean de Meun. Andreas instructs his student Gualterius in the art of love, but he also stridently warns him away from practicing this art. The duality of Andreas's text (a feature he himself points out) re-creates the gap between the *Ars* and *Remedia*, and, like that gap, presents an opportunity for the reader to take responsibility for understanding the text as a fiction. Because it is so vehemently moralistic, the *De amore* cannot be seen as a text that encourages non-marital love, but neither can it be seen simply as love's condemnation. Andreas is in fact inviting his readers to distinguish between art and experience, between fantasy and reality; his text shows that even within a society whose ideology condemned both secular literature and erotic love, amatory fiction could make a place for itself.

Andreas's follower Jean de Meun is arguably the most important writer in the medieval French tradition of Ovid's amatory works. Jean refashions both Ovid's *Ars* and Guillaume de Lorris's courtly *Roman de la Rose*,[34] on which his own text was firmly based, but the relationship among these authors is not an easy one: Jean wants both to be and to conquer his predecessors, to imitate their works and to supersede them. His multifaceted work displays the interaction between the *Ars* and *Remedia* from a series of varied perspectives, each of which opposes the others. Yet despite the complexity of the *Rose*, it teaches its readers the same lesson Ovid first offered in the *Ars*. At the end of the romance, Jean consummates the Lover's desire for the Rose, and so simultaneously brings dream and poem to an abrupt end, pushing illusions of love to their breaking point; yet even this gesture has already been prefigured by Ovid. The end of the *Roman de la Rose* shows us that even a text that goes on for 22,000 lines and contains reflections of all the arts and sciences of the Middle Ages is still an Ovidian text, a literary re-creation of conventional, illusory love.

For a very long time, then, Ovid provided a basis—perhaps even the principal basis—for the Middle Ages' view of the relationship between love and fiction. He showed that love, at least as represented in literature, was a work of art—a work that required the reader's active participation, and which could exist only within limits designated by literary conventions. These limits made it possible for readers to imagine love freely—a possibility that was particularly important in the intellectual and moral confines of medieval Christianity. The model proved to be amazingly durable and productive, and was, in good part, responsible for one of the Western tradition's greatest flowerings of literary love.

1. The Illusion of Love, the Love of Illusion: The *Ars amatoria* and *Remedia amoris*

Strange things happen when one reads Ovid's *Ars amatoria*.

At first, Ovid's instruction manual in the art of love seems to be a useful, practical guide to what everyone knows is a tricky subject. The narrator, the *praeceptor amoris*, offers a hand to the inexperienced reader:

> Si quis in hoc artem populo non nouit amandi,
>   hoc legat et lecto carmine doctus amet.
>
> $$(1-2)$$

(If anyone here does not know the art of loving, let him read this; after reading my poem, he will be an expert lover.)

These lines politely suggest that interested readers can be helped by the preceptor's superior knowledge, and that, by reading the text, they will be enlightened. The preceptor reassures his readers that he is not a frivolous poet who has produced a work of fiction; he is rather a *uates*, a prophet, who will sing the truth: *uera canam* (*Ars* 1.30). This reassuring sales pitch is immediately followed by practical hints on the first step of the process: finding a young woman to love.

As one makes one's way through the text, however, what appeared to be solid ground is gradually revealed to be quicksand. Expecting truth, the would-be lover is encouraged to mislead and to exaggerate. He is told to beware of the dangerous power of female lust; he learns how to defend himself. Such advice seems reasonable, and it is offered, as always in Ovid's texts, with humor; but on reflection it is hard not to see the *uates* chipping away at his own credibility. These tips are followed by lessons on cheating, along with instruction in the arts of seducing, creating illusions, and even of accepting deception in hopes of eventually ending up with some semblance of what one originally wanted. Further on, things become even more complex: after two books of instruction devoted to his male students, the preceptor, announcing that it is now time for him to arm the enemy, addresses his advice to women. Then, in the fourth book of the series, the *Remedia amoris*,[1] the poet offers antidotes to the very lessons he has been teaching. Each reversal, however, though witty, poses marked reading problems for the reader in the text by revealing that the world of the *Ars* is unstable and deceptive. The true experience the preceptor claims ("usus opus mouet hoc," *Ars* 1.29) turns out to be nothing but a compilation of literary experiences drawn from Ovid's *Amores*, and the preceptor himself is shown to be only the *Amores*' inept narrator, grown to a cynical middle age. The love he teaches is shown to be nothing but seduction and illusion, whether perpetrated on an unwilling victim or on oneself.

Even the reader's identity in the text is problematic: though the reader is at first depicted as a trusting, if ignorant, pupil of the preceptor, it becomes clear by the end of the work that he or she may need to have become a well-read student of elegiac poetry, a sophisticated *rhétoriqueur* whose analytical skills far outweigh his trust. In Book 3, the inscribed reader's identity is further complicated as he becomes female; then, in the *Remedia*, he/she is again transformed—this time into a suicidally depressed victim of obsessive, unrequited passion:

> cur aliquis laqueo collum nodatus amator
>   a trabe sublimi triste pependit onus?
> cur aliquis rigido fodit sua pectora ferro?
>   (*Remedia* 17–19)

(Why did one lover, tied around the neck with a noose, hang—a depressing burden—from a beam? Why did another pierce his chest with a stiff blade?)

This disturbing image could well depict the despairing readers who believe the preceptor's claims. In the world of the *Ars*, people handle themselves and one another by creating and destroying illusions; falsehood and truth (in its rare appearances) are both threatening. At the end of Book 3, the *Ars* declares that it is only a game; in the *Remedia*, this game has become a deadly illness. The *Ars* is indeed a dangerous text.

In the present chapter, I will outline a reading process that allows readers of the *Ars* to find a balance between the truth and falsehood, the illusion and disillusionment of the text. By working through the multiple conflicts and contradictions in the *Ars*, the reader learns that his or her task is not to believe what the text says but to understand it, despite its claims to the contrary, as a literary fiction, a work which is false to itself in so many ways that it cannot possibly be read as true. The only way to come to terms with the preceptor and his treatise is to see them both as fictions.[2] This is not an easy accomplishment, since the *Ars* explicitly denies that it is a poetic creation, but it is a necessary one if the reader is to avoid the fate of disappointed lovers. By inviting, and then destroying, the reader's trust, the preceptor shows him or her how to set limits on belief, how to create a barrier between his or her emotions and experience and their literary representation. This barrier serves as a frame that sets the text apart, and lets it, within carefully defined limits, describe imaginative experiences that would be impossible in a literal world. The *Ars* teaches its audience how to create this frame and the illusions within it: how to read, how to write, how to imagine—in short, the art of poetry. This lesson in literary theory illuminates not only the *Ars amatoria* but also Ovid's *Amores* and its literary context (elegiac poetry): Ovid shows how these fictional texts on love are constructed and how they can be read. The insights the *Ars* and *Remedia* provide, I will argue, form a theoretical framework for medieval authors—particularly Andreas Capellanus and Jean de Meun.

The following discussion of the *Ars* will draw at times on the *Amores*, from which many of its characters and motifs are taken. There are differences between these two works, of course: the *Amores* are a sequence of elegiac poems in which the *amator*[3] describes his love for a certain Corinna, whereas the *Ars* is a didactic poem in which the *praeceptor amoris* instructs his readers in how to construct love affairs of their own. The works' similarities, however, are much more significant than their differences. The *praeceptor* is, in fact, the same *amator*, though older and apparently wiser (or at least more cynical); as he was a poet in love in the *Amores*, now he is a poet who writes about love. A relationship develops between narrator and reader, as the preceptor shows his student how to perform actions like those of the preceptor—how, in a sense, to become the *amator* the *praeceptor* used to be.

If, however, the lover-narrator of the *Amores* was distinguished by his experience, the *praeceptor amoris* recommends himself to his readers by the power of his art—the center of this text. The preceptor uses *ars*, he explains, to dominate both Cupid (1.17) and the woman the reader desires: "arte mea capta est, arte tenenda mea est" (2.12) (she is captured by my art, and by my art retained). The preceptor teaches his students that they need *ars* (which has a broad range of meanings in classical Latin: skill in workmanship, physical or mental art, scientific theory, moral character—even cunning, artifice, and fraud[4]) for every aspect of love: to find it, to retain it, and even to give it up (1.3–34, 2.121–22, 3.791–92; *Rem.* 15–16). *Ars* is harmful only when it is lacking, as Dido and other women find out to their sorrow:

> quid uos perdiderit, dicam: nescistis amare;
> defuit ars uobis: arte perennat amor.
>
> (3.41–42)

(I will reveal the cause of your downfall: you did not know how to love. You lacked art: it is only by art that love endures.)

Ars gives power in love by teaching one how to manipulate others, seduce them, and hold their affection. It is useful, the preceptor teaches, not for being in love but for causing others to be in love: the *Ars amatoria* is about using art to take advantage of others. The preceptor instructs his students not in how to feel but in how to look, how to see, and how to behave. Art is necessary in every circumstance, at every moment—and so, therefore, is the preceptor, its possessor—as he points out:

> Naso legendus erat tum cum didicistis amare;
> idem nunc uobis Naso legendus erit.
>
> (*Rem.* 71–72)

(You needed Ovid's works when you were learning how to love; you will need them just as much today.)

And just as Ovid's readers used the preceptor both in the *Ars* and in the *Remedia*, so they need *ars* in all of its manifestations, from mental ability to fraud. Nothing in the *Ars amatoria* is what it seems to be, and the reader must learn to be constantly on guard, seeing every character from both sides, finding the ulterior motive in every conversation, discovering the exceptions to every principle. The poet plays a complicated game with his readers: he constructs images, then tears them down; he solicits his readers' trust, then shows them that this trust is unmerited. The results of this process are not entirely predictable. Some readers—like the hapless lover depicted in the opening of the *Remedia amoris*—may become discouraged, and even despair of finding a meaning in the text. One need not, however, reach such a hopeless end. Ovid repeatedly shows that the kind of love the *Ars* represents is built on illusion, but this fact offers some benefits. Readers can learn to see literary love and the fictions that discuss it as a game, which they can enjoy as long as they set limits on their belief. Fantasy, whether literary or imaginative, can be a pleasure, provided that one recognizes it for what it is.

This ability to recognize—and even to help to create—the limits of fantasy is a skill the inscribed readers of the *Ars* learn only gradually. First, following the preceptor's invitation, they take the text literally; bit by bit, they learn to refrain from trusting; then they learn to trust not the preceptor but themselves. This exercise begins with the preceptor himself. Though he invites the confidence of his readers, they come to recognize that he is fallible and that his advice is sometimes dishonest, even insulting. The experiences on which he claims to base his precepts are often failures or mistakes: "Do what I say, not what I do," he recommends.[5] Though the preceptor claims to be a conqueror of women, he acknowledges in Book 3 that he will be their victim (3.590), and, despite his pose as a witty and emotionally impermeable *roué*, he reveals that he has been a victim of the art of seduction he tries to teach: "medicus turpiter aeger eram" (*Rem.* 314) (It's so embarrassing: I'm a doctor, but I fell sick).

The preceptor's hints reveal, bit by bit, that his background in love comes strictly from the classroom of literature—from Ovid's own *Amores*, in fact.[6] His advice about picking women up at horse races, for example (1.135–62), comes from *Amores* 3.2; his discussion of seducing one's mistress's maid (1.375ff.) is a reworking of *Amores* 2.7–8; the mentions of *militia amoris* (2.233, 672, 709ff.) are echoes of *Amores* 1.9 and 3.8. The image of writing secret messages in wine on a dinner-party table (1.571ff.) recalls *Amores* 1.4, 3.11A; his observations on wigs (3.165–66 and 3.245–46) are also found in *Amores* 1.14. The preceptor's protestation that he never loves unless he has been hurt ("non nisi laesus amo" [3.598]) echoes the *amator*'s masochism ("nil ego, quod nullo tempore laedat, amo" [3.19.8]: I love nothing which never causes injury). Even the remarkable exposition of Corinna's fictional status in the *Amores*, which will be discussed below, is recalled at *Ars* 3.358. Many other references back to the *Amores* could easily be cited. These regular and almost casual allusions, as well as the continuity of meter and style between the *Amores* and the *Ars*, easily set the didactic poem squarely within the context of elegy,[7] and encourage its readers to recall some of the principal lessons of the *Amores*: that the *amator* is far more successful at composing poetry than he is at loving, and that, while showing that his elegies are profoundly conventional, Ovid asserts through their very fictionality their value as an artistically satisfying work. The *praeceptor amoris*, like the *amator*, is a bungler at love whose experiences repeatedly belie his successful pose;[8] the lessons he can successfully teach are lessons about literature, not about love. (His precepts, he admits, are far less effective at acquiring love than are money and gifts [3.650–52].) Thus example will be no teacher to the alert reader of the *Ars*, who, if he is as *doctus* (or she as *docta*) as he or she should be, will see the weaknesses in the preceptor's record.[9]

Beyond casting doubts on his own experience, the preceptor also calls into question his students' ability to learn from it. He hints, from time to time, that their very need for him shows how inadequate they are: in the Golden Age, he informs men, no teacher was needed for love (2.479). His female readers, too, are failures: if beautiful women need no *praecepta*, as he proposes (3.256–57), one can infer with Ovid's translator Peter Green that those who must read the *Ars* are like "the clientele of a marriage bureau or lonelyhearts column," who are "not drawn, by and large, from the well-heeled, the well-favoured or the well-adjusted."[10] Instruction and abuse go hand in hand. The preceptor's insincerity is patent,[11] as is his low opinion of his readers, yet somehow he manages to persuade them (us) to continue to read, trusting and mistrusting him simultaneously, accepting the profound conflicts the *Ars* and *Remedia* contain. How Ovid convinces his readers to perform this complex act is the true lesson of the *Ars*.

The lesson is in fact a lesson in literary theory. The *Ars* and *Remedia* reveal (though often in indirect ways) that the love described in elegiac poetry is essentially the same as the poetry itself: both are artistic fantasies, constructed by the reader and the poetic lover together. Elegiac love depends for its existence on the presence of recognizable conventions, which help the reader situate it within a literary context, to recognize it as fiction. Through such conventions the poet involves the reader in the act of literary creation, which is itself an amatory relationship and, in fact, the most intimate relationship in these texts;[12] the preceptor's true task is to teach the reader how to be a creator, like himself.

In order to understand how this process works, it will be necessary first to investigate the rôle of artifice and convention in the *Amores*, on which the *Ars* is based. Despite the *Amores'* pose of sincerity, well-informed readers will recognize that each of their characters and situations are conventional. Their persona, for example, is less a lover than a poet in love,[13] and so the *Amores* do not recreate a real love affair but rather provide their readers[14] with a literary fiction of love, revealing their artistry as they go along. While his elegist predecessor Propertius opened his book of poems by having his persona fall dramatically in love,[15] Ovid begins the *Amores* by showing himself writing elegiac verse (1.1.1–4). The *amator* is little more than a convention himself, a reuse of the traditional Roman poetic "I," which derives from Propertius, Tibullus, Gallus, and Catullus, as well as Catullus's Alexandrian model, Callimachus. This poetic "I" is a ventriloquist's voice, a literary echo of an echo of an echo.[16] Even the sincerity that post-Romantic readers, at least, traditionally attribute to the poet-lover is undermined by the *amator*'s confessions of infidelity and multifarious desire. His affirmations of love are "sincere" not in the sense that they unify the *amator*, the poet, and the historical Ovid, but in the sense that they create an effective illusion of a poet in love.[17]

And though she is the ostensible raison d'être of the *Amores*, Corinna is no more real than her lover. Historical identities have been found for the women in earlier elegy,[18] but literary history is silent on Corinna,[19] and efforts to re-create her are not only fruitless but even irrelevant to an understanding of the *Amores*. Rather than existing as a person in her own right (in fact, she speaks only once [poem 2.18]), she is the object of the *amator*'s desire, the grain of sand that provokes the poetic oyster to produce a string of literary pearls ("te mihi felicem materiem in carmina praebe" [1.3.19] [Offer yourself to me as fortunate raw material for poems]).[20] Poetry, not Corinna, is the true star of the *Amores*. Only after four elegies about poetry and love does Corinna make a real entrance (1.5); Ovid does not call her by name even once;[21] and at the close of Book 3 it is to Venus, rather than to his mistress, that the *amator* bids farewell (3.15). The tenuousness of Corinna's position is revealed, in fact, in poem 2.17, where the *amator* threatens to replace her as his source of inspiration if she will not behave according to his wishes:

> et multae per me nomen habere uolunt:
> noui aliquam, quae se circumferat esse Corinnam;
> ut fiat, quid non illa dedisse uelit?
>
> (2.17.28–30)

(Many women want to make a name with me: I've heard of one who spreads the word that she's Corinna; what wouldn't she want to give, to become her?)

The *amator* threatens to annihilate Corinna, pointing out that her name is a literary cipher, a floating signifier that has no fixed connection to any particular person. Corinna is "Corinna" because Ovid needs her to be. She is his *amator*'s ideal counterpart, a literary mistress for an elegiac lover.[22] Even the *amator*'s jealousy of her turns out to be merely conventional: he begs to be made jealous because he can be in love only when he is hurt.[23] The lover, his mistress, fidelity, and infidelity are merely *topoi* in the *Amores*, whose integrity is poetic, not emotional: Ovid creates situations in order to have something to write about. "Omnia pro ueris credam, sint ficta licebit," the *amator* tells Corinna (2.11.53): "I'll believe everything is true, even if it's made up." The art of the *Amores* (as of the *Ars amatoria*) is the poet's art of creating literary fictions in cooperation with his audience.

On a few occasions in the *Amores*, the poet shows this audience how he wants it to participate in the creative process. On the one hand, readers should believe absolutely in the fictional creation: a young man, wounded by love, should be amazed by the accuracy with which the text depicts his feelings ("'quo' dicat 'ab indice doctus / conposuit casus ista poeta meos?'" [2.1.9–10][24] [What witness taught that poet how to write about my case?]), and pretty young women should be drawn to the *amator* by his writings (2.1.37–38). The audience is an inspiration to the poet;[25] similarly, the poet inspires readers to fill in the gaps in his text with their own feelings, as in his provocative but incomplete description of his first sexual encounter with Corinna.[26] The poet's invitations to belief, however, are limited. Ovid is careful, for the most part, to keep a prophylactic barrier between the fantasy world he creates and the reader's own experience. The pseudo-Corinna discussed above suggests that a female reader, taking the poetic fiction too much to heart, has shown how naïve she is; male readers are presented as being similarly gullible. In poem 3.12, the *amator* laments that because of his poems' success, Corinna has become so popular his love is overcome by his readers' competition.[27] "Et mea debuerat falso laudata uideri / femina; credulitas nunc mihi uestra nocet" (3.12.43–44) (It should have been obvious that I was over-praising my mistress—*you're* gullible, and now *I'm* in trouble!).[28]

Here Ovid re-creates the paradox of the Cretan liar,[29] and calls into question the way in which his poetry is to be taken. Readers must learn that their *credulitas* is invited by the text, but only within the limits of fiction—only within the literary frame which the poet clearly signals by using familiar conventions. Male readers, as represented in the text, may knock on Corinna's door; women in the *Amores* may try to seduce the poet and be immortalized by him. But real readers must learn to flirt with these possibilities without actually believing in them. *Credulitas* is not, in fact, what the *Amores* ask for; rather, they encourage their readers to maintain a conscious understanding of the fact that these poems play out a conventional game.[30] In the style of René Magritte, one might draw attention to the fact that the *Amores* are only a representation. Both Magritte's apple (which, as the painter puts it, "n'est pas une pomme") and Ovid's love poems are works of art about art which make the audience's rôle explicit: not to believe, but to see how the work of art leads them to imagine.[31] In order to accomplish this task, the audience must always be conscious of its rôle in the artistic process, and it is for this reason that Ovid sometimes makes a negative example of overcredulous readers going where they have no business to go. Ovid shows that the *Amores* are both a text to be read and a text about reading, both love poetry and an exposé of love poetry's techniques.

The readers' rôle in the *Ars* and *Remedia* is perhaps even more complex. The preceptor plays with his readers, persuading and dissuading them, offering opportunities to love and taking them away, seducing, deceiving, and betraying them, and finally teaching them how love poetry works. As in the *Amores*, the audience is characterized in various ways. At times the inscribed reader is ignorant of love; at other times he or she is sophisticated enough to recognize both how the preceptor manipulates him or her and how conventional the situations he creates really are. In the *Ars*, the reader seeks to learn how to love; in the *Remedia*, he or she needs to know how to *stop* loving. And, as in the *Amores*, the audience is described as being both male (in Books 1 and 2) and female (in Book 3). Even within these ostensibly segregated camps, however, members of the other side are occasionally present.[32] Though one may explain this polymorphous audience as a collection of men and women, each of whom may extract the parts appropriate to him- or herself, no individual reader is at once male and female, capable of always being the preceptor's student and never his laboratory specimen. Since Ovid continually requires his readers to connect the four books, to understand each piece of advice in relation to others, individual readers are always to some degree the losers in the text's battles between men and women. Each real reader must move from one book to the next, from one gender to the other, as he or she moves through the work.

This process creates obvious difficulties. Female readers must learn to live with the knowledge of male duplicity taught in Books 1 and 2; male readers must do the same with Book 3. The reader who seems to learn how to become master or mistress of the illusions that control love in the *Ars* suddenly finds, in the *Remedia*, that he or she has become their victim. These reversals, coupled with the preceptor's own inconsistency, produce a deliberately disorienting reading experience. Ovid exploits this vertigo in a variety of ways, even taking it to a point at which the real reader must separate him- or herself from the image of the reader the text constructs. The following discussions of female readers, illusions, and poetry will show the increasing pressure Ovid puts on the reader's relationship with the *Ars*, and will reveal how resolution finally becomes possible.

The preceptor's attitude toward women is highly ambivalent. At the beginning of Books 1 and 3, he restricts his female readership to unmarried women, ostensibly in the interests of public morality.[33] By excluding married women, who were legally defined as chaste, Ovid seems to suggest that all others are both aggressive and sexually voracious, a stereotype his rhetorical treatments reinforce. Men (who are naturally restrained, says the preceptor [1.281–82]) are taught that women are seducible, lustful, and dishonest, and that by learning about these traits, men can exploit them (1.269–76). As usual, Ovid's *exempla* provide surprising, even alarming, illustrations of his precepts: he talks about the incestuous Byblis and Myrrha, and the unnatural Pasiphaë, who became enamored of a bull and viciously sacrificed her bovine rivals at the altar.[34] The ostensible lesson is that women are so lustful that men need little effort to conquer feminine reserve. As usual, however, the text's literary allusions conspire against its surface meaning. The women the preceptor cites as examples of ordinary female desire are in fact the women Ovid will describe in *Metamorphoses* 10, the book of profane and perverse loves. Beyond Byblis, Myrrha, and Pasiphaë, one finds the treacherous Scylla; Clytemnestra, the husband-murderer; Medea, who killed her own children; Phoenix's stepmother, who blinded him out of jealousy; and Phaedra, whose lustful desires for Hippolytus eventually led to his death. The lesson the preceptor draws from these stories—"ergo age" (1.343) (Go ahead!)—is not one a sophisticated male reader would be likely to take.

The misogyny of Books 1 and 2 emerges in other ways. The apparently commonplace agricultural metaphors Ovid uses, for example, have a lurid quality. The preceptor, encouraging men to adultery, reminds them that the grass is greener on the other side of the fence: "fertilior seges est alienis semper in agris / uicinumque pecus grandius uber habet" (1.349–50)

(The grain in someone else's fields is always more abundant, and the neighbor's cow has a bigger udder than one's own has). Though the bucolic scenes of the *Georgics* may here come to mind,[35] the recent mention of Pasiphaë and her love affair's savage fruit, the Minotaur, suggest that even cattle can be frightening. Women are consistently represented as being closer to nature than men, while, as Eleanor Leach correctly notes, men are expected, as they are in the *Georgics*, to dominate and control their natural environment, a lesson which suggests that nature and the feminine are inherently threatening.[36] Finally, men should know that women's vanity makes them highly vulnerable to flattery. "Nec credi labor est: sibi quaeque uidetur amanda," the preceptor explains (1.613) (The trick is *not* to be believed: every woman thinks she's seductive); and the honorable behavior to which men should adhere in their business affairs has no place in their dealings with the inherently dishonest opposite sex (see 1.641–46, esp. 645: "fallite fallentes" [Deceive the deceivers!]). What women say has so little meaning that even their protests against violent seduction are lies, the preceptor affirms (1.673–74): they *like* it rough.

Though the preceptor appears to restrict his sympathies entirely to his male readers, in Book 3 he reverses this stance, making it clear that he is willing to abuse the less-than-fair sex as well. The preceptor justifies his turnabout by explaining that he is obliged to accede to Venus's request to protect women, who are inherently virtuous and honest (3.31–32, 45–48), but here as elsewhere he is not to be trusted. While every bit of advice in Book 3 of the *Ars amatoria* is designed to help women seduce men, its effect is also, of course, reciprocal: if women are having more sex, then men are, too. Thus the preceptor's *carpe diem* urgings to women (3.59–60) are actually no defense against lustful male aggression; instead, they make women sexually available to their adversaries. The preceptor assures his female readers that he is not dishonoring them—"nec uos prostituit mea uox" (3.97) (Nothing I've said has made you into whores)—yet this is precisely what he is doing. To seduction is added lying: women are encouraged to mislead men (3.616), just as men mislead them.[37] The preceptor is amoral to the point of immorality; he will teach anything to anyone as long as he is acknowledged as master. He asks male and female readers to commemorate their debt to him in identical inscriptions: "NASO MAGISTER ERAT" (2.744, 3.812). "Divide and conquer" is the preceptor's rule. Each group of readers thinks it has conquered the other, while the preceptor is really the master of both.

And yet, of course, this division of the audience is completely fictitious. Male readers are as unlikely to ignore Book 3 as female readers are to ignore Books 1 and 2. The temptation to see ourselves as others see us is far too strong. The individual reader must recognize both the deceptions he or she is told to practice and those that will be practiced upon him or her. Thus Ovid, in attempting to include all kinds of readers (men, women, those seeking love, those seeking to escape from love), puts each individual reader into an extremely awkward position—one that requires belief and disbelief at once. The preceptor is on the reader's side and also opposed to him or her, confiding and yet untrustworthy. The reader is made to trust and mistrust, to be male *and* female, and to be aware that these splits are occurring.[38]

Rifts between appearance and reality, surface and content, trust and the lack of trustworthiness are pervasive in the world of the *Ars*. The preceptor often actively cheats his readers, dismantling the assumptions of honesty that are the basis of communication. By doing so, he teaches them how greatly their perceptions depend on shared assumptions of truth, and how much depends on their fabrications. Deception can be practiced in many ways: the range of techniques the preceptor offers covers a wide range of amatory situations. Some of these techniques are nonverbal. Men who have been unfaithful may allay their mistresses' suspicions by the convincing proof of intercourse (2.411–14); women, similarly, can use their bodies to proclaim their reciprocal desire, whether that desire be true or feigned (3.769–804). Men can cry real or false tears (1.659–62); so can women (*Rem.* 689–90). Pretended drunkenness may be a useful tool in seduction (1.597–98). The key to success is to be a successful performer, keeping one's focus on one's audience: "miserabilis esto, / ut qui te uideat dicere possit 'amas,' " (1.737–38) (Look pitiable, so anyone who sees you can conclude, "You're in love!"). As long as the other person believes the constructed image, it does not matter that "love" is merely sexual desire wrapped in illusions. By acting as if one is in love, one can be received as a lover, and gain whatever one's true objective is, whether this be sex, money, or power. Believing is not necessary, except in an artistic sense: performance is the key.[39]

Verbal performance in the *Ars* is ambiguous, too, particularly on the textual level—one which corresponds directly to the medium of instruction. Composers and readers of written texts discussed in the *Ars* (letters and poems, for the most part) must always be aware that these texts may contain double meanings, and must therefore be interpreted with caution. Thus women can write letters which, beneath an innocuous surface that will not arouse a husband's suspicion, carry a lustful message to their lovers (3.468–89, 619–30). As readers, on the other hand, women must avoid being seduced by feigned passion (3.471–72). Interpretation is a function of context, Ovid notes: as time passes and situations change, old love letters may become dangerous either because they may reveal past indiscretions (3.395–96, 495–96) or because they may remind their readers of passions they are trying to forget (*Rem.* 717–20). Poetry, too, has a range of possible meanings. At times it is literary, at times magical (*carmen* means both "lyric" and "charm"); it can be trustworthy or dangerous.[40] In every case in which meaning is called into question, the fundamental issue Ovid debates is how literature is related to the world of phenomenon and experience.

On this subject preceptor and poet disagree. The preceptor bases his appeal to his students on the claim that his poems are efficacious (1.205–6, 3.533–34, *Rem.* 361–98). The poet, however, repeatedly undermines this assertion by creating situations that show—as the *Amores* did[41]—that poetry cannot persuade, and that it is to be valued only as art. Thus while the preceptor advises men to send verses as a token of their affection to educated or pretentious women (2.281–86), Apollo himself points out that reciting one's own poetry is *never* sexy (2.507–8), and even the preceptor eventually acknowledges that the Muse should remain outside the bedroom door (2.704). Poetry does not seduce. It *is* effective, however, in permitting its reader to imagine him- or herself as a successful lover: within its limits, the reader is transformed. Thus the preceptor's opening promise ("lecto carmine doctus amet" [1.2]) (After reading the poem, he will be an expert lover) is made good, since, when one reads the *carmen*, its literary magic takes effect. This game begins at the opening of the poem and ends at its close (3.809; compare *Rem.* 814). Ovid demonstrates that the concept of a frame and the limitation of the reader's trust and belief are essential to the free play of fiction. The *Ars* both offers this experience and shows how it works.

The device of the unreliable narrator, which Ovid uses to demonstrate how limiting belief can reveal artistry, is also found in the dramatic monologues of more modern writers. By briefly examining their practice, we can gain deeper insight into the *Ars*. Robert Langbaum elaborates a model of how these monologues function. Florence Verducci has applied it to the *Heroides*; it works equally well for the *Ars*. According to Langbaum, the relationship between narrator and reader is developed in four stages. First, the reader identifies with the speaker's ethos; second, the meaning of the monologue unfolds in the reader's experience, leading to both sympathy and resistance; third, the narrator exposes his moral failings; and last, the reader comes gradually to understand that, during the course of the monologue, the speaker has led him or her to depart, in Verducci's words, from "the conventional norms which have shaped his own understanding." Through this "outrageous perspective," the reader's consciousness is enlarged to accommodate that of the speaker, and, in this process, the reader takes on a creative rôle like that of the poet himself.[42] This is precisely what happens in the *Ars* and the *Remedia*. Ovid's preceptor beguiles his readers into the text, but in the process he disrupts their images of themselves by splitting their consciousness into fragments—members of each gender see themselves from the others' hostile perspective. The audience of the *Ars* is seduced, misled, and divided against itself.

By leading his readers to lose their complacency, Ovid permits—but does not oblige—them to gain a new perspective by revolting against the preceptor, denying his claims of truth and working with the poet in constructing, out of the fragments of broken poetic images, a new world that is clearly fictional. Readers who fail to recognize the fictionality of the text and the limits it imposes on their belief will be unable to read with satisfaction. Those readers who learn to distinguish truth from poetic invention, however, learn to classify it not in the categories of truth and falsehood, but in the intermediary place of fiction.[43] The preceptor's method of teaching this lesson is often indirect and confusing. His common phrase "crede mihi" (Trust me!), for example, is usually a hint that he is about to say something misleading. There is no guarantee that readers will find a successful path through this labyrinth of illusion, but if they do so, they have learned to take responsibility for their part in both creating and interpreting the literary text. The preceptor's lies, his unflattering portraits of men and women, and the highly conventional nature of love in the *Amores* and the *Ars* all work together for two purposes: to vitiate the readers' belief that the work of art is an accurate and trustworthy representation of anyone's experience (the preceptor's, the poet's, or their own); and to create an understanding that another world can exist outside of that of experience—the world of art. This world is limited; indeed, it is dependent on its limitations, which form its borders. Without these limits, readers of the *Ars* find, encounters with fiction and fantasy are dangerous and destructive. Within them, however, art has meaning and gives pleasure.[44] Thus the artist's first job, and perhaps his or her most important one, is to create those limits, to set aside a space for the work:

a space like that of fantasy in which—since rules, belief, mutual emotion, and complete emotional involvement are not necessary—it is possible to play. This is how Ovid's reader learns to use the signs that designate fiction as such (literary conventions, the preceptor's self-contradictory instructions, etc.): with them he or she can create a framework that separates the literary world from his or her own experience. What happens within the frame may mirror what has happened or can happen in the outside world, but it need not be limited by these things: the possibilities of fiction permit the reader to play and imagine freely.

Ovid, in fact, makes this point in terms related to those we have been using. When the preceptor asks for the reader's *fides*, for example, what he asks for is faith not in his truthfulness but in his artistry.

> sed neque Phoebi tripodes nec corniger Ammon
>   uera magis uobis quam mea Musa canet;
> si qua fides, arti, quam longo fecimus usu,
>   credite: praestabunt carmina nostra fidem.
>
> (3.789–92)

(Neither the Delphic oracle nor the ram-horned Ammon will reveal greater truths to you than will my Muse. If you can trust at all, believe in my art, which I have built up with years of practice: my poems are a guarantee of credit.)

The reader's trust must always be self-limiting, recognizing the poet's fictions for what they are. The *amator* proposed this idea smilingly in his attempts to woo Corinna in the *Amores*: "omnia pro ueris credam, sint ficta licebit" (2.11.53) (I'll believe everything is true, even if it's fiction). Years later, in the *Tristia*, Ovid was to make the same point, though in a more desperate, defensive mood: "magnaque pars mendax operum est et ficta meorum" (the greatest part of my work is lying fictions)[45]—an evocative line which would be echoed, eleven centuries later, by one of Ovid's medieval followers, Baudri of Bourgueil. Poetry, the preceptor shows us, is effective less as seduction than as entertainment; and those who give it some measure of belief are not so much the characters in the text as those outside of it—namely, we, Ovid's readers.

Readers are taught more about the workings of poetic fiction when the preceptor teaches his students about the illusions of love—and, simultaneously, about the poetic process. The pre-eminence accorded to illusions in the *Ars* is jarring at times because the preceptor regularly shows how insubstantial they are; and since the love he teaches is entirely based on illusion, this love, too, is proven to be without any basis in fact. But this process of creating impressions and then destroying them, of inviting and then rejecting the reader's trust, reveals more clearly than any traditional elegy the way in which poet and reader work together. If the reader is able to understand the distinction between illusion and reality, between precept and example, he or she may learn to find pleasure in creating illusions for their own sake, in learning how to participate in the process of art and in recognizing it for what it is.

Illusion has many meanings in the *Ars*. It may refer to beauty, seduction, or deceit; it may lead to truth; it has its dangers, but also its own esthetic appeal. Love and poetry are both closely linked to illusion, as are the relationships the poet creates among his characters and between himself and his readers. By refusing to offer his readers anything but illusion, the preceptor gives them a difficult reading experience, but he also shows them again and again how art is made.

His method is often less than gentle. The preceptor urges his readers to lie and commit adultery whenever it is convenient or appealing to do so. For him, creating illusions is a valuable way of manipulating people, morality notwithstanding. Even the gods are bad examples.[46] Men may use false promises, feigned generosity, pretended drunkenness, and lying oaths (1.442–43, 449, 597, 634–35); the point is to make women believe they are in command (2.193–232). Women, too, should try to manipulate their lovers by stimulating their jealousy, whether it is merited or not (3.603–8). Precepts and their applications multiply almost without end, until the preceptor makes his most sweeping warning: a man should trust no one, no matter how close a friend he may be. "Friendship and trust are only empty words," he warns: it is dangerous to praise one's mistress's beauty even to one's best friend, cousin, or brother (1.740–53).

The preceptor suggests these principles as guidelines for dealing with others, but it is hard for the reader not to apply them to their originator as well, since his insistence on lies as a means of communication and his frequent reversals of posture solicit the reader's mistrust.[47] This uneasiness grows every time the preceptor encourages the reader to be deceitful or unfaithful. He insists, for example, that adultery is perfectly normal, as mythological *exempla* prove (for example, the stories of Helen and Menelaus and of Venus and Mars: 2.371–62, 554–600). Readers are urged to commit adultery if they have the chance to, or to accept it if it is their beloved who takes a fancy to someone else.[48] This advice is hard to accept, since the more the preceptor encourages his readers to break faith, the less able they are to find a safe place for themselves within the text. This insecurity reaches a critical level when, in Book 3, the preceptor warns his female readers that they, too, must trust no one: his *exemplum* makes it virtually impossible for the inscribed reader to maintain a relationship with him.

> haec quoque, quae praebet lectum studiosa locumque,
> > crede mihi, mecum non semel illa fuit.
> nec nimium uobis formosa ancilla ministret:
> > saepe uicem dominae praebuit illa mihi.
> quo feror insanus? quid aperto pectore in hostem
> > mittor et indicio prodor ab ipse meo?
>
> > > (3.663–68)

(She too—your friend who happily offered you her bedroom—we've done it more than once, believe me! And don't employ the services of too pretty a maid: she's frequently offered herself to me in place of her mistress. Wait—I must be crazy to tell you this! Why am I rushing on the enemy's sword with my armor open, betrayed by my own confession?)

By claiming to have had a sexual relationship not only with his inscribed female reader but also with her friend and with her maid, the preceptor creates a vortex of mistrust. Deceit is piled up on deceit: the preceptor will sleep with anyone, lie to everyone, in order to have his way. And, disorienting his readers even further, he admits that he is both an adulterer and a liar, and that he cannot be trusted. Beyond manipulating words in this cratylistic universe in which friendship and trust are empty nouns ("nomen amicitia est, nomen inane fides" [1.740]), the preceptor also teaches readers how to create illusions by manipulating appearances. In so doing, he demonstrates the importance of conventions. He teaches his students how to make their public personae conform to those ideals that will make those who see them fall in love. As usual, *ars* is the key: whatever nature gives, *ars* can improve on. As with the preceptor's urgings to lie and to commit adultery, so here his advice to create a persona that is entirely artificial seems at first selfishly appealing. Gradually, however, this advice becomes more and more distasteful, as the reader finds that taking the preceptor's advice literally is not only immoral but impossible as well.

To conform to the rôle of the perfect seducer, or of the perfect inscribed reader, one must sacrifice all one's integrity.

The lessons on illusion in the *Ars* are among Ovid's most elaborate and memorable forms of instruction. By instructing first men, then women, and finally (in the *Remedia*) all those who wish to disengage themselves from love, the preceptor shows his students both how to influence others' perceptions and how to resist such influence—how to be illusionist and spectator, poet and reader in turn. Both men and women must learn to use reason to arouse the objects of their desire to passion. Whoever can guide perceptions, in the world of the *Ars*, has all the power.

Often the *Ars* presents the creation of illusions as a female domain. This representation seems to be a compliment to women, but in fact it is not: women are artists not so much because they are inherently creative, but because they have little to rely on except beauty, and so must learn to control their sole asset. "Cura dabit faciem; facies neclecta peribit," the preceptor menacingly reminds his female readers (3.105) (It takes work to look good; if you neglect your looks, you'll lose them). Furthermore, he suggests, anything that will enhance women's appearance is fair play—no surprise this, from the author of a treatise on cosmetics, the *Medicamina faciei femineae*. Even hair dye and wigs are acceptable (3.163–68). Many of the preceptor's examples of beautifying techniques are amusing—"si breuis es, sedeas, ne stans uideare sedere" (3.263) ("Sit, if you're short, lest standing you seem to be sitting"[49])—but the underlying message, which neither women nor men can fail to perceive, is deeply critical of the female sex: "rara tamen menda facies caret" (3.261) (Rare indeed is the face with no flaws). As Green paraphrases the preceptor, "Women in their natural, unmasked state are fundamentally not just uncivilized but actively disgusting."[50] Women have something to sell; men, if they can be successfully tricked, will buy; but the rule of *caveat emptor* always applies.[51] In arming women (the mission of Book 3[52]) the preceptor teaches them how to cover up deficiencies but warns them not to let men know what they are doing. "Multa uiros nescire decet," he urges (3.229) (There are many things men are better off not knowing); the goal of using cosmetics and other adornments is to appear *naturally* beautiful (3.210; see also 3.153–55).[53] It is clear that this advice conceals a threat, particularly when the inscribed female reader knows that she has men looking over her shoulder at the text. Women are pleasing only if they adhere to the preceptor's standards of *cultus* (style, elegance, refinement); those who do not conform will fail to attract or hold men. Ariadne is a striking example of this rule. At first her distress at losing Theseus is said to enhance her beauty (1.533–34), but when her emotions impinge on her appearance, the preceptor loses all sympathy with her, mordantly noting that "et color et Theseus et uox abiere puellae" (1.551): without her beauty and her voice, persuasive tools of seduction, Ariadne cannot keep her man. A word to the wise is sufficient: female readers and male readers alike can easily take the lesson that appearances are all-important.

Even in this area, Ovid divides his readers from one another, for while women must adorn themselves, the preceptor's male students must not. Men ought, of course, to be clean, healthy-looking, and well dressed, but some of the preceptor's hints are so basic as to be insulting—"keep your nails clean, trim the hair in your nostrils, avoid bad breath and perspiration" (see 1.509–22). Ovid, it appears, does not trust that his male readers know even these fundamentals of grooming. Elegance, on the other hand, is ruled out, since an excessive concern with appearance suits only women and those men who seek to attract their fellows (1.523–24). The preceptor repeatedly warns his readers against those men who are too intimate with the secrets of the toilette (see also 1.505–8); they may, he hints, be wanton seducers, homosexuals, or even dress-stealing transvestites (3.433–66)— i.e., men who transgress the boundaries of sexual propriety. These comments, however, like all the preceptor's confidences, have a suspicious ring. The ambiguous and immoral gender-switching of dandies is not far from the preceptor's own knowing familiarity with the secrets of both men and women, or, in fact, from the regularly changing gender of the inscribed reader of the *Ars*. (Later, we will see similar ambiguities emerging among the male and female allegorical figures who represent sides of the woman's character in the *Roman de la Rose*.) The preceptor's fear of those who depart from social norms both mirrors the reader's increasing alienation from his or her inscribed rôle and reveals the dependence of the *Ars* on a strictly established system of gendered behavior. Without conventional morality, there can be no *nequitia*;[54] without rules and boundaries, the fantasy of elegiac love cannot exist.

The text's relationship with social conventions is analogous to its treatment of literary ones: it inverts and exposes them while maintaining them as a framework. All the disillusioning work of the *Remedia*, for example, serves not to condemn illusions but to show that they are only ways of seeing whose magic is found in the fact that they can exist at all.[55] When the preceptor tells men to see a woman who is "nigrior Illyrica . . . pice" (blacker than Adriatic pitch) as "fusca" (suntanned) (2.657–59) or one who is "fusca" as "nigra" (*Rem.* 327), it is not the woman who changes. She is only, like Corinna, poetic *materia*; it is by viewing that the man becomes a true artist. To conquer the deceptions of feminine artistry, men must become discriminating viewers, learning to see women as they truly are— "improuisus ades," the preceptor advises (*Rem.* 347) (Visit her when she doesn't expect you). But even this principle—like every other provided by Ovid—has its exceptions, because sometimes women really *are* beautiful, and this true appearance may be even more dangerous than a false one.

> non tamen huic nimium praecepto credere tutum est:
> fallit enim multos forma sine arte decens

(Don't trust this precept too far: natural beauty has tricked many a man),

men are cautioned (*Rem.* 349–50). False appearances are dangerous; true ones are, too. Natural beauty and deeply held emotions are more powerful, and more threatening, than any advice.[56]

The *Ars amatoria*, as we have seen, is full of contradictions. It frequently promises readers that it can teach them to manipulate others to their advantage, and then reveals that the readers themselves may be seduced. The preceptor insists on being trusted, then reveals that he is a liar. The inscribed reader is male, then female, then male again. He (or she) first wants to fall in love, and is taught that love is nothing but a game; then, as the *Remedia* begin, he or she finds out how distressing love can be, when what were merely illusions have become painful realities. The reader is constantly misled, seduced, de- and re-gendered, taught to see him- or herself from contrary perspectives. To be the text's inscribed reader, to trust the *praeceptor amoris*, to take the *Ars* at its word—any of these acts makes one lose all sense of oneself. The *Ars* demands impossible things of its readers, who, as they read, go from illusion to illusion, from lie to lie. The reader who truly believes the text finds him- or herself ravished and helpless, betrayed by the preceptor, and deprived of all faith in the reading process.

There is, however, a way out. The preceptor frequently uses the term *lusus*, which means anything from "game" to "trickery" to "(non-marital) sexual intercourse":[57] one can recognize that his text, and the love it teaches, are a kind of game. Each of these meanings has a place in the *Ars*. Women, for example, are advised to play games (3.368), men to "play around," as long as they keep their playing discreet and delude only those in the opposite camp: "ludite, si sapitis, solas impune puellas" (1.643; see also 2.389) (to avoid retribution, trick only girls, if you're wise). When the *Ars* ends, as we have noted, it describes itself as a completed game: "lusus habet finem" (3.809). Sex, love, pretending, and cheating are all part of a literary game, one that the preceptor's students must learn to play. If they take it too seriously, they will find themselves in serious trouble, as the *Remedia* witness; but if they know how to set limits on their belief, they will be successful players and readers.[58] Thus, while recommending that women learn to gamble, the preceptor shudders at the thought that a fight may break out on the gaming table (3.367–76). Here the preceptor is ostensibly warning his female readers of the risks of taking dice, backgammon, or checkers[59] too seriously, but the ambiguity of *lusus* can readily be exploited here as elsewhere: love is a game, as well. In board games and in the game of love, the risk lies in taking play so seriously that one may lose control. Of the preceptor's many lessons, this is the one he most consistently teaches: that one must never entrust too much to love.

Learning to see the text as a *lusus* also means learning to read it like the highly conventional *Amores*. Each time the *Ars* refers to the *Amores*, Ovid shows his readers that the love affairs his elegies describe are strictly poetic, and that they should be read as such.[60] The *Ars*, despite its claims, has no real advice to give about love.[61] The preceptor would like his students to forget this fact, but the poet never lets them. By making the preceptor constantly declare the importance of *ars*, the poet exposes the real meaning of the text, which glorifies Ovid's verbal artistry[62] and exposes the reader's rôle in the creative process. The art of elegiac love is the art not of taking the text at face value, but rather the art of recognizing and constructing fantasy (the art of reading and writing), since it is fantasies of unrequited love that give rise to poetry.[63] Many of the characters of the *Ars* (like Pasiphaë, who falls in love with an animal, and Procris, whose husband accidentally kills her when she pursues him with a jealousy that is born of misinterpretation) never learn this lesson, and suffer in consequence. But we have seen often enough that Ovid's mythological allusions require careful reading to be properly understood, and that many of them are examples of what *not* to do. Ovid, the poet behind the *praeceptor amoris*, is a skilled and subtle teacher who makes his students learn their lessons by experience. If readers fall too readily into believing the text, they will suffer some hard knocks; but if these lessons permit them to learn the boundaries between truth and fiction, then the lessons are well worth the discomfort they inflict. The *Ars* claims to teach its readers about love, and, in a way, it does, but its focus is not on constructing a real and lasting love affair between two people who tell the truth and understand one another. Rather, it teaches about the love that resembles and constitutes literature and fantasy, and how this process of creation works.

The process of obtaining such a reading of the *Ars amatoria*, though somewhat complex, provides an interpretation of the poem that I find more complete and more satisfying than most others, particularly those that attempt to see it as a consistent, univocal poem. (This question of interpretation will be of particular importance in regard to the two medieval works we will be reading in later chapters, where the Ovidian opposition between illusion and disillusionment gives way to a weightier ideological conflict—that between Christianity and non-marital love.) To obtain a satisfying reading of the *Ars*, one must recognize its humor and its limits, heeding "the poet's unspoken warning: 'Not To Be Taken Seriously.' "[64] To read the *Ars* not as a treatise on love but as a self-conscious, critical discussion of elegiac love poetry involves certain risks: many readers, no doubt, will not take the poem this way. But Frederick Ahl, in his book *Metaformations: Soundplay and Wordplay in Ovid and Other Classical Poets*, reminds us that classical poetry in general may be subversive rather than supportive of order, and that, for Ovid, "reality is not reducible to unity."[65] Ahl proposes that classical poetry in general may often be ambiguous, requiring careful interpretive efforts which may nevertheless not yield a single, fixed meaning. Rather than being as clear as possible, he suggests, ancient writers

> preferred to play the Delphic oracle with their readers: to challenge them to engage in dialogue, to solve riddles. Without men to answer her riddles, and to ask what they are, the Pythia is dead. So too is the ancient poet or the philosopher. At the other extreme, once the riddle is solved, the poet, like the Sphinx, is of no further use. So the poet must always try to insert an insoluble element into the poetic texture.[66]

Thus the reading I propose, which sees the *Ars amatoria* and the *Remedia amoris* as a treatise on the art of love poetry, can never claim to be uniquely correct. Nevertheless, to see these two texts as an exposition of the world of Roman love elegy, of the literary world that the reader can never fully enter but can always enjoy imagining, is an approach that explains much about how the poems function. Read in this way, Ovid's treatise teaches its readers that they are participants in the poet's art, that love poetry is an exercise in fantasy that works only within a setting strictly defined by the rules of convention, and that fiction depends on these limits to establish a place for itself outside the world of experience, outside the realms of truth and falsehood. The *Ars amatoria* and *Remedia amoris* show, as they claim to teach love, that what they teach best is how to read and write, how to appreciate and to create a world of fiction—a lesson the poets of the Middle Ages were to learn and follow.

2. From Rome to France: Under the Sign of Ovid

The previous chapter of this study used Ovid's *Ars amatoria* and *Remedia amoris* to establish a model of reading love poetry, a model I will apply to two French texts, Andreas Capellanus's *De amore* and Jean de Meun's continuation of *Le Roman de la Rose*. We will see that, in a context very different from Ovid's, these two treatises teach very much the same lessons on the relationship between literary love and the creation of fiction. Before studying the medieval texts, however, we need to investigate the literary culture into which they were inscribed. This culture—which was largely ecclesiastical—valued sacred writing but was deeply rooted in classical, pagan literature; it extolled the love of the divine, but could not rid itself of a fascination with a worldly love (often described as "courtly") that had little to do with marriage, let alone with God. Ovid's amatory texts, which were almost universally read, were directly implicated in these controversies, and were sometimes at their very center. This intermediary chapter, then, will first provide a survey of the place of secular fiction in medieval literary culture and then, as the most pertinent case in point, study the literary history and reception of Ovid's amatory texts (particularly the *Ars* and *Remedia*) in the Middle Ages.

Medieval Literary Culture and the Place of Secular Fiction

The literary culture of the Middle Ages derived largely from two separate worlds: that of classical Greece and (primarily) Rome, and that of early Christianity, with its Jewish roots. Though both of these traditions had religious, literary, and philosophical strains that were often complementary, secular fiction was one subject over which they were inevitably in conflict. The literature of the Jewish and early Christian traditions was exclusively sacred and had long displayed a tendency to be canonical and authoritarian. Ovid's amatory works, on the other hand, were thoroughly secular. They were composed by an author who, at least in the classical period, late Antiquity, and early Middle Ages, did not have a particularly high moral standing (though, as we will see, he was popularly read); and they were expressly concerned with erotic love—a topic that became further and further removed from the lives of ecclesiastics (the Middle Ages' primary readers and writers) as the centuries passed[1]—as well as with problems of fiction and literary creation.

The status of the amatory texts in medieval culture, then, is a particularly useful index of the way in which sacred and secular, Christian and classical literatures were interacting—a *cas-limite* for medieval tolerance. Generally speaking, the amatory texts became increasingly popular in the Middle Ages, reaching their peak in the twelfth and thirteenth centuries (with an earlier crest during the Carolingian revival); but at almost all times they were also a battleground for two opposed schools of reading. One, the orthodox Christian school, scarcely accepted secular literature at all. When it did, it valued secular texts only for the moral truths they were seen as "containing"; their artistic elements were seen either as a worthless husk or as a seductive distraction from the work's moral core. The second school, on the other hand, validated the play of fiction as a literary fantasy within a poetic frame which, by its nature, excluded the moral concerns of everyday Christian life. Ovid's texts offered these writers an exceptionally important model for understanding how they could create fictions of their own.[2] Neither school was ever completely dominant, and individuals most often took positions between the two extremes, even when their religious or poetic ideologies pulled them more toward one or the other.

Let us examine the ways in which these two opposing tendencies influenced the development of medieval European literary culture. During the first few centuries A.D., Latin literature was scarcely an issue for Christianity, which was only a marginal part of Roman society; but when, in the fourth century, the Roman Empire first tolerated and then embraced the new religion, Christians were forced to confront the potential conflicts between their religion and the pagan culture in which it had been implanted. At issue specifically were the Latin language and its literature. Since Latin was the medium of culture and religion, anyone who received an education (i.e., anyone who was to take any part in the ecclesiastical hierarchy) had to be Latin-literate. This meant, in practice, receiving an education which was built on the works of the "classical" (because used in classes[3]) pagan authors, or *auctores*. In an effort to maintain a distance from the surrounding culture, Christians began to create their own schools as early as the fourth century,[4] but even these, due to the need to train students in the Latin language, were obliged to include secular literature in the curriculum.[5] And once Christianity became the official religion of the Roman Empire, it assimilated much of Rome's culture and language, along with its models of literary style—the poets and writers revered by Roman tradition. From this point on, the church was committed to a system of education that held the pagan poets up not only to be admired but also to be imitated.[6]

The conflict between the secular, classical tradition and the spiritual and exclusive Judeo-Christian tradition marked the whole of the Middle Ages' intellectual development. It is best and most familiarly illustrated in the thought of two of the most important Christian figures of the fourth century, Jerome (ca. 340–420) and Augustine (354–430).[7] These men were raised in the culture of the Roman Empire; "foreign" to them was not classical rhetoric but the simpler style of the Jewish and Christian scriptures, which they saw as ugly and uncultivated. Jerome, who frequently cited the pagan writers, felt tremendous guilt about his attraction to Roman literature,[8] but he could not abandon it. He thus ordained that secular texts could be used by Christians, provided that these texts were purified of their worldly affiliations.[9] Of particular interest to us here is the fact that he deemed love poetry acceptable reading matter for schoolchildren[10] but declared it sinful for their elders.[11] Augustine similarly tolerated pagan texts, as long as their readers sought in them truths that would lead back to those of the Gospels.[12] These compromises were based on a fundamental need—that of teaching Latin—and on three principles of accommodation: the idea of purifying the pagan writers, that of discarding the pleasurable aspects of their texts in order to concentrate on the moral truths that they were believed to "contain," and that of seeing the pagans as proto- or crypto-Christians. These principles constitute the orthodox model of medieval reading.

Strict Christian readers found numerous stumbling blocks in many classical texts. One was the absence of Christian references in these works; another was the presence of pagan gods and models of behavior, such as extramarital love, that directly contradicted Christian beliefs. And another, of great importance for our present subject, was their use of literary fiction. Fiction, of course, had a problematic heritage among the more stringently moralistic classical writers, since it was, by definition, distinguished from truthful narrative. Cicero's *De inuentione* and the pseudo-Ciceronian *Rhetorica ad Herennium* (texts that were fundamental to the medieval study of rhetoric) made this distinction plainly: *fabulae*[13] were false, *historiae*[14] were true. Christians, adopting this distinction, would put the Bible into the category of *historia*;[15] as a consequence, the status of any text not deemed to be part of this group was highly problematic. Some Christians, indeed, saw poetic *fabulae* as an audacious human challenge to the work of the divine Creator.

Despite these condemnations, however, other classical and late Antique critics saw a wider range of possibilities in fiction—a range that parallels the more liberal positions of later medieval readers and writers. Petronius (second half of the first century A.D.), for example, noted that while historians were limited by strict constraints on their writing, poets could tell their stories more freely, through myth and *ambages* (ambiguous indiscretion, another term for fiction).[16] For Servius (fourth century), *fabula* was a wide-ranging term with both positive and negative implications. As Paule Demats explains, it was

> a receptacle of ancient, disparate acceptances: artifice of the poet, from which philosophy is not completely excluded; ageless rumor born from the meeting of an event and a mistaken explanation of it; a lie linked on every side to a truth to which it is opposed, no one knowing which is the origin of which; scholarly knowledge indispensable to the understanding of texts and inseparable from other sciences; history, physics, and philosophy, it can be used for any purpose, and particularly for those undertaken by the grammarian or the medieval mythographer.[17]

Such a complex concept could not be entirely without value. And so while Macrobius (fl. ca. 400) claimed that *fabulae* were lies, both he and Martianus Capella (early fifth century) often used fables by reading them as allegories, because in this way they could discuss the latent truth behind pagan stories.[18] Gregory (540–604) took the positive view even further. He believed that creating fiction could be a valuable activity in itself.[19] That fiction was not based on truth was clear; whether it was desirable depended on the view one took of human creative activity.

As I noted above, those medieval writers who valued fiction saw it as a kind of play. One of the most notable of these was an eleventh-century writer and a close imitator of Ovid: Baudri of Bourgueil (1046–1130; abbot of Bourgueil from 1089, archbishop of Dol from 1107).[20] Though Baudri was not a major poet, his writings, in Gerald Bond's words, "deserve careful critical attention, for they bear witness to the important constructs of the collective imagination of his regional textual community"[21]— a community that foreshadowed the literary culture of the twelfth and

thirteenth centuries in which Ovid was to become so popular and so influential. Baudri discusses the question of imaginative writing in his fictive
epistles between "Ovid" and the poet "Florus," an exchange that is often
read as Baudri's apologia for his own writing. In this exchange, the two
writers discuss the moral relationship between life and art. "Florus" argues
that "Ovid"'s expertise on love is not evil, since it is merely an observation
of how people behave, and since love itself, as Bond paraphrases, is "an
integral part of nature (and human nature) directly attributable to God."
Baudri's "Ovid" more circumspectly claims (echoing Ovid's *Tristia* and
Martial's epigrams) that while his writings were impure, they did not reflect his life: "Garrula lingua michi moresque fuere pudici" (98.61) (My
tongue was loose, but my behavior was modest).[22] Such a defense may not
seem particularly courageous today, but it had important implications in
the world of medieval writing. By separating poetry and life, Baudri was
able to develop an idea of literature as fictional play. "Crede michi: non
uera loquor—magis omnia fingo," he pleads (85.39) (Believe me: I do not
tell the truth; it's all fiction); his use of the term *fingere* both excuses and
justifies his poetic creations. While Baudri did not directly challenge those
who believed that creating was the privilege of the Creator alone, he did,
by describing his amatory fiction in terms such as *iocus* and *ludere*, begin
to re-create these concepts in medieval Europe and thus helped to open
the way for a secular literature of love.

Attitudes toward fiction in the twelfth and thirteenth centuries varied. William of Conches (1090–1160) and Peter Abelard (1079–1142) believed that fables could embody truth, and that the human craftsman could
be analogous to the creator.[23] The more reactionary Conrad of Hirsau
(ca. 1070–ca. 1150), however, writing on Aesop, told his students that
poets were mostly liars: "poeta fictor uel formator dicitur eo, quod uel pro
ueris falsa dicat uel falsis interdum uera commisceat" (a poet is called a
writer of fiction or a fashioner, either because he says false things instead
of true ones or because he occasionally mixes truth with falsehood).[24] Even
Conrad, however, admitted that there were things very like fables in holy
scripture, and acknowledged that even impossible fables might serve a
good purpose.[25] This fact shows that medieval readers and writers, if they
chose, could see literary fictions as meaningful simply for their stories. In
certain ways, this approach showed humility, since it removed secular literature from the sphere of competition with sacred texts; but reading for
the literal sense alone was also a subtly audacious approach, since it pre-
supposed the idea that literature without moral meaning had the right

to exist and could in fact legitimately be read and written. If the pagan texts were, in fact, morally empty, and if Ovid, for his medieval French readers, personified this quality (Roger Dragonetti has referred to him as "O-vide,"[26]), then literature without a spiritual sense could and did exist. John of Garland (ca. 1195–ca. 1272), indeed, felt that the value of pagan fiction was to be found in its literal sense, and not in any supposed spiritual meaning.[27]

Others, however, held to the more conservative position that secular literature was to be valued only for its moral *sententia*, and not for its literal meaning. One example of this school was the thirteenth-century author of the *Ovide moralisé*, who explained his position as follows:

> [et] qui la fable ensi creroit
> estre voire, il meserreroit,
> et seroit bogrerie aperte.
> mes sous la fable gist couverte
> la sentence plus profitable.[28]

(And whoever would believe the fable to be true would go astray: it would be blatant heresy [or perversion]. But underneath the fable, the most useful meaning lies covered.)

Boccaccio, too, in expounding his own literary theory in the *Genealogie deorum gentilium* (*The Genealogies of the Pagan Gods*), held to the orthodox position that *fabula* was valuable only for its moral meaning.[29]

Despite these relatively conservative critical statements, however, twelfth- and thirteenth-century poets developed the art of fiction, to which the blossoming of the vernaculars was intimately connected. Troubadour and trouvère lyrics, for example, with their deep reliance on literary conventions and their use of *senhals* (character pseudonyms), maintained only an ambiguous tie to the lives of their composers, while courtly romance—particularly Arthurian romance—was clearly set apart from reality, as Jehan Bodel explained in his famous tripartite division of poetic subjects:

> Ne sont que trois materes a nul home entendant:
> De France et de Bretaigne et de Rome la Grant;
> Et de ce trois materes n'i a nule semblant.
> Li conte de Bretaigne sont si vain et plaisant.

Cil de Rome sont sage et de sens aprendant.
Cil de France sont voir chascun jour aparant.[30]

(There are only three literary subjects for any man of understanding:
France, Brittany, and Rome the Great; and these three subjects are not at
all alike. The tales of Brittany [that is, Arthurian literature] are empty
and fun. Those of Rome [the cycle of classical epics] are wise and instructive. Those of France [the cycle of epics about the founding of France]
are true, as is evident each day.)

The word "vain" in Bodel's categorization of the "conte de Bretaigne"
leads us to a further stage of debate about the hidden meanings of medieval fiction, often discussed in terms of allegory and *integumentum* (covering). Some writers, as we have seen, accepted the "emptiness" of fiction
as a positive quality; most often, however, fiction was read for what it was
thought to "contain."[31] When commentators considered a work inherently factual, they would read it as an allegory;[32] those, on the other hand,
who considered a text an *integumentum* (a covering) or an *involucrum* (a
wrapping) read it as a fiction that had been used simply as a vehicle for the
underlying moral truth.[33] Both of these tools, however, made fiction acceptable not for any pleasure one might find in reading it, but only for the
moral lessons the text could yield.[34]

The final element in this debate is the *accessus*, a sort of standardized
introduction to classical texts that accompanied them in many manuscripts. The *accessus*, as their name suggests, made classical texts approach-
able to interpretation, and, by and large, they are distinguished from
allegorical and other sophisticated kinds of criticism by their literalness.
As a rule, the *accessus* provided information about the *circumstantiae* of the
text: the author's biography, the work's title, the writer's intention, the
subject matter of the work, its utility, and its philosophical classification.[35]
Though they seemed to require their readers to interpret classical literature
in certain normative contexts, however, the *accessus* did not always seek to
set out a single path toward meaning: often, instead, they offered medieval
readers a variety of approaches to the texts they introduced.[36] This variety
gave readers a freedom that many other approaches denied them. We will
see its importance when we study the medieval reception of Ovid in the
later portions of this chapter.

None of these positions—the "moral" principles of the orthodox
school, the "creative" position of more play-oriented writers, nor the

literal, biographical approach often taken by the *accessus*—overcame the others: rather, they played off one another throughout the Middle Ages. Later on we will see how, in this highly debated field, certain writers composed texts that espoused Christian values to some degree but also encouraged the free play of amatory and erotic fantasy, and left the ultimate responsibility for determining the text's meaning and moral value up to their various readers. The relationship of *auctor* to readers and their interpretations—past to present, single to multiple, fixed to variable—made the literary text not a container for a particular meaning, but rather a basis for diverse, potential interpretations: the "text as possibility," as Hennig Brinkmann has put it.[37] And at least at times, it seems, readers wanted texts that did not require any moral interpretation at all.

While Christian points of view on medieval literature have been well documented, critics have less often recognized the place filled by morally "empty" texts, works that were simply entertaining. Secular works may not always have been smiled upon by the authorities, but they were nevertheless quite popular. Then as now, love was usually an element in these texts, often the most important one; and then as now, these texts did not necessarily document the experiences of their readers. Rather, they served as fantasy and as entertainment—in other words, as literary play. Other purposes, educative or moral, were subordinate to enjoyment.

This separation is the feature that makes any recreative activity most valuable, as Johann Huizinga demonstrates in his book on play, *Homo ludens*.[38] Separation, notes Huizinga, is established by setting limits and defining rules according to which the play will proceed, thus emphasizing the artificiality of the game and its distinctness from life outside the bounds. Sigmund Freud also remarks that the writer's relationship with fiction is characterized by a sharp separation from reality.[39] In literature, these boundary markers may take various shapes: vocabulary, imagery, and meter that signal language as poetic; subject matter that incorporates elements of fantasy; and literary conventions, which, as we have seen, indicate the text's place within an established genre. All of these traits mark the literary text as such. Their function reveals, as Huizinga observes, that *poiesis*, like love itself, is a play-function.[40] The rôle of texts on secular love in medieval ecclesiastical literary circles can be seen in these terms: not immoral but rather amoral, they were designated as a special activity by their poetic nature, and set apart from religious life by their subject matter. These texts were thus ideal recreation.

And though medieval theorists of various kinds did not always give

their blessing to secular literature as such, they were not necessarily opposed to the concept of play in general.[41] Aquinas himself wrote,

> The activity of playing looked at specifically in itself is not ordained to a
> further end, yet the pleasure we take therein serves as recreation and rest to
> the soul (ad aliquam animae recreationem et quietem), and accordingly when
> this be well-tempered, application to play is lawful.[42]

And as Glending Olson convincingly demonstrates in his book *Literature
as Recreation in the Later Middle Ages*, medieval medical theory generally
promoted the concept of play as being beneficial to physical and mental
states of well-being.[43]

It may well have been this place—that of diversion—that Ovid's love
poetry could occupy for and offer to medieval writers who were in search
of ways of creating fiction. Baudri of Bourgueil and his circle were among
the early Ovidian imitators who pioneered the concept of literary fiction
in the European Middle Ages. When, in the twelfth century, court life
(what C. Stephen Jaeger calls "literature operating in the medium of reality") developed in Europe, this new culture offered a much wider place
for secular literature, and people rushed to fill it.[44] This literature was immensely popular precisely because, as fiction, it found its meaning outside
of meaning. Just as Baudri used Ovid's term *ludere* to designate the composition of love poetry, and as Paul Zumthor, Laura Kendrick, and others
have seen in the poetry of the troubadours and trouvères a verbal game in
which love and playful writing are almost interchangeable terms, so other
medieval texts of love fiction are also a form of play.[45] By defining itself as
a world apart, an enclosed garden in which fantasy could grow, amatory
fiction was gradually able to establish itself outside the restrictive norms
of Christian morality.[46] Much of this success was due to the preeminent
classical model of amatory fiction in the Middle Ages, Ovid's *Ars*, and it is
to the history of this model that we now turn.

Ovid in the Literary Culture of the Middle Ages

The information we have about Ovid's place in medieval literary culture
comes from several types of sources: citations in the works of other writers, extant manuscripts that can be dated to a particular period, and the
catalogues of medieval libraries, which show the presence of manuscripts
at a particular place and time, even if these texts have since moved or

disappeared. (Detailed summaries of this information, and further references, can be found in the Appendix, "Medieval Reception and Transmission of Ovid's Amatory Works.") As we have noted, Ovid's popularity climbed considerably over the course of the Middle Ages, reaching its height in the twelfth and thirteenth centuries, a period commonly known as the "*aetas ovidiana*"[47] (the Ovidian Age) of European literature, when, as Frederick Adam Wright has noted, "Virgil and Horace were regarded with admiration, [but] Ovid alone was really read."[48]

Information about Ovid's readership during the early centuries A.D. is spotty. The poet's perceived affronts against Augustus—his *carmen* (the *Ars amatoria*) and a mysterious *error*[49]—caused him to be relegated to the Black Sea and his works to be banned from the public libraries.[50] Yet Ovid's works had some popularity among the learned and the general public alike: not only was he quoted by major first-century writers, but citations from the *Amores*, the *Heroides*, and the *Ars* have also been found among the graffiti at Pompeii[51]—an indication that these writings, accessible in style and appealing in subject matter, were widely read and may already have been taught in schools.

After the second and third centuries, we find a consistent increase in references to Ovid, and, eventually, an increase also in the presence of manuscripts. The *carmina amatoria* were cited often in the fourth through seventh centuries in Africa and in Spain, regions in which the traditions of Roman education continued for a long time; they were also commonly cited by the writers of the Bodensee (Lake Constance) area during this period. In addition, they were mentioned, and loosely imitated, by writers in Gaul in the sixth, seventh, and eighth centuries, who may have become familiar with these and other classical texts through contact with the erudite monastic culture of Ireland and the British Isles.[52] During this period, however, first-hand knowledge of the classics was generally sparse, and Ovid's name and poetry may have been known primarily through citations in florilegia rather than through the study of complete texts.[53] By the end of the eighth century, Ovid was clearly becoming better known than he had been in the early period. References to and imitations of his works are found in the writings of the major literary figures of the Carolingian Renaissance; among them, in particular, Modoin (bishop of Autun in 815) was called the "Naso" of Charlemagne's court.[54] Ovidian material is also found in the ninth-century *Carmina Sangallensia*[55] and, later, in the tenth-century *Cambridge Songs*.[56]

During the eleventh century the classical authors—Ovid chief among them—became rapidly more popular. This era saw the rise of the cathedral schools and the broadening of literate culture, which brought the classical authors into wider circulation. The *auctores* were an essential part of the school curriculum, of which manuscript production was a major part.[57] Amidst this resurgence of interest in the *auctores*, new hierarchies emerged. F. J. E. Raby suggests that the changing literary tastes of the eleventh and twelfth centuries were symptomatic of the times' increasing interest in the secular world, a world more fully represented in Ovid's poetry than in that of the more sober writers.[58] Thus in 1086 Aimeric of Angoulême's grammatical treatise, the *Ars lectoria*, placed Sallust, Vergil, and Ovid, the *aureum genus* (the golden race), in the first rank; Boethius, Cicero, Donatus, and Priscian were demoted to the second rank, the *argentum genus* (the silver race).[59] Gradually Vergil too slipped behind, while Ovid's popularity grew: eleventh-century German library catalogues list an increasing number of manuscripts of Ovid's poems, including the amatory works (see Appendix). As the century continued, it was in France (where vernacular literature began to blossom early) that the amatory poems were most widely imitated. French libraries contained numerous copies of these texts, and the most important poets of the day used Ovidian themes, meter, and genres.[60]

The eleventh century witnessed not only a growth of interest in Ovid, "the unchallenged master and instructor in love,"[61] but also an increasing concern about women, sex, and marriage, particularly in connection with members of the clergy; one may well imagine that Ovid's writings may have seemed highly topical in this context of changing attitudes. It was during this period that clerical celibacy was affirmed as the norm;[62] the nature of relationships between the sexes was changing as well. Marriage, formerly an association of equals, became a state in which men dominated women, and as they exercised more control over their wives and the process of reproduction, they began to fear those whom they oppressed.[63] And even when women were not feared, considered a source of corruption, or reviled for witchcraft, they were excluded from rôles of power in eleventh-century culture.[64] This fear of and revulsion toward women would grow stronger in the following centuries,[65] a fact readily noted in the fierce misogyny voiced in both the *De amore* and in the second *Roman de la Rose*.

Extramarital sex, a key element in Ovid's amatory works, was another issue that became a major preoccupation of this period—particularly in its texts. Outside of marriage, men's sexual liberties were often lightly treated,

but adultery, which troubled the dynastic concerns of genealogy and in-
heritance, was the object of heavy penalties in the written codes.[66] The
relationship between law, social practice, and literature in this area, however, is unclear. John Benton has noted that it is difficult to know how
often the penalties in the legal codes were actually imposed,[67] and medieval
literature, like Ovid's amatory works, often treats adultery with complacency, or even approbation. We cannot assume that courtly literature, in
this or in other details, is an accurate depiction of medieval life, nor can
we assume, as some scholars have done, that "courtly love" is a modern
invention that has no basis at all in medieval texts.[68] Rather, this disparity
may be good evidence that medieval literature about love, rather than re-
flecting social practice, provided a realm in which ideas and desires that
could not be actualized in life could be played out in fantasy. Amatory
fiction, which Ovid developed so effectively in the *Amores* and the *Ars*,
seems to have been an important basis for much medieval writing about
erotic love, particularly by clerical writers such as Baudri of Bourgueil,
Andreas Capellanus, and Jean de Meun.

In fact, many of the major writers of the eleventh century in France
were, as Raby states, "men who knew their Ovid as well as their Bible by
heart."[69] These included Hildebert of Lavardin (1056–1123), Godefroy of
Reims (d. ca. 1095), Guy (Bishop of Amiens from 1058 to 1076), and Raoul
de la Tourte (b. ca. 1063), as well as Marbod of Rennes (1035–1123), who
revived the poetic letter and adopted, perhaps for the first time in Europe,
the fictive first person so important in Ovid's amatory works.[70] But of all
the poets of the Loire school, the one whose work is closest to Ovid's own
and is most indicative of the tone and subjects of the two texts we will be
studying is Baudri of Bourgueil. I have already discussed Baudri's treatment of fiction; we will now pause briefly to examine how he dealt with
with another central Ovidian focus—the relationship between love and
literature. Leo Pollmann describes Baudri as "the first poet of the Christian
West who took the positive step of setting profane love in the path of
Christian literature,"[71] and the balance between the secular and the sacred
is one of the most noteworthy, if at times one of the most ambiguous,
aspects of his writing.[72]

Baudri closely connects fiction with love. At times, for example, he
uses the term *spetialis amor* to mean a special kind of love that finds its
chaste fulfilment (see also 200.79) in literary exchange rather than in physical consummation,[73] an idea related to the concept of love Ovid wrote
about in the *Amores* and the *Ars* (of which Baudri seems even to have had

his own manuscript copy).[74] In Baudri's poetry, then, as in Ovid's amatory works, reading, writing, and being in love are activities so closely related that they are sometimes indistinguishable. In his poetic epistles, for example, Baudri interchanges the terms for these activities, and the language of passion often modulates into the language of literature.[75] Writing, like loving, is a mutual, reciprocal activity in this poetic world; it is also one in which the body, the imagination, and the page blend into one another.

Reading, too, is an interactive process in Baudri's poetry that resembles the act of love (compare 153.24).[76] Even more importantly, we see that Baudri invites each individual reader to find his or her own meaning in the text, an Ovidian gesture we will see repeated and developed in the *De amore* and the *Roman de la Rose*. Thus at the end of poem 144, he asks his readers to add their own meaning to the written word: "Quicunque hos uersus legitis, imperfectum meum uideant oculi uestri et uos imperfecti mei supplementum estote" (Whoever you are who read these lines, may your eyes see my imperfection and be yourselves its fulfilment).[77] Baudri's poetic epistles—modeled after the *Heroides* and possibly after the *Amores*, which were often read as letters in the Middle Ages—show clearly that the relationship between reader and writer is not unidirectional but reciprocal, and that both are responsible for the process of finding, even making, the meaning of the text.

Baudri's poetry, then, re-creates certain important aspects of Ovid's writing: the concept that love poetry is play,[78] or fiction, rather than reality; the close relationship between loving, reading, and writing; the concept of the fictional voice;[79] and the importance of the reader's involvement in finding the meaning of the literary text. This technique and other devices found in Ovid's poetry conferred on medieval letters the freedom to live within their own fictive domain, to create and reflect on themselves, and to find material and ideas in the classical tradition that would permit them to develop new strengths and liberties as they moved forward in time.

If Baudri was a relatively unusual figure in the eleventh century, his interest in love and fiction became more common in the increasingly sophisticated and cosmopolitan twelfth century. This new era saw the development of intellectual, social, and economic life in Europe, the importation by the Arabs of exotic merchandise and previously unavailable scientific and philosophical texts, and the movement of culture from the rural abbeys to the wider audience of courts and urban cathedral schools. It witnessed revivals in all areas of learning—law, theology, philosophy, mathematics,

astronomy, art, architecture, commerce, and letters; as Charles Homer
Haskins notes, one-fourth of the works in Migne's *Patrologia latina* were
written during the twelfth century.[80] In both the religious and secular
domains (in many ways two aspects of a single culture), intellectuals concentrated much of their attention on a single subject—love.[81] Here Ovid
was the primary classical authority, and one whom virtually everyone with
an education knew extremely well. Ovid's key position in the literature of
the age was due in large part to the deep roots of the twelfth-century
Renaissance, which derived its nourishment both from a direct interest in
the classical world, and from the heritage of the restoration of Roman
letters for which Charlemagne had been responsible.[82] And the literary and
ethical concept of courtliness, so much a part of twelfth-century culture,
has been traced back to the study of the classics in German cathedral
schools. "We misunderstand the nature and intellectual origins of medieval
courtesy," writes Jaeger, "if we fail to see it as a survival or revival of ideals
from classical antiquity."[83] Courtliness and a new Latin literature developed together through classical education, and the vernacular literatures
began their era of great growth at this stage.[84]

The popularity of love as a subject of sacred literature was probably
also connected with the increasing exchange between the cloister and the
secular world at this time. As Jean Leclerq has shown, monastic popu-
lations changed in the twelfth century in important ways. While the older
orders were populated largely by oblates (religious who had been offered
to the monasteries as children and had been raised and educated in the
cloister), the newer orders recruited their membership from the adult
population. Many of these recruited monks and nuns (*conversi*) had been
married; all had belonged to secular society; some were even troubadours
and trouvères.[85] The popularity of Ovid, the worldly experience of these
religious, and the church's belief that secular love was purely and simply
sexual produced a literature of the cloister that was by no means strictly
spiritual; indeed, Leo Pollmann suggests that obscene texts may have been
acceptable precisely because they reinforced commonly held ideas about
the nature of secular love.[86] Some famous parodies placed Ovid among the
dignitaries of the church; even a Pope Ovid is humorously described.[87]

All this is not to say that the cloister had been completely taken over
by an interest in secular literature and profane love. The *Song of Songs* was
tremendously influential; the works on love of Bernard of Clairvaux
(1090–1153) still exist in a remarkable 111 manuscripts;[88] and Aelred of Rievaulx (1109/1110–1167; his *De amicitia spirituali* [On Spiritual Friendship]

would be translated into French by Jean de Meun), Richard of St. Victor (d. 1173), and Gérard of Liége (mid-thirteenth century) all worked hard to elaborate Christian concepts of love and friendship.[89] But even this trend displayed a preeminent concern with love and perhaps constituted an attempt to offer a Christian alternative to Ovid's increasingly prevalent influence. Whether copied, imitated, or opposed, Ovid was an essential part of twelfth-century literary consciousness.

Closely tied with these cultural developments were changes in the study of the *auctores*. Their rôle in the twelfth century is not a simple one, for while they attained their greatest popularity at this time, they were beginning to lose their status in intellectual circles, a change that foreshadowed their coming decline. In general, the pagan authors were recognized and valued during the twelfth century. John of Salisbury, bishop of Chartres (ca. 1115–80), wrote in his *Policraticus* that the classical writers' wisdom was indispensable for culture, the liberal arts, and moral conduct, and Alain de Lille (1115/28–1203) even approved the use of classical citations in preaching.[90] But the critical spirit of the times was beginning to weaken the reverence the classical writers had formerly received. John of Salisbury complained that his students preferred to draw knowledge from themselves rather than recognizing the ancients;[91] Alain de Lille flippantly noted that *auctoritas* "has a nose of wax, which can be bent in various directions";[92] and Abelard even compiled in his *Sic et non* the contradictory sayings of the church fathers in order to stimulate his readers to develop their critical sense.[93]

Perhaps because they fit in with the skeptical spirit of the times, Ovid's amatory works permeated the literary culture of the twelfth century, as evidence from manuscripts, libraries, and adaptations makes clear. The literate classes became familiar with Ovid early in life: he was read in the schools with little hesitation on the part of teachers,[94] though often his texts were presented in excerpted form.[95] Florilegia used for private study and instruction show unusually high numbers of Ovidian citations during the ninth century (after the Carolingian revival) and in the twelfth and thirteenth centuries, with the amatory works (particularly the *Remedia*) furnishing a substantial proportion of the citations offered for classroom use.[96] Large numbers of the extant manuscripts of the amatory poems date from this period; the library catalogues also witness the popularity of Ovid's works. In addition, various non-Ovidian texts began to gravitate toward the poet's name, a sign of his growing prestige.[97] Ovidian material also formed part of a more popular culture, as witnessed by the

Carmina burana,[98] and two stories based on Ovid's amatory works, the *Pamphilus* and the *Geta*, survive in sixty and sixty-seven manuscript copies, respectively[99]—as opposed to a mere six copies of the *Chevalier de la Charrette* of Chrétien de Troyes, who himself translated into French (in versions that have, unfortunately, been lost) the *Ars* and the *Remedia*.[100] The *Ars* and *Remedia* were adapted into other medieval versions, Latin and vernacular, in a tradition that began in the twelfth century and blossomed in the thirteenth.[101] This broad trend shows clearly how popular the *carmina amatoria* were, not only for educating the young, but also for the perusal of more advanced students and scholars.

One of the better-known, if odder, developments in the twelfth-century reception of Ovid was his transformation into a moral authority. As Franco Munari recounts,

> Humanists like Hildebert de Lavardin and John of Salisbury, mystics like Hugh of St. Victor and Bernard of Clairvaux, scholastics like Alain de Lille and Roger Bacon and many others referred to him as a leading authority on problems of morality and other related issues of great seriousness.[102]

Even Ovid's critics were more ambivalent about his works than unremittingly opposed to them. Abelard condemned lying and immoral poets, but he recognized that literary writers could be inspired in the same way as philosophers, and both the *Heroides* and the *Ars* are cited in his correspondence with Heloise.[103] William of St. Thierry (ca. 1085–1148) condemned Ovid in his treatise *De natura et dignitate amoris* (On the Nature and Dignity of Love), but made excuses for the poet as well: in the section entitled "About False Love and the Doctors Who Teach It," he claimed that Ovid's contemporaries forced him to write the *Remedia amoris* as a recantation, but asserted that the poet "surely did not intend to do evil."[104] Even Conrad of Hirsau, the "sworn enemy of Ovid,"[105] while condemning secular learning (including the *Metamorphoses* and the amatory poems) in harsh terms, advised tolerance for the *Fasti*, the *Pontics*, and the *Nux*.[106] The work of Ovid and the other secular authors was considered to have merit if it was oriented toward good; the profitable part of it, moralists believed, could be used to educate the young and even to adorn the style and souls of Christian writers.[107] And while Alexander Neckam (1157–1217) warned the young against the dangers of the other *carmina amatoria*, he recommended the *Remedia amoris* as salutary.[108] Typically, Ovid's amatory works were seen as representing models of "good love" and "bad love," as one introduction to the *Heroides* defended the poet, "quia bonorum morum est instructor, malorum uero exstirpator" (because he is a teacher of good morals and an uprooter of bad ones).[109] This kind of explanation was easily reconciled with Christian concerns, since it put morality first, but it left that morality to the conscience of the individual reader.

A similar freedom of interpretation was provided by at least some of the *accessus* to Ovid's works. The biographies these introduction contained (like the *vidas* of the troubadours) were often somewhat fanciful and tended to be based on the assumption that a poet's life could be read directly from his or her works.[110] The *accessus* to the *Amores*, for example, thus suggest that Ovid was describing his own love affairs in them, though one of them astutely notes that "he called *each* of his girlfriends 'Corinna.'"[111] His name was read etymologically to betoken either his philosophical and moral sagacity or his aptitude for love.[112] Various explanations were given for the poet's exile: his literary immorality, his witnessing the emperor sleeping with a male lover, or rumors of an adulterous affair between Ovid and the Empress Livia.[113] Other commentators, however, took the opposite tack, Christianizing him through an invented conversion recorded in a poem called *De vetula* (The Old Woman), a pseudo-Ovidian work ostensibly found on the poet's tomb in Sulmo.[114] And one even more surprising story, found in a manuscript note, explains that Ovid was converted to Christianity by the preaching of Saint John.[115] The literalness of these readings, combined with their variety, suggests that the *accessus* were compiled from a variety of sources, and that the interpretations they proposed were not meant to be definitive. Poetic facts were not carefully separated from historical ones.[116] And when the *intentio* of the *Amores* is discussed, it is often summed up very simply: *delectare* (to please).[117]

Questions of morality do come up at times in the discussion of the *Ars* and the *Remedia*—not surprisingly, given that these texts were often used in medieval schools. Even here, however, the commentators give the poet a good deal of credit. One *accessus* thus categorizes the *Ars* as having a dual purpose: its use for the author was entertainment, and for its readers, the acquisition of a knowledge of love.[118] When the *Ars* is criticized, it is not in the work's own *accessus*, but in the introductions to the *Remedia* and the *Heroides*. In these more moral books, the commentators explain, Ovid attempted to make up for errors he had made or harm he had unintentionally caused. Because his overenthusiastic male readers had practiced the art of love not only with virgins but also with matrons and even with their own female relatives, they suggested, the poet had become extremely unpopular. He therefore wrote the *Remedia*, in penance, to deter illicit love.[119] Even these highly literal moralizing gestures, however, seem unlikely to discourage potential readers from enjoying the poems.

What is most notable about the *accessus*, in fact, is their diversity. Though they frame the text, they do not appear to coerce their readers into holding a single interpretation. An *accessus* to the *Heroides*, for example, offers a good example of interpretive freedom by proposing that the letters were written for one of several purposes: to praise the chaste and condemn the incestuous, or to continue the instruction of the *Ars* by demonstrating techniques of epistolary solicitation, or to exhort virtue and condemn vice, particularly after the poet had been condemned by Caesar.[120] Each new explanation is introduced by *aliter* (alternatively): the writer does not espouse one theory or another, but simply relates all those that have been proposed. These explanations of Ovid's intention in the *Heroides*, like the use of allegory and other techniques of reading that produced multiple meanings and Baudri of Bourgueil's request that his readers complete their texts for themselves, suggest that medieval strategies of reading often provided varying interpretations that depended on the reader's intention, desire, and circumstances.[121] Thus the model I elaborated earlier for the *Ars*, in which readers are made a part of the poetic process, would have been readily comprehensible to twelfth- and thirteenth-century readers and writers.

The twelfth century saw Ovid becoming increasingly popular while the prestige of other *auctores* declined, and in the thirteenth century, these opposing trends intensified. Ovid's works were in many ways central to the literary culture of the new and earthier era.[122] Manuscripts and school versions of the amatory works increased in number; the *Ars* and *Remedia* were adapted and translated into the vernacular;[123] commentaries and interpretations proliferated.[124] The opposition and reluctance shown toward Ovid by twelfth-century authors such as the German Benedictine Conrad of Hirsau largely declined, though some writers, like the English Franciscan Roger Bacon (1214–94), denied any moral value to Ovid's "mad fables."[125] In the *Tesoretto* (compiled in France, 1262–66) of Brunetto Latini (1220–95), Ovid played the guiding rôle that Vergil was to have in the *Divina commedia* of Latini's student, Dante,[126] and, as we will see in Chapter 4, as much as 10 percent of the combined *Roman de la Rose* is composed of citations from or borrowings inspired by the amatory works.[127] Fragments of one thirteenth-century Latin "pseudo-*Ars*" and "pseudo-*Remedia*" remain,[128] and five French versions of the works are

extant, produced by Maistre Elie, Jakes d'Amiens, Guiart, and two anony-
mous authors.[129]

Each of these versions attempted to accommodate the *Ars* to the literary conventions of the day. One of the most striking changes they made
was to eliminate *Ars amatoria* 3—a symptom of the period's growing uneasiness toward women, as noted above.[130] The adapters of the *Ars* were
careful to enclose their material within various frames: a dream in the *Clef*,
fictional dialogues in the works of Jakes d'Amiens and Guiart.[131] And every
medieval version of the *Ars* is accompanied in its manuscript by a version
of the *Remedia*, even in cases in which the two texts were composed by
different authors.[132] No evidence suggests that Andreas Capellanus or Jean
de Meun worked from these translations, but their texts are similar to
them in many essential features: the close focus on Ovid, the misogynistic
anxiety, the literary frame, the adherence to the structure of an opposing
diptych. Andreas and Jean clearly formed a part of this tradition of trans-
lating and adapting the *Ars* and *Remedia*.[133]

But though Ovid's works remained popular in the thirteenth century,
their scholastic authority decreased, largely in response to changes in society and intellectual culture. Courtliness lost some of its hold as an ideal,
at least within the Church,[134] and moral strictures were tightening, often
severely.[135] These phenomena made manifest the century's increasing in-
tolerance and its desire for conformity, both social and intellectual.[136] Ecclesiastical and university authorities grew notably more repressive in the
face of their loss of certainty, for the thirteenth century was a period of
intellectual disruption: Europe was being flooded with greco-arabic philosophy; returning crusaders had been affected by the artistic richness of
Constantinople, which revealed how limited European culture was in certain areas; and the relative stability that had characterized the European
world-view until the twelfth century was being lost.[137] In the face of increasing ecclesiastical resistance, it is not surprising that Ovid's works
should have become less popular. Some new manuscripts were still produced, and the Sorbonne's 1338 catalogue lists almost all the works of Ovid
(though not the *Ars*).[138] But even the *Remedia* were eliminated from the
school handbooks by the fifteenth century, when these collections became
known by a name that explained Ovid's exclusion from them: the "auctores octo morales" (the eight moral authors).[139]

Ovid remained a tremendously important source for the major vernacular poets of the late Middle Ages, such as Boccaccio and Chaucer, but
his texts were being read in new ways. By the fourteenth century, as Alas-

tair Minnis notes, "Scriptural *auctores* were read literally . . . ; pagan *poetae* were read allegorically or 'moralised'—and thus the twain could meet."[140] Such allegorical reading was a new development for Ovid. Vernacular versions of Ovid's text and of other treatises began to be seen as works of hermeneutics,[141] and, in the fourteenth century, two heavily glossed versions of the *Metamorphoses* were produced: Pierre Bersuire's *Liber de reductione fabularum et poetarum enigmatum* (known as the *Ovidius moralizatus*) and the 70,000-verse French *Ovide moralisé*, mentioned above.[142] As these works allegorized, explained, and enclosed the *Metamorphoses* in commentary, they also distanced readers from a direct experience of the text; or perhaps, as Hexter proposes, their immense exegesis was "a sign of the loss of status of the secular text as an authority in its own right, since for the first time in nearly a millennium it required such extraordinary measures to be saved."[143] The unwieldiness of these explicated works showed that old ways of understanding Ovid were losing their appeal. His texts were valued more for their moral and philosophical truths than for the pleasure they offered: the Ovidian Age had come to an end.

Over the millennium from the fourth century to the fourteenth, Ovid's rôle increased from that of a minor figure to that of the most important classical writer the Middle Ages knew. Yet his poetry, while highly attractive as entertainment, had to fight for a place in a system of thought that placed everything under the sun in the domain of the sacred.[144] Readers who adhered to the orthodox, Christian model of interpretation had little use for Ovid, but his popularity and his place in the educational system meant that they could not easily live without him; more humanistic readers, though they enjoyed the ludic freedom Ovid showed them, could not forget that they belonged to the Church and owed allegiance to its morality. To resolve (or avoid) this conflict, some writers, such as Baudri, developed the concept of literary fiction, a realm which explicitly did not exist in the divinely created world, and which, for this very reason, could contain descriptions of events and emotions that could never have found a legitimate place in it. For clerical authors, including Andreas Capellanus and Jean de Meun, the emotional and sexual experience of love was inappropriate, even impossible, but love as a literary fantasy was not. By borrowing the familiar models of Ovid's *Amores*, *Heroides*, and *Ars amatoria*, they were able to find ways to express desire and cultivate fantasy, while the restrictive presence of the *Remedia amoris* conveniently made clear the limits of such imagining. The *Remedia*, in a Christian setting, were thus not an infringement on the erotic fantasy of the *Ars* but were in fact essential to its success. The pairing of these two works made it plain that the love they described was only a fiction; but as a fiction, it was a literary subject medieval writers could readily use.

In conclusion, then, we can see that Ovid's amatory works were central in the medieval literary tradition, providing ways of thinking about love and fiction that were widely influential. Ovid's works were particularly well suited to the medieval literary world in this regard. As we have seen, they were widely available and, at least in excerpted form, almost universally studied. In content, they were more "modern" (that is, less tied to the ideology of a past culture) than, for example, the works of Vergil.[145] And the reflexive literariness of the *Ars amatoria* and the *Remedia amoris* also provided the ideal model of a closed text in which love needed to mean no more than love poetry. It was, of course, still a challenge to Christian ideology, but it was much less a challenge than any other expression of sexual desire would have been. Thus the *Ars* and *Remedia* were profoundly formative in the development of European love poetry in the Middle Ages: as Salvatore Battaglia has written: "Under the sign of Ovid were formed, at the dawn of the modern literatures of western Europe, new poetic aspirations and cultural openings that were absolutely original."[146] This long and complex tradition of literary suppression and tolerance, of sublimation and transformation, of openness and closure, was the Ovidian background for the two works we will next consider: the *De amore* and *Le Roman de la Rose*.

3. The Diligent Reader and the Twofold Text: Andreas Capellanus and the Rhetoric of Love

At the beginning of the *De amore*, Andreas Capellanus wonders aloud whether he should accede to his friend Gualterius's requests to instruct him in the art of love. Andreas obliges: the first two books of his text teach his readers what love is, how it is obtained, and how it is kept.[1] But as all readers of Andreas's peculiar work are well aware, the third book (*De reprobatione amoris*) flatly repudiates love and condemns it as sin. Andreas acknowledges that the two parts of his text offer a *duplex sententia* (a double meaning), speaking both for love and against it; yet, in the face of this double message, Andreas invites his reader to employ his talents toward a *lectio assidua*, a consistent and diligent reading which will presumably reveal that which the text is meant to teach.

The basis of the conflict in the *De amore* is that discussed in the preceding chapter: the split between medieval Christianity and classically-inspired secular love literature. Unlike most medieval texts, whether *accessus* or romance, the *De amore* does not seek to reduce or resolve the dissension posed by these opposing ideologies. Instead, it dramatizes the opposition. Andreas's Christian evangelism is too strident for any reader to see his text as comfortably secular, but his instruction in the art of love is too blatant and too worldly to be successfully covered over by the pious sentiments of the preface and Book 3. Andreas's narrator goes too far in both directions to be a trustworthy spokesman for either cause. In the face of this highly unreliable narration, it becomes the reader's task to develop a strategy that will make the book readable for himself. (I describe in this chapter a male reader. Though there were Latin-literate women in the twelfth century, Andreas's inscribed reader, "Gualterius," is a young man, and the history of the text's reception suggests that its public, for centuries, was essentially male.[2]) I will argue that in the *De amore* Andreas draws on the tradition of Ovid's *Ars* to open up a place for secular fictions of love in the very heart of twelfth-century Christian literature.

A key to the relationship between Andreas and Ovid is the *De amore*'s structural imitation of the *Ars*. The split between the pro-love and anti-love sections of Andreas's work, though it seems motivated by Christian concerns foreign to the *Ars*, is in fact essentially and fundamentally Ovidian. The experience of reading the medieval text, like that of reading the classical one, is a tricky, sometimes dangerous procedure involving illusion, credulity, and contradiction; and like the *Ars*, the *De amore* has proven to be a difficult problem for many readers.[3] But for those who are prepared to have their expectations challenged, the *De amore* is a seductive and exciting game that offers moral and literary lessons in plenty, and a valuable demonstration of how fictions about love could find a place even in the ecclesiastical world of the Latin twelfth century.

Before proceeding to a more detailed discussion of the *De amore* and the reading experience it offers, I will provide a brief summary of the text. The beginning of the treatise is quite ambiguous: while dedicating his instruction in love to Gualterius, Andreas warns him that the advice he gives is something his friend is ill-advised to follow, and offers his teaching not to encourage Gualterius in his pursuits, but to keep him safe from their consequences. The treatise starts with a preface to the young man, warning him against the teaching Andreas is about to convey.

> Cogit me multum assidua tuae dilectionis instantia, Gualteri venerande amice, ut meo tibi debeam famine propalare mearumque manuum scriptis docere qualiter inter amantes illaesus possit amoris status conservari, pariterve qui non amantur quibus modis sibi cordi affixa valeant Veneris iacula declinare. . . . Quamvis igitur non multum videatur expediens huiusmodi rebus insistere, nec deceat quemquam prudentem huiusmodi vacare venatibus, tamen propter affectum quo tibi annector, tuae nullatenus valeo petitioni obstare; quia luce clarius novi quod docto in amoris doctrina cautior tibi erit in amore processus, tuae prout potero curabo postulationi parere.

> (My revered friend Walter,
>   My most sedulous and insistent affection for you compels me to publish for you in my own words and to instruct you by my own hand how the condition of love can be maintained inviolate between lovers, and equally the means by which those whose love is unrequited can shift Venus's shafts lodged in their hearts. . . .
> So though dwelling on such topics seems hardly advisable, and though the man of sense shows impropriety in making time for such hunting as this, the

affection that binds us makes me utterly unable to oppose your request. I shall do my best to obey your demands because I realise more clearly than daylight that your progress in love will be more circumspect if you are learned in its lore.) (*Praefatio* 1, 4)

After this cautionary preface, the following two books are a mixture of Ovidian precepts and medieval allegory, romance, and social comment. Book 1 shows how love is acquired; it is composed mostly of dialogues that ostensibly teach men of various classes how to court women of lower, equal, or higher social status, from the bourgeoisie to the highest nobility. One dialogue includes an allegorical narrative of what happens to the three kinds of women—the judicious, the promiscuous, and the reluctant—in their afterlife, and reveals twelve precepts promulgated by the God of Love.

Book 2 contains helpful hints about maintaining the tender passion, as well as judgments on love pronounced by notable historical women such as Countess Marie of Champagne and Queen Eleanor of Aquitaine. One chapter of Book 2 is a courtly tale in which a British knight discovers a scroll containing the King of Love's rules for loving, which teach, among other useful principles, that "marriage does not constitute a proper excuse for not loving," that "true jealousy makes the feeling of love grow," and that "there is nothing to prevent one woman being loved by two men, or one man by two women" (2.8, rules 1, 21, 31, pp. 282–85). These provocative statements have been part of the reason this work has attracted critical attention, particularly by those who study the phenomenon of courtly love: Andreas appears to promote some of the most extraordinary, contradictory, and even immoral aspects of twelfth-century literary love with neither a hesitation nor a blush. The final book, on the contrary, dramatically reverses this indulgent stance: it consists of a detailed, vitriolic condemnation of love and of women, and a fire-and-brimstone sermon that exhorts Gualterius to abhor sin and prepare himself for the Second Coming of Christ. At the end of this book, Andreas explains that the *De amore* contains two contrary views: it teaches love as an art, but also shows that renouncing love will give the reader all worldly success and glory. Andreas does not explain, however, why he has taken so much time and trouble to instruct his friend in an evil art, nor how the reader is meant to reconcile his erotic desire with a concern for the well-being of his soul.

The two views of love Andreas's treatise contains appear to be squarely opposed to one another. Book 3's sermonizing conclusion pays homage to ascetic Christian views of love, sex, and strict control of meaning and interpretation; it also invokes the authority of medical science and philosophy to force the reader to accept it as absolute truth.[4] But much, if not most, of the *De amore* flouts Christian ideas of sexual morality and draws not only on the ethical disciplines but also on recreational, secular texts for its material.[5] (The courtship dialogues of Book 1 and the judgments on love in Book 2, for example, are elaborations of the rhetorical casuistry found in such poetic genres as the Provençal *tenso* and *partimen*;[6] the King of Love's "Rules for Loving" are presented within the framework of a miniature courtly romance.) One can see—and many have seen—the *De amore* as a partial or total failure because of the contradiction of its two messages. I propose, however, that we read it as a medieval re-creation of Ovid's treatises, and so view the *De amore*'s apparent gap of meaning as a clue to the text's greatest significance.

Like the *Ars* and *Remedia*, in which illusion and disillusionment play off one another, so in the *De amore* Christian and secular views of love conflict, and through this opposition Andreas's readers become able to understand how they can participate in creating fictions about love. By using a context of both sacred and secular texts, Andreas invites his readers to imagine a world in which ecclesiastical morality has a limited domain and in which literature may function as fantasy, provided that it is kept within limits. The whole of Andreas's instruction on love, in fact—Books 1 and 2—is contained within a moral parenthesis ("Although I shouldn't teach you this, nevertheless I will") opened by the preface and never closed until the *Reprobatio*. The art of love is a finite, fictive domain that, if readers are sophisticated enough, they may isolate from the moral strictures of everyday life. Outside its borders Christian views of marriage and celibacy hold sway, but in the imaginary realm of fiction—for those who recognize it—love is possible even for clerics. Like Baudri of Bourgueil, Andreas uses Ovid as a model for creating literary incarnations of love in a context in which such creation was frowned upon, but not impossible.

By seeing the *De amore* as an Ovidian treatise, we can recognize that "Andreas" and "Gualterius," whether or not they had historical identities, function first and foremost as textual constructions, masks, embodiments of rhetorical or poetic situations. "Andreas" defines himself as a character who suffers from hopeless love but who is also a chaplain at the royal court—"Andreas amator aulae regiae capellanus" (1.6.385, p. 152; compare also 2.12, p. 260). This ambiguous description may indicate that Andreas was chaplain to the court of Philippe Auguste, as Alfred Karnein has suggested,[7] or, as Ursula Liebertz-Grün has proposed, it may present

Andreas as a (fictional) servant of the (literary) God of Love; perhaps the description is a pun, meaning both at once.[8] But whatever his historical identity may have been, "Andreas" is clearly a medieval incarnation of the Ovidian *praeceptor amoris*,[9] who teaches love as a poetic art.

Like Andreas, Gualterius is also a character with a function. He is a representative of every reader who wants to learn the art of love.[10] And Andreas's instruction in this art—like Ovid's—doubles as instruction in the skills of reading and interpretation, which, in fact, can easily be viewed as the *De amore*'s principal theme. Andreas frequently advises his pupil to be suspicious of love and of the deceptions of women (1.4.3–4, p. 38; 1.9.16–18, p. 218). Gualterius will learn to interpret women by being trained in his careful reading (*assidua lectio*) of the *De amore* itself (1.9.20, p. 218; see also 2.5.10, p. 236). In Book 2, Andreas further conflates the art of reading and the art of love, telling Gualterius how careful he must be in interpreting the very text that instructs him.

> Multa praeterea tibi possemus de amoris attenuatione narrare, quae tuae sollicitudini penitus derelinquimus indaganda. Nam adeo te videmus negotiis omnibus aliis derelictis amoris exercitio deditum et in amandi proposito confirmatum, quod nil te poterit in amoris arte latere, quia in ea nil indiscussum relinques.

> (There are many other points which I could make to you about the diminution of love, but I leave them entirely to your diligence to seek out. For I see that you have so abandoned all other business, and are so committed to the practice of love, and so firm in your decision to love that none of the techniques of love will be able to escape you; you will leave nothing in the realm of love unexamined.) (2.3.7–8, p. 232)[11]

By speaking to Gualterius in this way—and, through Gualterius, to his other readers—Andreas invites them to make the text their own, to look under the surface in order to find hidden meanings. Repeatedly, Andreas urges his readers to upset his text's balance, to analyze rather than to accept: this is the challenge of the *De amore*.

Andreas also demonstrates the importance of speaking, reading, and interpretation through characters other than the narrator and Gualterius. These are divided into three groups—men, women, and clerics—which are differentiated primarily by their relation to the question of love:[12] lay men are constantly questing for love, but without success;[13] women are manipulators, seductresses, gold-diggers, or prudes; and clerics—Andreas's probable intended audience[14]—read the text and learn its lessons, whatever these may be.

By and large, Andreas's women pose more interesting problems than his laymen, about whom there is little to be said beyond courtly clichés. Men should be eloquent (1.6.171, p. 88), well-to-do, of an appropriate age to love, and, as Ovid also cautions, careful to avoid effeminate excess (1.5–6, pp. 38–46). Unlike corruptible women, men are not harmed by being unfaithful in love (2.6.10–17, pp. 240–42), but since, in this book, their desires are rarely requited, their liberty is of little practical interest. The book's women, on the other hand, are varied and ambiguous. Sometimes they are noble and ennobling; sometimes they are contemptible. Their most important characteristic, in fact, is precisely this lack of consistency, which constantly requires men to interpret, to decode, and to be on guard against them. It is important to note that the *De amore*'s women are not unequivocally bad. They may be teachers (1.6.54–55, p. 54, and 1.6.148, pp. 80–82) or innocents who need advice so they can learn to avoid the snares of male deceit (for example, 2.6.3–9, pp. 238–40—a rare echo of *Ars amatoria* 3). But more often women are a source of trouble for laymen and clerics alike. Women's appearance is deceptive, particularly when it is enhanced by cosmetics (1.6.171, p. 88; 1.9.12, p. 212). A constant temptation, and often a threat, women in the *De amore* represent both the dangers and frustrations of masculine lust. They have virtually no existence outside of male rhetoric, fantasy, and fear.

Andreas's women are, in fact, closely tied to the text's central concerns with rhetoric and interpretation. Book 1 contains many instances in which women are the objects of male persuasion. As usual in the traditions of medieval misogyny, male discourse in the *De amore* is structured so as to coerce women into the rôles men wish them to occupy. These rôles are highly constraining even in the seductive discourse of Book 1, of which we will consider an example in a moment; by the time Andreas adds the misogynistic sermons of Book 3, it is clear that women can never satisfy the demands the narrator imposes on them. Like love, women in the *De amore* are clearly creatures of fantasy who cannot exist beyond the boundaries of the text.

As we have noted, Andreas's first book consists in large part of dialogues between men and women of various social classes. In each case, the man is trying to persuade the woman to accede to his love; in each case, the discussions end inconclusively. Male rhetoric, though it tries hard to control its objects, is only a fantasy, a fiction: despite extraordinary efforts to produce an effect, it remains as ineffectual as the machinations of the Ovidian *praeceptor amoris*.

One of the most memorable demonstrations of the rhetorical struggle between men and women is found in the dialogue of two members of the aristocracy ("Loquitur nobilis nobili," 1.6.196–280, pp. 96–120).[15] The nobleman begins by explaining that he is obsessed with the noblewoman, whose image never leaves his thoughts; the only consolation he receives is another fantasy, the "falsa demonstratio" offered him by sleep (1.6.201, p. 98). His interlocutor grants him the right to contemplate her directly, rather than staring at the empty air. Despite the lover's protestations that he is dying from his passion, however, the woman announces that she has no intention of subjecting herself to the painful servitude of love.

In hopes of persuading her to change her mind, the lover offers an allegory that describes the palace of love and the rewards and punishments it accords to women for their attitudes toward men: the discriminating but cooperative are rewarded, while the promiscuous and the prudish are accursed. The same tripartite classification is developed in greater detail as the man continues his story, recounting an excursion in which he sees a vision of the God of Love and the armies of the dead. Here again women are rewarded or abused according to criteria that are explicitly rhetorical: virtuous women are those who have given appropriate responses to men's requests for love (whether true or feigned: 1.6.243, p. 108), whereas the vicious are those who have refused to respond to men according to their merits. The torments of these unfortunates range from the disagreeable (some women are clothed in wolves' skins, mounted on inferior horses, and forced to breathe the dust kicked up by the armies of men who precede them) to the sadistic (others, their bare feet resting on the burning ground, are seated on bundles of thorns that are constantly readjusted to new and more painful positions). But though the suitor draws out the lesson, and though the lady appears to consider herself appropriately warned, she nevertheless refrains from making any commitment to him, agreeing only to grant her love once she finds a suitable recipient. The man is cheered that the woman he loves is no longer sworn to chastity, but is scarcely any closer to physical satisfaction. All he can hope is that God will permit her to share his fantasy ("ita de me absente divina vos faciat cogitare potentia" [1.6.280, p. 120] [So may God's power make you think of me in my absence]). Men's attempts to dominate women through speech are, in fact, nothing but fantasy and empty words.

If men's rhetoric is ineffectual, women's is often actively deceptive, as Andreas insists again and again (for example, 1.6.319, p. 130).[16] Women never speak truly of love, Andreas explains, with the voice of experience.

For money or gifts, they will say anything to a man (3.66, p. 306; 1.9.12–14, p. 216). And if some women pervert speech, others are entirely immune to it. It is pointless, explains Andreas, to waste fine words on prostitutes and peasant women (to treat them in literary fashion): rather, men should either speak bluntly of love (that is, sex), or simply abandon language and communicate their desires by force (1.6.21, p. 46; 1.9.3–4, p. 222). In every case, Andreas links women closely with abuses of speech and the trust it represents.

> Ad haec mulier omnis non solum naturaliter reperitur avara, sed etiam invida et *aliarum maledica*, rapax, ventris obsequio dedita, inconstans, *in sermone multiplex, inobediens et contra interdicta renitens*, superbiae vitio maculata et *inanis gloriae cupida, mendax*, ebriosa, *virlingosa, nil secretum servans*, nimis luxuriosa, ad omne malum prona et hominem cordis affectione non amans.

> (Again, every woman is by nature not only miserly but also *an envious backbiter of other women*, a grabber, a slave to her belly, fickle, *devious in speech, disobedient, rebellious against prohibitions*, marred with the vice of pride, *eager for vainglory, a liar*, a drunkard, *a tongue-wagger who cannot keep a secret*. She indulges in sexual excess, is inclined to every evil, and loves no man from the heart.) (3.70, p. 308; emphasis added)

This wide-ranging list, which Andreas expands seriatim in the paragraphs that follow it, has two principal themes: the lusts of the female body and the falseness of the female tongue. But while it is easy for Andreas to criticize the female sex as Other, the *assiduus lector* must contemplate the hidden meanings and applications of these accusations. The "female" physical vice of gluttony is, in fact, a sin often attributed to members of the male monastic community,[17] and the vices of deceptive language—oral crimes as well—are the sins which Andreas and every other writer perpetrate upon their readers, as R. Howard Bloch has pointed out.[18] Women's inherent and perverse tendency to misinterpret and refuse male authority is crystallized in a disturbing but compelling fabliau Andreas recounts about a man who, to rid himself of his loathsome and perversely disobedient wife, warned her not to drink a fine wine he said (hoping she would disbelieve and disobey him) he had mixed with poison. She did; he had; she died (3.90–91, p. 314). Andreas's readers face similar problems. If they follow the text's instructions on loving, they will be condemned by its moralizing; if they disregard them, they read without purpose or comprehension. Should one interpret? Should one not? Who is woman, who is writer, who is reader? To become involved with Andreas and his text is as dangerous as to seek out love.[19] Once having embraced the text-as-woman, one can never disentangle oneself from it.

As the *De amore* proceeds, the chaplain's irony entwines itself also around the complicated problem of the clergy's relationships with language, love, and sin. Chapter 7 of Book 1 is entitled "De amore clericorum" (On Clerics' Love), and like every other part of the text it contains a *duplex sententia*. Andreas piously intones and elaborates upon the traditional reasons why churchmen, ennobled by their service to God, should refrain from loving. But Andreas's piety gives way to humor—or hypocrisy. Since hardly any man has lived without sin, the chaplain concedes, and since the leisure and abundance of food in their life make clerics especially susceptible to corruptions of the flesh, those among them who do choose to love may follow the patterns set forth in the dialogues appropriate to men of their social class (1.7.4, p. 210). Thus moral problems are resolved on the level of etiquette. (Lest there be any confusion on this subject, Andreas has already declared that all clerics are by nature members of the highest nobility [1.6.20, p. 46].)

Andreas's gentle teasing of the first estate gradually sharpens into satire as the *De amore* progresses, a development that complicates the narrator's relationship with his readers. The dialogue between the two members of the upper-upper class recalls various similar medieval debates,[20] as the male *nobilior* (a clergyman, of course) argues that clerics are better suited to loving than laymen. His central thesis in this entertaining but morally troubling debate is that a cleric's main duty to God is only verbal. If a clergyman carries out his special responsibility of preaching the faith, Andreas argues, his sins will be judged no more harshly than those of other men: it is a cleric's words, not his deeds, that should serve as an example.[21] Later in the *De amore*, Andreas praises even so cardinal a virtue as monastic chastity less because it is divinely ordained than because it serves as a cloak for other aberrations and offenses:

> "Et si aliquis in se ipso illam [sc. abstinentiam] constat habere, multi per eam in homine excessus operiuntur, et varia quoque crimina tolerantur."

> (And if anyone claims to have abstinence in himself, many of a man's excesses are covered by it, and various crimes are tolerated, as well.) (3.55, p. 302)

Women distort human language and law, but clerics surpass them in hypocrisy by perverting the divine word. And no one can be more justly accused of such twisting than Andreas the Chaplain: his ambiguous irony, once released, works against his readers and himself alike.[22]

It is as difficult for readers to trust Andreas, as narrator, as it is for
them to trust the Ovidian *praeceptor amoris*. At the beginning of the text,
Andreas lets himself be swayed from good judgment by his affection for
Gualterius; in the middle, he readily provides instruction that is clearly
immoral, in terms of Christian teaching; at the end, the chaplain fulminates as dogmatically as any modern revivalist preacher. Obviously, the
reader cannot develop a consistent relationship with this narrator. Andreas's statements about the clergy, as we have seen, suggest that he has
no fundamental code of values; yet, when he wishes to coerce his reader,
he is not at all reluctant to use Christian rhetoric. Even more confusing
than these didactic inconsistencies are the few hints Andreas drops about
his own past. He explains that he has experienced the suffering of hopeless
love (2.6.22, p. 244), a confession that makes the teaching of Books 1 and
2 more persuasive but undermines the moral high ground on which he
stands in Book 3. And if these insights make the narrator seem inconsistent, the lesson of chapter 1.8 is even more troubling. Immediately after
excusing the love of male clerics (1.7, pp. 208–10), Andreas unreservedly
denounces the man who would love nuns: "ab omnibus meretur contemni
et est tanquam detestabilis belua fugiendus" (He deserves the contempt of
all and is to be avoided like an accursed beast) (1.8, p. 210). This fierce
attack, however, is immediately rendered suspect when Andreas confesses
that he once almost violated this interdiction:

> Nam tempore quodam quum quandam monacham nobis pervenerit oppor-
> tunitas alloquendi, monacharum sollicitationis doctrinae non ignari facundo
> artis eam sermone coegimus nostrae acquiescere voluntati; et nos tanquam
> mentis caecitate prostrati et quid deceret nullatenus recolentes, quia "Quid
> deceat, non videt ullus amans" et iterum "Nil bene cernit amor, videt omnia
> lumine caeco", statim coepimus ipsius attrahi pulchritudine vehementi et dul-
> ciori facundia colligari. Interim tamen eam qua ducebamur vesaniam cogi-
> tantes a praedicta mortis dormitione summo sumus excitati labore. Et
> quamvis multum credamur in amoris arte periti et amoris praedocti remedia,
> vix tamen eius novimus pestiferos laqueos evitare et sine carnis <nos> con-
> tagione removere.

> (There was once an occasion when the chance of making advances to a nun
> came my way. I was not ignorant of the theory of importuning nuns, and
> through the eloquence of my art I compelled her to accede to my will. I was
> smitten, as it were, with mental blindness and utterly forgetful of right con-
> duct, for "of conduct seemly fair no lover is aware" and "Love's vision is awry;
> he sees all with blind eye" [Walsh, n. 205: Ovid, *Her.* 4.154, Ps-Ovid, *Rem.*
> 51.]. So at once I began to be drawn by her forceful beauty and enchained by

her still sweeter eloquence. However there was time for me to reflect on the mad course I was following, and by the hardest of struggles I was wakened from that sleep of death just mentioned. Though considered abundantly experienced in the art of love, and well-versed in love's remedies, only with difficulty could I avoid its baneful snares and withdraw without contamination of the flesh.) (1.8.4–5, p. 212)

Andreas will not end a chapter by taking blame on himself, however. As he continues warning his inexperienced friend, the focus shifts. After a shudder at the memory of sin avoided, the narrator subtly transfers responsibility for his near-lapse to his usual scapegoats—women—and then moves on to belittle the intelligence of Gualterius, and, by implication, that of his other readers as well.

Cave igitur, Gualteri, cum monialibus solitaria quaerere loca vel opportunitatem desiderare loquendi quia, si lascivis ludis locum ipsa persenserit aptum, tibi non crastinabit concedere quod optabis et ignita solatia praeparare, et vix unquam poteris opera Veneris evitare nefanda scelera sinistra committens. Nam quum nos, omni astutos ingenio et qualibet amoris doctrina vigentes, earum coegit vacillare suavitas, qualiter sibi tua imperita poterit obstare iuventus? Amor igitur talis tibi sit fugiendus, amice.

(So be careful, Walter, not to visit isolated spots in the company of nuns, nor to seek an opportunity of addressing one of them, for if she realises that the place is suitable for wanton sport, she will not hesitate to grant what you desire, and to devise consolations that burn; you will hardly ever avoid the wicked acts of Venus and you will commit ill-omened crimes. Seeing that the charm of nuns forced me to waver, with all my clever brain and the advantage of infinite learning in love, how will your inexperienced youth be able to confront them? So you must avoid such love, my friend.) (1.8.6, p. 212)

Just like the preceptor of the *Ars*, the narrator of the *De amore* is not to be trusted. His protestations, his confessions, his sermonizing are all rhetorical poses; his relationship with his readers is highly inconsistent. The more closely one reads, the more one realizes that one must watch out for oneself, sifting the text for its many contradictions and keeping for oneself the responsibility of making its meaning.

The ambiguity of the *De amore*—its *duplex sententia*—affects not only the way the book treats women and presents its narrator, but, even more, the way it describes its central subject, love. If we take the *De amore* at face value, we find love presented in ways that are bluntly incompatible: it is both commended and condemned. A close examination, however, shows that the reader of the *De amore* can find a way to reconcile these attitudes if he sees love both as a powerful force and as a controllable function of the imagination. In the *De amore*, love cannot exist in the public world. It belongs only to two people, or even to one alone. Thus the first chapter of Book 1 defines love as a suffering that comes from "immoderata cogitatio" about the beauty of the other sex: love is an obsession composed of and abetted by fear and jealousy. It may, in fact, be a completely closed circuit that exists only within the lover's mind. Beauty in the eye of the beholder is not only love's cause, but also its result (1.6.181, p. 90). Love is a secret that can scarcely be revealed to the beloved, and must on all accounts be concealed from others, as the preceptor repeatedly insists (for example, 2.1.1–6, p. 224). Those suitors who use "fatuae et indiscretae sermones" (2.3.5, p. 230) will find that such foolish speaking diminishes rather than magnifies women's love for them; blasphemy, another verbal crime, also weakens love (2.3.6, p. 230). "Amor raro consuevit durare vulgatus," declares Rule 13: "Love does not usually survive being noised abroad" (2.8.46, p. 282). Love must be kept secret, the text informs us, hidden behind the veil of language, available only to the initiated.

One of the most important reasons for this concealment is that love, as the *De amore* defines it, clearly and blatantly violates religious, legal, and moral codes. Love is completely incompatible with marriage, as Andreas's characters assert in both Book 1 and Book 2.[23] And the third book of Andreas's treatise defines love (along with women) as the source of all ills. Love comes from the devil; it violates God's will; it harms one's neighbors; it destroys marriages, damages friendships, and pollutes the soul and body; it is a state of servitude that makes one contemptible and causes suffering and eternal torture; it leads to murder, adultery, perjury, theft, false witness, incest, and idolatry; it stains women, makes lovers idle, and leads to war (3.1–47, pp. 286–300). "Cur, stulte iuvenis, quaeris amare?" (Why, stupid boy, do you seek to love?), Andreas asks the hapless Gualterius (3.48, p. 300); and indeed, after this harangue, he—or anyone else—would be hard put to reply.

But if the chaplain is so firmly opposed to love, why has he spent so many pages teaching it? An answer to this question can be found in the passages that open and close the third book of the treatise: they hint (albeit obliquely) that love can be seen as a form of imaginary entertainment, a fantasy or fiction. Andreas opens Book 3 by stating that he has composed the *De amore* in response to Gualterius's urgent request to learn about the art of love. Nevertheless, the chaplain does not recommend that Gualterius practice this art, since doing so would be a dangerous waste of time.

Rather, his pupil should study the book for recreation, and, having learned how to sin, should please God by abstaining from doing so.

> Taliter igitur praesentem lege libellum, non quasi per ipsum quaerens amantium tibi assumere vitam, sed ut eius doctrina refectus et mulierum edoctus ad amandum animos provocare a tali provocatione abstinendo praemium consequaris aeternum et maiori ex hoc apud Deum merearis munere gloriari.

> (So I would have you read this little book not with the intention of yourself adopting the life which lovers lead, but rather to obtain recreation by the learning in it. Then, once instructed in how to rouse women's hearts to love, you may by refraining from such action win an eternal reward, and deserve by this conduct to take pride in greater blessings in God's presence.) (3.2, p. 286)

This paradox has been the major crux in the history of the text's reception, both medieval and modern. Some medieval translators simply omitted Book 3 from their vernacular renderings; others transformed it, like Drouart la Vache, who drastically toned down Andreas's attacks on women.[24] Some Latin versions of the text went to the opposite extreme, excluding the first two books or developing to an even greater length the third book's anti-feminist tirade.[25] Modern critics have displayed no less varied responses to the divergent *sententiae*. In a remarkable review sentence, Bruno Roy encapsulates a sampling of explanations of the treatise that have been proposed since the 1940s:

> The solutions which have been proposed to overcome this dilemma come from an infinity of directions: philosophical (the Averroistic double truth [Denomy]), theological (*agapè* against *eros* [Schlösser]), moral (poison followed by antidote [Frappier]), psychoanalytic (attraction/repulsion of the man towards the woman [Askew]), rhetorical (irony followed by clear discourse [Robertson]), dialectical (a confrontation of two aspects of the medieval soul [Singer]), political (heterodoxy ending in orthodoxy [Rajna]), autobiographical (an author first in love, then disillusioned [Palumbo]), literary-historical (an initial plan supposedly modified along the way [Walsh]), and many others.[26]

The list could easily continue.[27] There is no denying that Andreas is responsible for this confusion: why teach love and then denounce it? But Andreas repeats the argument at the end of Book 3, a clear indication that it must be considered seriously; and, in the end, the chaplain himself provides a way to read the text's double message. "Haec igitur nostra subtiliter et fideliter examinata doctrina, quam tibi praesenti libello mandamus insertam, tibi duplicem sententiam propinabit," Andreas reminds us (So if you peruse with careful diligence this teaching of mine which I send you within the covers of this little book, it will present to you two differing views) (3.117, p. 322). The first lesson is that practicing the art of love will reward the reader with "omnes corporis voluptates" (all the pleasures of the body); but such practical application will also cause one to lose God's grace, the friendship of good men, and one's reputation and honors. The second part of the book, on the other hand, teaches that one should not waste one's time in love, since refraining from indulgence in vain activities will bring success in this life and glory in the world to come (3.119–20, p. 322). One may *read* about the art of love with impunity, but to *practice* it is a sin.

Is this a conflict? The answer depends on one's understanding of the relationship between literature and the world. Those who see the *De amore* as a description of or prescription for courtly behavior are easily—almost necessarily—troubled by the text, which appears to be either hyperpious or immoral, and usually misleading into the bargain.[28] But if we read the *De amore* as an argument not for or against love but for separating it from moral consideration by turning it into a text, we can begin to look at the *De amore* quite differently—not as a single-voiced pronouncement on how one should or should not behave, but as an affirmation that literary texts (and especially texts about love) can exist side by side with religious and moral discourse, as they do in the *De amore*. That Book 3 condemns the practice of love is not in question,[29] but this position need not exclude the possibility of accepting love in literature, as indeed the chaplain seems to do.[30] Andreas speaks both in the discourse of poetic love and in that of Christian morality; his treatise contains not an apparent but a real *duplex sententia*. Christian morality governs behavior, Andreas loudly announces, but he also hints that it does not govern desire and the imagination. His transgression is merely rhetorical, only literary, he assures us, but it is nonetheless significant, even audacious. For to assert that illicit love may exist in literature is to suggest that a secular world, a world not governed by biblical prohibitions, is conceivable even for Christian writers.

The *De amore* makes this exception only on the page and in the imagination, of course, but as the preceding chapter has shown, this literary space was the focus of much contention in the Middle Ages. Andreas's use of sources reveals him to be a participant in these debates. At first glance, his bibliography, like his moral point of view, seems hopelessly ambivalent, unwilling to commit itself to either a sacred or a secular affiliation. But we can see the *De amore* handling its literary context as it handles Christian and non-Christian views of love: the text recognizes both sacred and secular writing, and manages to build structures in which they can co-exist.

A closer look at the *De amore*'s relationship with its context will reveal just how broadly based a text it is.[31] Andreas draws material from most of the kinds of sources available to a medieval writer: the Bible (both Old and New Testaments); patristic writers; classical poets and philosophers; and medieval secular poets.[32] And though the orientation of the various parts of the treatise might lead one to expect otherwise, there is no shortage of allusions to sacred texts in the first two books. Indeed, as the following brief table shows, Book 1 contains more references to the Bible and the Church Fathers than either of the others. And of the non-Scriptural sources Andreas cites, Ovid is by far the favorite: the chaplain refers to virtually all his works, including the *Epistulae Heroidum*, the *Metamorphoses*, the *De medicamina*, the *Fasti*, the *Tristia*, and especially the *Ars amatoria* and *Remedia amoris*. And, like the Bible, Ovid is cited in each of the treatise's three books.

Given the popularity of Ovid's amatory works in the twelfth century, it is not surprising to find that Andreas often cites the *magister amoris*. But his reliance on Ovid goes far deeper than this. The *De amore* is in fact a far more faithful re-creation of Ovid's treatise in medieval Christian terms than its readers have usually seen it to be. Not only does Andreas fre-

Sacred and Secular Textual References in the *De amore*.[33]

	Book 1	Book 2	Book 3	Total
Sacred texts				
Bible				
Old Testament	19	2	11	32
New Testament	30	0	19	49
Patristic authors	10	0	2	12
				93
Secular Texts				
Classical authors (excluding Ovid)	31	3	11	45
Ovid	24	10	8	42
Medieval secular authors	19	6	3	28
				115

quently cite the Roman poet, but he repeatedly invokes the name and rôle of the narrator of the *Ars*, speaking frequently of *praecepta* (for example, 1.6.147, p. 80; 1.6.266, p. 114; 1.6.268, p. 116; etc.) and of *remedia* (*Praefatio* 2, p. 30; 1.6.327, p. 134; 1.6.352, p. 142); he also labels himself *magister* (2.6.18, p. 242). The matter of the *regulae amoris* and of many descriptions of love and lovers' behavior recall the *Ars*, leading scholars to note Ovid's particularly strong influence on Andreas, whose *De amore* one critic (perhaps with excessive enthusiasm) called "by far the most important and interesting Ovidian document of the Middle Ages."[34] But the most substantial, and perhaps the most important, parallel between the ancient and medieval treatises is found on the level of structure. Books 1 and 2 of the *De amore*, as many have noted, are patterned after the first two books of the *Ars*.[35] Except for a few comments directed toward women, Andreas follows common medieval practice in omitting *Ars* 3, but his third book, *mutatis mutandis*, provides an analogue to the extensive disillusioning of the *Remedia amoris*.[36] The structural similarity between the works is obvious and fundamental.

Even the complex strategies of reading that Andreas's text requires recall those I discussed in the Introduction and Chapter 1. Ovid's offer to teach love's rules in the *Ars amatoria*, as we have seen, is vitiated by the incompetence of the *praeceptor*, by the strictly conventional nature of the love described, and by the disillusioning force of the *Remedia*; what the *Ars* teaches is not the art of love, properly speaking, but the art of love poetry. Andreas, I believe, has a similar goal in the *De amore*: to teach his readers about the place and value of secular literary treatments of love. If Andreas had been truly interested in propounding only a Christian *simplex sententia*, he would not have written Books 1 and 2 at all.[37] His purpose, like Ovid's, is both to invoke the illusions of literary love, and, by purporting to dispel these illusions, to reveal the power of writing to create love as a textual phenomenon. Even though Andreas espouses and recommends the Christian viewpoint, neither side of the dichotomy conquers the other: both remain. Andreas endorses Christian principles, but also provides room for secular love poetry.

An *assidua lectio* of Andreas's treatise will show that both parts of the *duplex sententia* are there to be found, from the beginning, irreconcilable but coexisting; it is the reader's responsibility to learn to come to terms with their dual presence. Andreas's book creates an image of a world in which sacred and secular both have a place. He accomplishes this task by constructing a complicated text that seduces the reader into a literary love affair that is also a hermeneutic exercise. But the *De amore* is built in such a way as to make consummation impossible. There is no end to the interpretive process, no solution to the problem of duplicity. Andreas thus offers his reader the chance to learn that secular literature is a textual issue, a verbal fantasy that is, in the end, neither true nor false; it is a practice of mediation, interpretation, and exchange that simply continues. The constancy of an *assidua lectio* can never unify the author's double meaning, but this fact does not imply that there is anything wrong either with the reader's efforts or with the author's creation. The act of reading texts, and particularly texts about love, is the act of achieving a suspension of belief and disbelief, of finding some balance between truth and lies.

As we saw in Chapter 2, working out this balance in a twelfth-century literary context is a treacherous process, particularly when religion, with its emphasis on absolutes, is party to the negotiations. Andreas describes his text as teaching, *doctrina* (1.6.17, p. 44; 1.6.385, p. 152), but his curriculum consists largely of deceit and falsehood. Gualterius, Andreas teaches, must learn to avoid being deceived by women (1.6.9–10, pp. 42–44; 1.9.20, p. 218). The lovers represented in the text are obsessed by concerns about misuses and miscarriages of language. They talk about their fear of having their secrets revealed or of being misunderstood (1.6.119, p. 74; 1.6.292, p. 122, etc.). They also discuss the need for discretion in love and the deception practiced by men and women (2.7.50, p. 268; 1.6.130, p. 76; 1.6.319–41, pp. 130–38). The chaplain, too, emphasizes dishonesty: dissuading his student from love, he explains that there is no lie that lovers will refrain from telling (3.30, p. 294). What lesson can Gualterius and other readers draw from these confusing messages and this preoccupation with deceit? Ostensibly, the chaplain tells lies so that his student will learn about truth, but such a message is fraught with pedagogic and moral danger. (Augustine, for example, in his treatise *De mendacio*, condemns as the most heinous lies those that are used to teach religion: "Corrupta enim auctoritate doctrinae, nullus aut cursus aut recursus esse ad castitatem animi potest" [Once the authority of doctrine has been corrupted, no advance or return to chastity of the soul is possible].)[38] If we read the treatise in strict Christian terms, we must see it as completely sinful: Andreas's preoccupation with deceit makes the truth irretrievable. This approach mires the reader in confusion.

But if we try again to read the first two books of the *De amore* as secular fiction, a rhetorical construction that is not *im*moral but *a*moral, we can recognize that the text is not meant to be applied in practice. The text is not to be used but read, and the reader must share the responsibility for understanding it and supplying any moral meaning it may have. Andreas opens up this possibility in Book 3 when he notes that no one can be fully educated about love and its pains without being schooled by *magistra experientia* (Mistress Experience) (3.23, p. 294). Despite its claims, the text is incapable of really teaching. The meaning of the text and its lessons come not so much from the teacher as from his students. And in fact a near-contemporary of Andreas's, Petrus Cantor, head of the school of moral philosophy at Paris at the end of the twelfth century, made precisely this judgment, as John Benton recounts:

> Peter was asked about the art of love, whether about Ovid's work in particular or the genre is not clear. He replied that "the art itself is good but its use is evil." The next question was then "Does not he who teaches the amatory art use it and sin mortally?" To which he replied that the teacher "does not use it but transmits it. He who corrupts women by its means uses it. Nevertheless, the teacher transmits it, not for use but as a warning."[39]

The text and its *doctrina* may be used or not, according to the reader's inclination and moral disposition. It may be, as Petrus suggests, a warning; it may be simply a diversion. But in any event such questions are up to the reader to resolve.

As the discussions of literary theory in the previous chapter have shown, not all medieval writers believed that literature had to be read as moral or immoral. Some believed that there was a place for fiction, too. *Fingere* (creating) and *ludere* (playing) were, at least for some theorists, acceptable descriptions of poetic activity; some *accessus* acknowledged that a poet's intention might be simply to please. And we need not assume that the *assidua lectio* Andreas requests was expected to lead to a single, sanctified meaning that unified this text with every other. Indeed, Robert Guiette proposes that a residue of uncertainty may have been a quality medieval readers would have appreciated in literature, finding "a sort of esthetic delight resulting from mystery and obscurity: they perceived the mystery and, no doubt, did not ask that it dissipate."[40] The problems of Andreas's text are there, perhaps, to challenge the text's readers, to provoke them, and to train them to develop their own understanding and literary sense.[41] Andreas's work on love, like the tales of King Arthur, are "Ne tut mençunge, ne tut veir / Tut folie ne tut saveir" (not all lies, not all true, not all madness, not all wisdom), as Jehan Bodel wrote.[42] The *De amore* is a literary fiction that demonstrates that human artistry has a place alongside divine creation and the religious discourse of the church.[43]

This reading of Andreas's treatise has important consequences for our understanding of other twelfth-century writings on love. Courtly love itself has been seen as a medieval literary game,[44] and in this connection Andreas's work takes on meaning as theory. By inscribing the game of courtly love into a treatise that also includes theological discourse, Andreas accords a certain recognition and legitimacy to the secular love poetry of his time; by presenting both sides of the question of love, Andreas emphasizes the reader's responsibility to come up with his own interpretation of the literary text. And by modeling his treatise on Ovid's *Ars amatoria* and *Remedia amoris*, Andreas limits the scope of his Christian objections to love, since, like Ovid, he allows love to flourish as a fantasy within the bounds of a text which, though it claims to teach its readers about love in the external world, is fundamentally a meta-literary document. Andreas acknowledges the power and moral value of Christian teachings, but by turning these rules into a moral frame inside which he writes a treatise on courtly love, he manages to eat his cake and have it, too; as Salvatore Battaglia writes, "In him, cleric and layman cohabited."[45] If they choose to, his readers may learn to do the same: to see through the conflict between the first and second part of the treatise two extreme positions that come together to form the *duplex sententia* Andreas urges his readers to look for. His text reflects the literary world in which he writes, a world in which secular writing was beginning to make a place for itself. While drawing on all the traditions available to him, placing them in opposition to one another, Andreas provides a way for readers to accept the dichotomy. The *De amore*, in possibility and imagination, creates a space for itself that is isolated from Christian morality, and then plays inside these limits.[46]

It is through the use of fiction that we can best understand the relationship between the *De amore* and other twelfth-century texts about secular love. Andreas's book is neither a Christian condemnation of courtly love nor a *summa* and a "glorification" of extra-marital sex;[47] rather, it situates medieval secular writing about love in a fictional mode that developed from Ovid's writings. Such fiction asserts itself against the dominant ideology of the medieval church, but not in an attempt to overthrow it. The struggle of medieval fiction is simply to find a way to exist at all. By figuring this fight, the *De amore* sets itself forth as a work of literary theory, a medieval treatise on the poetic practice of love.[48] And by giving Gualterius and his other readers the freedom to come to this understanding themselves, Andreas teaches them about their abilities and responsibilities, about their power and limitations. Medieval writers and readers, we have seen, could use language to construct books or interpretations. These works of art were not seen as the equivalent of divine creation, but they could be a respite or a diversion from the constraints that religion imposed. Their very limitations were the elements that made them inviting for recreation and the free play of the imagination. And, in the primarily sacred world of the twelfth-century Latin text, such creation was itself a triumph, inspired by Andreas's Roman master, of secular fiction and the verbal art.[49]

4. Through the Looking Glass: Jean de Meun's *Mirror for Lovers*

Jean de Meun's continuation of Guillaume de Lorris's *Roman de la Rose,* the final work this study will examine, was written nearly one hundred years after Andreas Capellanus's *De amore.* Jean's and Andreas's works have many important features in common: both transpose the *Ars* and *Remedia* into a context of medieval literary forms, both are concerned with fantasy, and both address the conflict between secular, sexual, non-marital love and Christian morality and philosophy. Jean de Meun, moreover, is one of the few French writers who cite Andreas; the texts are also linked by the fact that in 1277, just about the time when Jean was completing his controversial work, Etienne Tempier, the Bishop of Paris, condemned the *De amore,* a few other texts, and a wide variety of ideas he considered theologically dangerous.[1]

These connections show that Jean de Meun was writing squarely in the medieval tradition of Ovid's amatory poetry. Yet Jean was less easy in his relationship with Ovid than his predecessors were: while earlier medieval writers used the content, style, and structure of the *Ars amatoria* as a model that permitted them to write fiction in a challenging and even hostile environment, Jean actively challenges Ovid's authority in the work he calls *Le Miroër aus amoreus*[2] (*The Mirror for Lovers*). In his struggle to absorb, rewrite, become, and overthrow his predecessors, Jean gives us invaluable insights into the literary world of the thirteenth century, a period in which both the influence of the classical *auctores* and the courtly literature that had blossomed in the twelfth century gave way to new forms and interests.

This chapter will investigate the ways in which Jean used and fought with Ovid.[3] Its major concerns are those we have been studying since the beginning: sex and love and their relationship with writing and reading. In particular, we will look closely at how Jean defines himself and his text in relation to authors and texts of the past; at the ways in which Jean recreates the *praeceptor amoris* in his text's varied allegorical personae; at the connection between illusion and literary and fantasy love; and at the ways in which Jean discusses the relationship between literary art and interpretation. Many of these aspects of the text will be reminiscent of others we have seen, though, given the length of Jean's poem, they are often more complex. But while Ovid's treatise valorizes first and foremost the pleasure of writing, and the *De amore* makes a tentative and ambivalent effort to write fiction in the face of ecclesiastical prohibitions, Jean de Meun discourages his readers from being content to remain within the literary world.[4] He ends his dream-vision—extended and elaborate as it is—with a boisterous orgasm, bringing dream, poem, and reading to an abrupt end, and plunging his readers back through the looking-glass[5] and outside the literary frame that had kept medieval amatory fiction safe, and into the outside world. And yet Jean's text, in the most fundamental of ways, is no different from its predecessors, if only because it is still a text. The goal of this chapter will be to see what happens when a subversive author, writing in a period that, as we have seen, is uneasy with authority, challenges a brilliant master at his game.

Authorship and Authority

Auctoritas is an obvious locus of conflict in Jean de Meun's *Roman de la Rose*. The most obvious example of this strain is in the dual authorship of the text itself: rather than writing a work of his own, Jean chooses[6] to continue a text that belongs to another writer, borrowing subject, story, characters, and style. From the beginning, then, Jean's text is parasitic, even predatory. And the referential structure (both overt and covert) of Jean's text also draws our attention to the importance of *auctoritas*. Thus, while Guillaume de Lorris names only a single *auctor* (Macrobius, in line 7), Jean de Meun mentions no fewer than forty-four of them,[7] and also borrows enormously: 2,100 verses of his text derive from Boethius's *De consolatione philosophiae* (*The Consolation of Philosophy*), more than 5,000 from Alain de Lille's *De planctu naturae* (*The Complaint of Nature*),[8] and 2,000 more from Ovid (largely following the progress from Book 1 to Book 3 of the *Ars*).[9] All in all, 12,000 of Jean's 17,500 verses represent the work of other authors, in Ernest Langlois's estimate.[10] The bulk of Jean's literary output, moreover, representative of the popularizing of classical culture so typical of the thirteenth century,[11] consisted of renderings of Latin literature into French: he translated Vegetius's treatise on chivalry, the letters of Heloise and Abelard, Aelred of Rievaulx's *De amicitia spiri-tuali*, and Boethius's *De consolatione*.[12] Yet though Jean relies so much on the writings of other authors, he is highly selective in the ways in which he attributes his borrowings in the *Rose*. He never, for example, refers to medieval authors by name.[13] And though his text clearly owes more to the *Ars* and to the first *Roman de la Rose* (to which, following Paul Zumthor, I will refer as "R_1,"[14]) than to any other works, Jean is quite reluctant to acknowledge openly his debts to Ovid and Guillaume de Lorris.

This absence is no oversight. It is, rather, a challenge both to Jean's sources and to his readers to puzzle out how writing and reading overlap and interact. Let us begin this puzzle by examining how Jean treats Ovid. The statistics just cited (and, even more important, the structural similari-ties we will be studying below) reveal Jean's debt to Ovid; yet this debt is perceptible only to those readers who are knowledgeable enough to look below the surface of the text, which bears scarcely any visible trace of the Roman poet's presence. Despite his full-scale use of the *Ars* and *Remedia*, Jean mentions Ovid only five times, and these references are, without ex-ception, deprecatory. Three of the instances in which Jean names Ovid discuss the incompatibility of love and poverty. In each of these cases, Jean belittles the ancient writer by identifying him with his narrator's conven-tional self-portrait as a poor elegiac lover.[15] In a fourth instance, Jean praises Ovid for teaching techniques on how to win the love of old women—but then immediately warns his readers *not* to do what Ovid advises, since, he says, old women are far craftier and more dangerous than one might suppose (21409–20). In none of these instances are Jean's readers left with the impression that Ovid might have anything worth-while to teach them on the subject of love: the *Ars*, the *Roman de la Rose* seems to imply, has been superseded.

Yet Jean is not content simply to ignore his *auctor*; instead, he kicks him out of the way. Jean's most important reference to Ovid—and his only mention of Guillaume de Lorris—comes at a crucial moment, the dis-cussion of authorship at the midpoint of the conjoined texts of R_1 and R_2.[16] At first reading, this passage appears to contradict the others by ex-pressing Jean's admiration for his predecessors. But on closer analysis, we realize that in assigning Jean the tasks of teaching the art of love and of completing the *Roman de la Rose*,[17] the God of Love has killed off Jean's competition: both Ovid and Guillaume are dead and gone. It is worth pausing for a moment to investigate this scene, both because it reveals a good deal about Ovid's place in thirteenth-century literature and because

it presents a model that Jean may invite his own readers to follow in dealing with the *auctor* in whose footsteps they will have to tread—namely,
Jean himself.

In urging the reading public to revere the *Miroër aus Amoreus* and
its creator, the God of Love appears to honor Ovid by paraphrasing his
verse. Yet the lines he cites, from *Amores* 3.9 (Ovid's lament on the death
of Tibullus[18]), sound more like a eulogy than an encomium:

> Gallus, Catillus et Ovides,
> qui bien sorent d'amors trestier,
> nous reüssent or bien mestier;
> mes chascuns d'aus gist morz porriz.
> Vez ci Guillaume de Lorriz,
> cui Jalousie, sa contraire,
> fet tant d'angoisse et de deul traire
> qu'il est en perill de morir,
> se je ne pens du secorir.
>
> (10492–96)

(Gallus, Catullus, and Ovid, who knew well how to discuss love, would
have been very useful to us now, but each of them lies dead and rotten.
Behold Guillaume de Lorris, whom Jealousy, his enemy, causes such grief
and sorrow that he is in danger of dying unless I choose to rescue him.)

Amor's polite thoughts about rescuing the imperiled Guillaume are in fact
undercut by his choice of rhyme: the link between "porriz" and "Lorriz"
makes it clear that Guillaume is already in a state of decay.[19] And since
Ovid's corpse has been shoveled out with those of Gallus and Catullus,[20]
Amor goes on to predict that Jean will become (like his forebears Modoin
and Baudri) a *Naso nouus* who will write a new *Ars* and *Remedia* for the
Frenchmen of his day.

> Endoctrinez de ma sciance,
> si fleütera noz paroles
> par carrefors et par escoles
> selonc le langage de France,
> par tout le regne, en audiance,
> que ja mes cil qui les orront
> des douz mauz d'amer ne morront,

por qu'il le croient seulement:
car tant en lira proprement
que tretuit cil qui ont a vivre
devroient apeler ce livre
le *Miroër aus Amoreus*,
tant i verront de bien por eu[s].
(10610−22)

(He will pipe our words to listeners at the crossroads and in schools in
the language of France, throughout the kingdom, so that those who hear
them will never have to die from the sweet pains of love, provided only
that they believe him; for he will read so correctly that all those who are
yet to come should call this book the *Mirror for Lovers*, since they will see
so much good in it for them.)

Jean de Meun has killed off Ovid and Guillaume[21] in order to usurp
their voices. He has also described their texts and his own in the standard
form of the *accessus*, thus canonizing both his predecessors and himself:
according to Amor, Jean de Meun is no less an *auctor* than any Roman
writer.[22] And if Jean is a latter-day Ovid, then his readers will have to
employ precisely those reading skills they developed in studying the *Ars*.
They will need to interpret the discourses of Jean's many speakers with
insight and caution, become willing to refute authority, and learn to rely
on themselves to determine the meaning they will take away from the text.
The few marks of overt respect Jean shows to his forerunners are overshad-
owed by his audacious tendency to appropriate their rôle, their accom-
plishments, and their texts.

The unusual nature of the relationship between R_1 and R_2 parallels
the relationship which is the basis of this study: that between the *Ars* and
the *Remedia*. R_1 begins by recounting the experience of the narrator-as-
lover, and by teaching the art of love; R_2 completes this instruction by
keeping lovers from dying from les "douz mauz d'amer" (10616) (the sweet
pains of loving). As the *Ars* picks up the themes and motifs of the *Amores*,
and as the *Remedia* do the same for the *Ars*, so Jean's continuation takes
the situations, characters, and story of Guillaume's romance, examining
them, developing them, and turning them inside-out. By bringing the
Lover's self-centered love to fruition, R_2 reveals it to be a fantasy, a literary
construction that can exist only within the confines of the dream, the page,
or the mind of the reader. Jean suggests that the world outside this frame

is more important than the one inside it: like Andreas, he is fundamentally a Christian. But, like Andreas also, Jean is a creator of amatory fiction, and his massive textual construction asserts both his own power as an author and the continued force of Ovid's and Guillaume's texts, on which Jean's power depends.

One of the methods Jean uses to subvert his textual models is to complicate the identity of the narrator. Not only does the "I" of the *Roman de la Rose* represent Ovid, Guillaume, and Jean;[23] it is also the dreamer in whose mind the allegory takes place, the young man who went through the experiences prefigured in the dream,[24] as well as the poem's narrator;[25] and since, by the nature of language, "I" is anyone who says "I," it is also every allegorical speaker in R_2.[26] The speaking voice of R_2 also represents other poets, recalls elements of a variety of other texts and genres (including troubadour and trouvère lyric,[27] treatises on the art of love, and courtly romance), and espouses (through the allegorical characters) many different points of view on love. The result of this fragmented narration is that the reader, alternately seduced[28] and belittled (compare 15104–290) by the shifty poet-narrator, receives little consistent or reliable guidance,[29] and must therefore take increasing responsibility in finding or making meaning in his or her reading experience.

Sex Relations, Points of View

The continuous process of reinterpretation Jean requires of his readers often focuses on a single subject: sex. Each of the allegorical speakers has an opinion about this topic, and these opinions vary widely. Jean de Meun presents a spectroscopic range of views. Thus Reson[30] despises sexual love; Ami, on the other hand, sees sex as fun. The Vielle considers it a useful way for women to manipulate men, while Genius believes that sex is the primordial concern of the human race and the manifestation of God's will. Jean offers his readers no guidance with which to choose among the ways sex is packaged (marriage, "free love," celibacy, homosexuality[31]): none receives unqualified approbation, and many are advocated in such a cynical way that it is difficult not to take the endorsements as ironic. The end of the poem, of course, gives exemplary support to heterosexual intercourse (assuming that the Rose actually figures a woman), but even this plug entails an explicit rejection of Reson, and marriage is nowhere in the picture. R_2, by showing that each character's view on sex calls into question that of the previous speaker, offers a reading experience is a continual process of auto-interpretation—a process which, gradually, readers learn to use in order to read the text as a whole, its author, and, in the end, themselves.

The first speaker in R_2 to discuss the question of sex is Reson. Though not an original Ovidian figure, she is one of Jean's incarnations of the *praeceptor amoris*, and she fulfils several other functions, as well: she provides the link between R_2 and R_1, and she serves as a Christian and philosophical disillusioner of fantasy love, which she condemns as nothing but *"folie"* (3025–29)[32] and "maladie de pensee" (4348) (mental illness), citing the *De amore* almost word for word.[33] Reson has her own vision of love, one that is philosophical, altruistic, and even wise, but it is completely out of place in a courtly romance. Her proposals demonstrate little understanding of human nature, and the discordance between her message and its situation and audience shows how much she misses the mark. The narrator and Reson part company because of irreconcilable differences. And though the narrator, on parting from her, is, for at least a moment, "pensis et morne" (7200) (depressed), he is not swayed by her cautions from his loyalty to the God of Love.[34] Reson receives no gratitude from the narrator, and is unable to teach him a single lesson.

What conclusions are readers to draw from this treatment? On one level, Reson is a Boethian figure whose advice the narrator ignores at his peril; his inability to understand her is, as Winthrop Wetherbee puts it, "a way of illustrating the disfunction suffered by man's nature with the loss of Paradise."[35] But the style of Reson's discourse and the structure of R_2 as a whole deny her the authority her moral position might seem to give her.[36] She is a poor rhetorician and a bad psychologist;[37] she is garrulous and—in a very genteel way—seductive (she tries to get the narrator to enter into an intimate relationship with her); she is ignorant of love;[38] and, finally, she is rejected in favor of more sympathetic counselors. Jean uses Reson to point out the weaknesses of R_1: a disillusionist, she disrupts the narrator's subjective vision. But Jean does not stop, as Andreas does, at providing a pairing of pro- and anti-love views: instead, he encloses this *Ars/Remedia* dichotomy within a series of other oppositions, thus providing an increasingly complex structure through which his reader will have to make his or her way.

This path leads the reader and narrator to a series of other allegorical figures who also discuss their philosophies of love and sex. Once reason has been abandoned, the next teacher the narrator encounters is Ami, who is, of all the characters in R₂, the most like the Ovidian *praeceptor amoris*. At first, Ami seems like a true ally and a proper antidote to Reson's preachy morality. He is a master of the tricks of his trade who will clearly help the narrator attain his true goal—sex with the Rose. But, like his Roman model, Ami gradually reveals his reliance on duplicity, and the reader eventually learns that this character is not to be trusted. In many ways, Ami seems immoral,[39] and the misogyny of his close associate, the Jealous Husband, is deeply disturbing to modern readers. But since the *Rose* lacks a solid moral center, it is difficult to be comfortable judging Ami.

And in fact Ami has a lot to teach his students about the art of love, which, like Ovid's narrator, he sees as a game in which morality is absolutely relative. He approves of whatever works and looks down on whatever does not. Thus his "arz et sciences" (8285; 9651) serve a practical purpose: advancement toward the sexual fulfilment of a love affair. For Ami, as for Ovid's *praeceptor*, love is essentially equivalent to sex,[40] and emotions—the man's emotions, at least—and ethics are no more a part of the process than marriage is.[41] Recognizing these facts makes it possible to understand Ami's highly practical advice, even if one does not approve of it. The rules he offers are few and simple: respond in kind to Bel Acueil, lie to those who would lie to you, respect the power of money but avoid ruinous extravagance, and do not dominate your *amie* (presumably not because Ami's disciples are feminists *avant la lettre*, but because smooth and seductive men are more likely to gain sexual satisfaction than violent ones—though this principle is belied by Ami's actions, as we will see). Deception is the primary principle he recommends. "Par barat esteut barater" (7357) ("Pour it on!"), he declares,[42] advising the narrator to mirror the lady's moods (compare 7692–7706). All is fair in love and war, according to Ami: "si sachiez que cil font bone euvre / qui les deceveors deçoivent" (7312–13) (Know that they do good work who deceive deceivers).[43] Illusion, he argues, is simply part of the "jeu d'amors" (8404); the influence of the *Ars* is nowhere more literal or more clear. While Reson worries about money because it symbolizes the vicissitudes of Fortune, Ami is troubled primarily because seduction by wealth, though effective, requires neither his *art* nor his *doctrine* (7859). Ami himself (like Ovid's *amator* and *praeceptor*) has had misfortunes in this area (7975–92), and warns the narrator that the exchange of love for money always benefits women far more than it does men.

This concern about women is fundamental to the discourse shared by Ami and his close associate, the Jealous Husband (never explicitly named in the text), whose outrageous anti-feminist comments have been at the center of *querelles* since Christine de Pizan and Pierre Col argued about the *Rose* at the turn of the fifteenth century.[44] The Husband's lecture (which is related to the diatribes of Andreas Capellanus's third book[45]) bears analysis not only for the picture of women that it paints, but also for the way it exposes a seamy underside of Ami and thus complicates still further the question of love in the *Rose*.

If one is able to see the humor in caricatural misogyny, the Jealous Husband's discourse can provide a cynical laugh at the dark side of heterosexual relationships, much like the preceptor's instructions in *Ars* 2 and the *Remedia*. In his long speech (8425–9390), the Husband traps women in all the traditional misogynistic paradoxes. Poor women are costly to keep, but rich ones are proud and haughty; beautiful women are pursued by all, while ugly ones want to make everyone happy. The only good women the Jealous Husband can name are those who are even readier to condemn themselves than he is: Heloise, who proved by her learning and experience that men should not marry, and Lucrece, who, even though pardoned by others for having been raped, could not forgive herself, and so committed suicide. Completely convinced that beauty and chastity cannot occupy the same place at the same time, the Jealous Husband compares women to dunghills that, even when covered with silk cloths or colorful flowers, continue to stink as they did before. Women's sexual immorality is constant throughout time, he proclaims. "Toutes estes, serez et fustes, / de fet ou de volenté, pustes" (9125–26) (You women are, will be, or were, in fact or in intention, whores).

Despite this incendiary invective, however, the Jealous Husband does not even threaten violence until the very end of his speech, and the violence that does occur is in fact narrated by Ami, of whose personality the Jealous Husband seems to be an embarrassing side that slips out from time to time.[46] And though Ami protests at length against dominance, which he presents as a rebuttal of the Jealous Husband's arguments, he has already let slip some highly misogynistic—if traditional—advice of his own. "Pluck the rose with all your force, to show that you are a man," he advises the narrator: "women want to give by force that which they will not give freely" (7656–70; compare *Ars* 1.664–79). Much of what Ami says—like much of the advice offered by the Ovidian preceptor—is highly objectionable; yet readers must also acknowledge that Ami's advice is part of what permits the narrator to reach his goal, and is therefore an effective art of love.

The dubious morality of the *praeceptor amoris* appears again in the discourse of the Lover's next teacher, the Vielle. Her speech invites cautious analysis, for though she appears to speak on behalf of women, she often condemns them in the traditional terms of male misogyny.[47] Even her pronounced misandry is a parallel to the anti-feminism of Ami's Jealous Husband, and her venality is the counterpart of Ami's repugnance toward the *chemin de Trop Doner* (the road of Giving Too Much), her past failures an analogue to his. These characters are two faces of the Ovidian teacher who leads his students toward a single goal: the satisfaction of physical desire at the expense of the Other. Ami and the Vielle are not only echoes of one another, but are also images of the relationship between the *Rose* and its sources. Like Jean, as he claims to supersede Ovid and Guillaume, the Vielle likes to see herself as an anti-preceptor whose instruction is more valuable than that offered by male teachers:

> Bele iere, et jenne et nice et fole,
> n'onc ne fui d'Amors a escole
> ou l'en leüst la theorique,
> mes je sai tout par la practique.
> Experimenz m'en ont fet sage,
> que j'ai hantez tout mon aage;
> or en sai jusqu'a la bataille,
> si n'est pas droiz que je vos faille
> des biens aprendre que je sai,
> puis que tant esprovez les ai.
> Bien fet qui jennes genz conseille.
> . . . .
> Mes tant a que je ne finé
> que la sciance en la fin é,
> don bien puis en chaiere lire.
> (12771–81; 12785–87)

("I was beautiful, and young, and stupid, and foolish, and I never went to the school of Love, where people studied its theory; but I know everything by practice. Experience [of love], which I have had all my life, has made me very wise; now I know it all, up to the battle, and so it is not right that I fail to teach you the useful things I know, since I have tested them so much. Whoever advises young people does well. . . . But there is so much of it that I could never finish telling all my knowledge, about which I could certainly lecture from a chair.")

She is a highly critical reader who exclaims, as she rejects Amor's commandments of generosity and fidelity, "C'est faus texte, c'est fause letre, / ci mant Amors" (13002–3) ("This is a false text, a false letter: Love's lying here!"). Rather than repudiating *auctoritas* altogether, however, what she truly wants is to have her own *doctrines* (12959) on love replace those of others (13469–86), much as Jean's *Miroër* is meant to appropriate the place of Ovid's and Guillaume's treatises on the art of love.

Yet for all her claims of experience, the Vielle teaches nothing new. She is a highly derivative and literary character—Jean de Meun's recreation of many figures, but most importantly the transvestite *praeceptor amoris* of *Ars amatoria* 3,[48] and she is no more trustworthy than the two-sided Ami. Her advice to women, like his to men, is based on deceit and manipulation: she teaches women how to substitute false hair, skin tones, bust size, and even orgasms for real ones if what Nature has provided is unmarketable. And her pupils, she says, should be no more honest about their ties to men than they are about their appearance. She urges women to be unfaithful, and to hold on to their sexual *franchise*, even though we know from *Ars* 3 that women's sexual liberty tends to serve male needs at least as much as it does female ones.

It is in espousing free love that the Vielle is at her most eloquent. She argues that Nature gave women liberty, but that the law has imprisoned them. The limitations of marriage are no more valid for women than those of clerical celibacy are for men, she explains, and all of them are contrary to nature. Nature, she argues, made all women for all men, all men for all women, and even if they are married, women will always try to revert to a state of freedom.

But behind all the powerful, strident, and sometimes humorous feminism of the Vielle is a painful history of injuries received and a deep pessimism about the fate of women in the amorous universe the *Rose* describes. Like the Jealous Husband's Heloise, whose condemnation of marriage derives both from learning and from her own experience, the Vielle sees no happiness in traditional love and matrimony. "N'am peut fame a bon chief venir" (13143) (Never can woman come to a good end), she explains, illustrating this grievous lesson with the sorrowful stories of Dido, Phyllis, Oenone, and Medea, which are taken, not surprisingly, from Ovid. The scarcely inappropriate moral she draws from this selection of tales is that men are endlessly deceitful, and that women, therefore, must never trust them, and must never confine themselves to one man alone. The men in her own life have followed Ami's lessons all too faithfully:

Trop sunt tuit espert menteür,
plus m'ont menti, li fouteür,
et foiz et seremenz jadis
qu'il n'a de sainz en paradis.
                    (13757–60)

("They are all truly expert liars; the fuckers have told me more lies and
false oaths than there are saints in paradise.")

The Vielle, like Villon's Belle Heaulmière and many other such figures, is
an old woman who has been a failure in her own life and who begs others
to learn from her experience.[49] Her lack of success in love demonstrates
both her kinship with other literary characters (the *praeceptor*, as well as
Ami) and the very real limitations of her wisdom. Though—like R_2 itself—she tries to replace others' *auctoritas* with her own, her exemplary
unwillingness to believe and submit to others is perhaps the most important lesson she offers her students.

The unstable relationship of sexuality to the text and the non-literary
world remains a central theme in the discourses of the last two figures to
be discussed in this section, Nature and Genius (who represents Nature's
generative forces[50]). It is through their power that the narrator attains
sexual union with the Rose and the romance is brought to its conclusion,
yet their vigorous endorsement of sexuality[51] leaves many questions. Are
these two figures the text's final authorities, as some medieval and modern
readers of the *Rose* have argued?[52] Or, as others propose, are they limited
figures whose views on sex carry little or no moral weight,[53] particularly
once the dream-vision has ended? The answer I will suggest is that Nature
and Genius are not simply Christian, nor simply (like Venus) incarnations
of sexuality. By offering yet more points of view on love and by using sex
to disrupt the Lover's and the reader's experience of the romance, they
serve as further disillusionists who, again in Ovidian style, reveal that the
Roman de la Rose is only a fantasy about love.[54]

Part of the reason it is difficult to tell what message these two figures
offer is that their relationship embraces many questions about life and
art—the root of the problem Ovid poses—without resolving them. One
would assume that Nature and Genius would be philosophically opposed
to art and all its manifestations, yet in fact they endorse a variety of arts,
from alchemy (16053–81) to cooking (20136ff.), and Nature herself is described as a figure art has created[55]—which indeed, being copied whole-

sale from Alain de Lille's *De planctu naturae*, she clearly is. And, even more startlingly, Genius compares the "natural" implements of sex—the male genital organs—to artisans' tools (another image borrowed from Alain). Thus, in urging men to fulfil their nature and propagate the human species, he tells them to use these tools to "plow," to "hammer," and to "write." [56] Yet Genius fears that the (nearly equivalent) activities of sex and writing can go wrong: homosexuals, for example, "write" incorrectly, breaking the rules of Nature. No matter how enthusiastically Genius promotes sex, it is for him closely linked with the ambiguous world of art, and hence a troubling topic.

Nature and Genius also have mixed feelings about many of the varied manifestations of love and about human behavior in general. They are the forces of life, but they believe in life only if it is lived in accordance with their views, and they are much more inclined to criticize their creatures than they are to praise them. Nature thus criticizes women, including herself ("Fame sui, si ne me puis tere" [19188] [I am a woman, and so I cannot be silent]), but her real venom, like that of the Vielle, is reserved for men, whom she castigates in a list of accusations whose vehemence is equaled only by Andreas Capellanus's denunciation of the vices of the female sex. Genius returns from misandry to misogyny, attacking women for avarice and for their loquacity; his attack on the female sex, however, is itself so voluble, so hysterical, and so repetitive (compare particularly 16547–53 and 16627–30) that it far exceeds any loquacity of which women might be capable. [57] Nature, in slandering men, and Genius, in tarring women, cannot help besmirching both themselves and one another, and though these two figures enunciate a moral message, their perverse rhetoric casts doubts on what they say. Even if a reader agrees with these two figures' points of view, he or she can scarcely take them as exemplary characters whose advice should be accepted simply on the basis of their moral standing. Like the *praeceptor amoris*, who advises now men, now women, and speaks both for and against love, Nature and Genius are disturbingly inconsistent.

And yet these two characters teach an important lesson about love—one that is in accordance with those of the the other personae. By urging the narrator (and, by extension, all other readers) to sexual performance, they disrupt whatever might have remained of the self-enclosed, courtly hermeticism of Guillaume's text. Their obsessive concern with sex permits the narrator to break through the barriers of lyric love to reach a physical interaction with the Rose. Viewed from the female perspective, of course, this intercourse constitutes rape. [58] But if one looks at the poem with an interest in the psychology of the lover-narrator, one can see that this sexual act embodies the alternative to art that love poetry perpetually hints at but can never reach—that is, a love affair in which the Other is not just an imagined object but a subject like the lover.[59] Ovid plays with this possibility in his amatory works but always restricts his understanding of love to play. Other medieval writers, as we have seen, find even that approach risky. Jean, alone among the writers we have considered, tries to go further. Nature and Genius, the voices of the body,[60] are major thirteenth-century additions to courtly ideology, and hence serve as challenges to the hermeticism of love literature. Yet it is not clear that even these challenges can overthrow the powerful Ovidian model, which molds the thinking of all its readers, including Jean. By making Nature and Genius speakers like the others, Jean gives them authority; yet his use of contradiction and dramatic irony undercuts any special privilege he may wish to lend them. If each speaker's views on sex deconstruct those of his or her predecessor, and if Jean rewrites Guillaume's rewriting of Ovid, there can be no finality: the process of undermining authority, once begun, can only continue. Love, in R_2, falls apart into its constituent elements, elements already isolated by Ovid. We have just seen how the romance treats sex, a prime Ovidian concern; let us now turn to another essential element of fantasy.

Love and Illusion

As it is in the *Ars*, illusion is a central concern in R_2. The love Jean's various preceptors teach is based on visual and emotional images, often deceitful ones. But illusions are most important in these texts because they are a figuration of literature itself. As we have seen, fiction is an artistic creation that has no substance in fact, but is simply an illusion made of words. Thus all discussions of illusion in R_2 can be read as ways in which Jean plays with his own art. And as its name implies, R_2 is a mirror that brings all kinds of images to its readers' view,[61] and a dream that has a deliberately ambiguous relationship with the dreamer's life, with those of its readers, and with the literary texts on which it is based.[62] The elaborate coding of the text,[63] and the complex chain of people (Guillaume-dreamer-lover-R_1 narrator-R_2 narrator-Jean-reader) through whom its experiences are passed and reshaped make it obvious that both characters and readers are bound up in subjective perception. Jean does not, strictly speaking, promote or condemn illusion; rather, he—like Ovid—demonstrates that it permeates every part of the sublunary world, and particularly the world of love.

The character who demonstrates this fact most clearly is Faus Semblant. In some ways he is an easy figure to condemn, at whom one can point as an incarnation of fraud: after all, he is the son of Barat (Deceit) and Ypocrisie (Hypocrisy); his heart is rotten; and he is a traitor (10437–44). Yet, like other *praeceptores amoris*, Faus Semblant permits the poet to reveal that every being—male or female, secular or worldly, aristocratic or common—is capable of dishonesty, too.[64] Faus Semblant can take on any human rôle, he announces:

> Or sui chevaliers, or sui moines,
> or sui prelaz, or sui chanoines,
> or sui clers, autre heure sui prestres,
> or sui deciples, or sui mestres,
> or chateleins, or forestiers:
> briefment je sui de touz mestiers.
> Or resui princes, or sui pages,
> et sai par queur trestouz langages;
> autre heure sui vieuz et chenuz,
> or resui jennes devenuz;
> or sui Roberz, or sui Robins,
> or cordeliers, or jacobins;
> . . . .
> Autre eure vest robe de fame,
> or sui damoisele, or sui dame;
> autre eure sui religieuse,
> or sui rendue, or sui prieuse,
> or sui nonnain, or abbeesse,
> or sui novice, or sui professe.
> (11159–70; 11177–82)

(Now I'm a knight, now I'm a monk; now I'm a prelate, now I'm a canon, now I'm a clerk, then I'm a priest; now I'm a student, now I'm a teacher, now I'm a lord, now I'm a forester: in short, I am in every walk of life. Start again: I'm a prince, now a page, and know all languages by heart; sometimes I'm old and bald, but then I become young again; now

I'm Robert, now I'm Robin, now a Cordelier, now a Jacobin. . . . Sometimes I put on a woman's dress. Now I'm a girl, and now a lady; sometimes I'm a religious, now a sister, now a prioress, now a nun, now an abbess, now a novice, now a professed nun.)

Faus Semblant provides an example of illusory images at their worst. He shows that illusion can lead to a bottomless abyss of deception, the same warning found in some passages of Ovid's amatory texts. Subjective images, however, do not always have a negative value in Jean's romance. The only true mirror, Nature explains, is God's, which reflects everything that has ever happened and everything that will come to pass. All other mirrors, like human vision in general, are subject to distortion.[65] Even Nature, though she scorns those who cannot distinguish between illusion and reality, is nothing but an image,[66] and the romance itself, as a *miroër* (in Old French, a looking glass, a lens, or an ideal), can provide only subjective reflections, whether these be edifying or immoral.[67] Within the world of the poem and the world of human love, everything is illusory. To illustrate this point, Jean retells a story whose presence in R₂ is overdetermined by its literary heritage—the tale of Narcissus, the boy who fell in love with his own image. Already recounted by Ovid and Guillaume,[68] this story provides a key to seeing how Jean confronts earlier amatory writers on their own turf.

Ovid's tale of Narcissus (*Metamorphoses* 3.339–510) is a story of transformation that serves as a warning about those who cannot distinguish between appearance and reality in love. Briefly, it goes as follows. Narcissus is the son of the river nymph Liriope. Tiresias, the famous seer, predicts that the boy will have a long life "si se non nouerit" (3.348) (If he does not know himself), a prophecy which, unfortunately, is fulfilled only in the breach. Young men and women alike fall in love with the sixteen-year-old youth. One of these is Echo, whose speech impediment provides an apt prefiguration of Narcissus's self-centered love: she can only repeat his words back to him, and, rejected, her beauty and her body waste away. Another spurned lover—this one male—prays that Narcissus himself fall victim to unrequited love, and Nemesis grants his prayer.

One day, tired from hunting, Narcissus lies down by a forest pool, sees his beautiful reflection, and falls in love; not understanding that what he sees is only an image, he tries to embrace it. The narrator explains that what Narcissus sees is an illusion, but, of course, he is heard only by his readers, and not by the boy.

quid uideat, nescit: sed, quod uidet, uritur illo,
atque oculos idem, qui decipit, incitat error.
credule, quid frustra simulacra fugacia captas?
quod petis, est nusquam: quod amas, auertere, perdes!
ista repercussae, quam cernis, imaginis umbra est:
nil habet ipsa sui: tecum uenitque manetque;
tecum discedet,—si tu discedere possis!

(3.430–36)

(He does not know what he sees; but what he sees, he burns for, and the same error that deceives his eyes incites them further. Gullible boy, why are you trying vainly to grasp a fleeing image? That which you seek does not exist in any place: turn away and you will lose the thing you love! What you see is the shadow of a reflected image: it has no essence of its own. It comes with you and stays while you are there, and leaves with you—if you could only leave!)

Though Narcissus eventually shows that he recognizes what has happened—"iste ego sum! sensi; nec me mea fallit imago! / uror amore mei" (3.463–64) ("I am the one! I have figured it out: my image no longer deceives me! I am on fire with love for myself")—his recognition does not release him from his suffering. Wasting away entirely, Narcissus's body is replaced by the white and yellow flower that bears his name (a symbol of artistry in nature[69]), and his spirit, Ovid notes with grim humor, continues to gaze at itself in the waters of the Styx. Narcissus's beauty is a trap, for others and for himself; the boy is a dangerous *exemplum* for those who would love.

Guillaume transforms the classical story into a medieval tale that is, by and large, more reassuring than its classical model. Echo is now "une haute dame" (1442) (an aristocratic lady) whose prayer (for it is now *her* prayer) that Narcissus learn to suffer is granted not by Nemesis but by God and Amor. The boy is turned not into a flower but into a literary text—the story Nature inscribes above the fountain[70]—and the fountain itself is redeemed by becoming the mirror in which the narrator sees, and falls in love with, the Rose.[71] The narrator manages to pass through the illusions of Narcissus's mirror and into a deeper experience of love than his classical predecessor had.[72]

Still, some unresolved elements of Ovid's story remain—in particular, the confusion of genders. Narcissus's male suitors are not mentioned by

Guillaume, but the boy's love for himself retains hints of blurred sexual and gender identity[73] that may carry over into the sexually ambiguous love for the Rose which the narrator conceives through looking into the fountain.[74] The sexual confusion of this passage culminates in the narrator's interpretation of Narcissus's story:

> Dames, cest essample aprenez,
> qui vers vos amis mesprenez;
> car se vos les lessiez morir,
> Dex le vos savra bien merir.
>
> (1505–8)

(Ladies who are unkind toward your lovers, learn from this example; for if you let them die, God will take care to give you what you deserve.)

It is far from obvious that one should derive such a moral from this version of the story: indeed, Rupert Pickens describes it as "absurd" and characterizes the narrator as an incompetent reader.[75] This tale is a warning more apt for lovers than for ladies.[76] But though Narcissus fails to attain love, Guillaume portrays his fountain as a risky but necessary rite of passage which, by transforming the narrator's vision, permits him to become able to love and understand his own experience.[77]

This positive interpretation of the tale does not last, however. When we meet the fountain again, in R_2, it is condemned by Genius as "la fonteine perilleuse," bitter and venomous, an ugly, unreflecting mirror that provokes men to madness (20379–408). Genius discusses the fountain of Narcissus as he creates his new image of Guillaume's garden—the park of the Lamb. Everything in the Garden of Deduit, says Genius, is illusory and corruptible; what *he* describes, on the other hand, is true (20319–24), and its beauty and pleasure inestimable. He portrays his garden and its fountain as a sort of moral mirror image of those in R_1. He comments ironically on the fountain of Narcissus:

> Dex, con bone fonteine et sade,
> ou li sain devienent malade!
> Et con il s'i fet bon virer
> por soi dedanz l'eve mirer!
>
> (20391–94)

(God, what a good and pleasant fountain, in which the healthy become sick! And how good it is to turn oneself toward it to look at oneself in its water!)

Guillaume claims that the fountain is clear, says Genius, when in fact it is so murky that those who lean over it for a reflection do not see a thing (20401–6). The fountain in the Park of the Lamb, on the other hand, which issues from itself and whose three streams are one, reflects not just half the park, as Guillaume's does, but the full, true, and eternal nature of everything that surrounds it.

> Si ra si merveilleus poair
> que cil qui la le vont voair,
> si tost con cele part se virent
> et leur faces an l'eve mirent,
> tourjorz, de quelque part qu'il soient,
> toutes les choses du parc voient
> et les connoissent proprement,
> et eus meïsmes ansement;
> et puis que la se sunt veü,
> ja mes ne seront deceü
> de nule chose que puisse estre,
> tant i devienent sage mestre.
> (20537–48)

(It has, indeed, such remarkable power that, when people go to see it, as soon as they turn toward it and look at their faces in the water, always, whichever side they are on, they see all the things in the park and know them truly, and themselves as well; and once they have seen themselves there, they will never be deceived by anything whatsoever, because they have become such wise masters.)

The old fountain, Genius says in summation, makes the living drunk with death; the new one brings the dead back to life (20595–96).

Yet, here as elsewhere, Jean insists that his readers take responsibility for their interpretations. The Christian rewriting of the scene and all its elements which Genius offers is undermined by his sexual licentiousness,[78] and readers are left to make their own meanings, as we see in the final sequence of Jean's poem, the assault on the tower and on the Rose. One can understand this scene as such only by a process of interpretation, since Jean describes sexual intercourse in allegorical terms. The assault, which is (once decoded) blushingly graphic, goes on for pages; we will examine only its climax. Once he has made his way through the defenses of the tower and all its guardians, including Poor (Fear) and Honte (Shame), the lover kneels down to kiss the "relics" between the two "pillars," then manages, after much effort, to penetrate the "narrow passage" between them (though his "hammers," hanging down, remain outside), and finally reaches his goal.

> Par les rains saisi le rosier,
> qui plus sunt franc que nul osier;
> et quant a .II. mains m'i poi joindre,
> tretout soavet, san moi poindre,
> le bouton pris a elloichier,
> qu'anviz l'eüsse san hoichier.
> Toutes an fis par estovoir
> les branches croller et mouvoir,
> san ja nul des rains depecier,
> car n'i vouloie riens blecier;
> et si m'an convint il a force
> entamer un po de l'escorce,
> qu'autrement avoir ne savoie
> ce don si grant desir avoie.
>   A la parfin, tant vos an di,
> un po de greine i espandi,
> quant j'oi le bouton elloichié.
> Ce fu quant dedanz l'oi toichié
> por les fueilletes reverchier,
> car je vouloie tout cerchier
> jusques au fonz du boutonet,
> si con moi samble que bon et.
> Si fis lors si meller les greines
> qu'el se desmellassent a peines,
> si que tout le boutonet tandre
> an fis ellargir et estandre.
>
>   (21675–700)

(I seized the rosebush by its branches, which were fresher than any willow; and when I was able to hold it with my two hands, I began to shake the bud very gently, without pricking myself, because I had wanted to have it without shaking it. But I had to move and shake the branches, without breaking any of them, because I didn't want to injure anything; and so I was obliged to damage a little of the bark, because I knew of no other way to get that which I wanted so much.

At the very end, I spread a little seed in it, when I had shaken the bud. This was when I touched it inside, to examine all the little leaves, because I wanted to look at everything, down to the base of the bud, because it seemed good to me. Then I mixed the seeds so well that it would be hard for them to be separated, in such a way that I made the whole tender bud enlarge and grow.)

As we have noted, none of Jean's narrative at this point is explicitly eroticized. But as the lover follows the path Genius has prescribed for him, and as the reader uses the interpretive tools he or she has acquired (and this simple allegory is hardly a challenge after one has read 20,000 verses of the *Rose*), it becomes abundantly clear that Nature and Genius, for all their puritanism, are at least as interested in carnality as any other characters in the text. They may disrupt the fantasies of Narcissus's mirror, Guillaume's text, and courtly love in general, but they do so with the most Ovidian of illusion-breaking tools—sex—rather than with the pure philosophy recommended, for example, by Reson. If readers reflect (as they can scarcely avoid doing) on Genius, they will see that his perspective, too, is subject to question. The more Genius condemns fantasy love, and the more explicitly the lover follows his path, the more readers are forced to recognize that the merits of any kind of love depend on the viewer's perspective.

The mirror of Narcissus, the mirrors of Nature, and the *Miroër aus amoreus* as a whole are representations of ways of seeing the universe and the love that both exists within it and constitutes its dominant force. All can be used *in malo* or *in bono*, and all will give a variety of reflections and views, depending on who is looking into them, and what he or she is looking at.[79] This variability is one of the mirror's most characteristic qualities: the multifaceted *Roman de la Rose*, as Gunn proposes, reflects "all the various and conflicting meanings and aspects of love,"[80] multiplying and transforming the appearance of things, representing its subject, love, from many angles, like a Cubist painting.[81] The optical nature of the *Rose* reflects the nature of poetry itself,[82] which represents the sublunary world with a vision that is always part illusion. The images found in Jean's text are invariably misrepresentative, but they are no more deceptive than any other kind of human sight or artistic vision; indeed, by permitting his readers to see the limitations of such characters as Reson and Genius, Jean reassures them of their own abilities. The romance is at once a metaliterary text, a lens for viewing the world, and a mirror for self-recognition.[83]

Art, Love, and Interpretation

We have seen that R_2 often treats love as a question of vision—as a product of images that may seem illusory or real, depending on the viewer. This question of love and its meaning is raised by another central theme of the romance—that of art. In this area, Jean again challenges his sources. Ovid, as we have clearly seen, presents his amatory works as a triumph of art: he is a proud creator who demands his audience's admiration. Guillaume de Lorris, like most courtly writers, creates a delicate fictional world deliberately distanced from the forces of everyday life.[84] Jean de Meun, on the other hand, seems to use his frequent references to matters in the world around him, such as the thirteenth century's mendicant crisis[85] and its scientific revolution, as well as to sex,[86] as tools for pushing his readers outside the framed world of courtly fiction. Jean's ability to throw his readers outside the frame is limited, of course, by his medium: R_2 is a fiction full of material borrowed from other fictions. Jean confronts these limitations by recounting a story that, though itself highly literary, focuses on a situation in which love transforms art into life: the tale of Pygmalion and his ivory maiden. This narrative, clearly of great thematic importance, is marked in numerous ways as a key episode of the romance, as many critics have observed. It is inserted at surprising length just before the romance's sexual allegory reaches its climax;[87] it is borrowed from Ovid; it is recounted in the narrator's own voice; and it seems to be offered as a corrective response to the tale of Narcissus, which we have just considered. If Jean wishes to show that Ovid and Guillaume were masters only of illusory love, and that it is he who will truly teach his readers how to break out of the framed world of fantasy love affairs, it is through Pygmalion and the sexualized conclusion of the romance that we will be convinced of his power. Let us see how Ovid recounts this story, and what Jean maintains and what he adapts in presenting his version.

The tale of Pygmalion is the story of a miracle of love performed by Venus. In the simple and relatively brief Ovidian version (*Metamorphoses* 10:243–97), Pygmalion, a sculptor, lives as a bachelor because he finds women immoral. Desiring a love-object without flaws, he creates a statue more beautiful than any human female, and, unable or unwilling to distinguish clearly between image and reality, falls in love with it. At Venus's feast, Pygmalion, too timid to ask the goddess to have his statue made into flesh, cautiously prays for a bride resembling his ivory maiden. Venus generously grants the request he did not dare to make, and when the sculptor, returning home, embraces the maiden, he finds her coming gradually alive.

In R_2, Jean de Meun retells Ovid's story at significantly greater length (366 lines [20787–21153] to Ovid's 54). He amplifies the tale not only by adding a substantial number of ornamental details, but also by giving the figure of Pygmalion a good deal of depth and self-consciousness. Having created a beautiful image and fallen in love with it, Jean's sculptor is assailed by self-doubts that take as their point of attack the very subjects we have been considering—the rôle of the spectator in creating the meaning of a work of art, the value and limits of fantasy, and the relationship between art and love. "Am I asleep?" he asks; "Am I crazy?" (20813, 20827). Even if he loved a queen, he muses, he could have some hope, whereas this infatuation is not only unnatural but completely incapable of fulfilment as well. Being a good medieval man, however, Jean's Pygmalion eventually consoles himself by finding *exempla* appropriate to his case.

> Puis que Pygmalion oi non
> et poi sus mes .II. piez aler,
> n'oï de tele amour paler.
> Si n'ain je pas trop folement,
> car, se l'escriture ne ment,
> maint ont plus folement amé.
> N'ama jadis ou bois ramé,
> a la fonteine clere et pure,
> Narcisus sa propre figure,
> quant cuida sa saif estanchier?
> N'onques ne s'an pot revanchier,
> puis an fu morz, selonc l'estoire,
> qui oncor est de grant memoire.
> Don sui je mains fos toutevois,
> car, quant je veill, a ceste vois
> et la praign et l'acole et bese,
> s'an puis mieuz souffrir ma mesese;
> mes cil ne poait avoir cele
> qu'il veait en la fontenele.
> D'autre part, en maintes contrees,
> ont maint maintes dames amees
> et les servirent quan qu'il porent,
> n'onques un seul besier n'an orent,
> si s'an sunt il forment pené.
> (20840–63)

(Since I have been called Pygmalion, and walked on my own two feet, I have never heard of such a love. But still I do not love too madly, for, if books do not lie, many others have been more foolish in love. Didn't Narcissus once, in the branchy wood, in the clear pure fountain, fall in love with his own face, when he thought he could quench his thirst? He was unable to stop himself, and then, according to the story, which people remember well, he died from it. So I am still less crazy than he was, since, whenever I want, I go to her and give her a hug and a kiss, and can thus endure my unhappiness better, whereas he [Narcissus] couldn't have the girl [*sic*] he saw in the fountain.[88]

Furthermore, in many countries, many lovers have loved many ladies and served them as much as they could, without receiving a single kiss, and have suffered a great deal as a result.)

Pygmalion refrains from asserting that he is as superior to courtly lovers as he is to Narcissus, but we can easily understand how he evaluates love: successful lovers, in his view, are not those who suffer profoundly or who create a beautiful fantasy world for themselves, like those portrayed in the courtly lyrics and romances of the twelfth century, but those who receive an answering love and consummate their desire. Yet the mere act of articulating his ideal does not constitute for Pygmalion a way out of his problem. He is still in love with a statue. He adorns it and offers it gifts, and even—an innovation—marries it, invoking Hymenaeus and Juno ("'the true gods of marriage'" [20990]) and rejecting the Christian participation of "'clerks, priests, prelates, mitres, and crosses'" (20988–89). It is only when the sculptor prays to the superior power of Venus and promises the goddess he will renounce chastity that his wish for a living partner is granted.

Upon returning home, Pygmalion expresses his fear that the image, though more lifelike than ever, is only a dream, but the maiden assures him that she is real: "'Ce n'est anemis ne fantosme, / douz amis, ainz sui vostre amie'" (21124–25) ("I am neither a demon nor a ghost, sweet lover: I am your beloved"). The story, read up to this point, has a happy end: the artist's fantasy transcends itself, and the sculptor not only enjoys his maiden's love but also, in congress with her, fathers a line of descendants.

In this positive interpretation of the Pygmalion story, illusion is successfully transformed into reality. Many critics have, in this vein, highlighted the contrast between Narcissus's unsuccessful and deadly self-reflexive passion and Pygmalion's other-directed, consummated love.[89]

Some scholars, however, have offered less affirmative readings of Pygmalion's love. Wetherbee, for example, suggests that his passion may be idolatrous;[90] Thomas Hill sees it as "ludicrous" and "obscene";[91] Leslie Cahoon sees it as a fantasy of what men wish love could be like;[92] and other readers suggest that Narcissus and Pygmalion are in fact quite similar, since they fall in love not with a true Other, but with images of the self.[93] Like many other aspects of Jean's poem, his treatment of Pygmalion is ambiguous: it shows the transformative and transcendent power of fantasy love, yet also hints at its dangers.

For Pygmalion has a negative side, a recessive trait that is expressed not in his life but in those of his unhappy descendants. Before returning from the *exemplum* to the assault on the Rose, Jean quickly mentions Pygmalion's offspring—his son Paphus; Paphus's son, King Cynaras; Cynaras's daughter, Mirra; and her son, Adonis—a long and famous line.[94] Jean closes the Pygmalion parenthesis with one of his many *occupationes*, resuming his main tale as he tells his readers that he has drifted too far from his subject, and assuring them that they will hear the meaning of this episode before the work reaches its end. Despite this promise, however, Jean does not elucidate the meaning of the story later on in the romance, and for a good reason: he has finished it earlier in his text.

The end of the Pygmalion story is found in the tale of Adonis, borrowed, once again, from Ovid (compare *Metamorphoses* 10.503–59), which Jean told in lines 15646–734—the only other myth Jean's narrator recounts in his own voice.[95] Though beautiful, we are told, Adonis was not wise, and by disregarding Venus's warning, he lost first his genitals and then his life to the boar he was hunting. And just as Guillaume gave an ambiguous moral to the story of Narcissus, so Jean follows his Adonis episode with a caution:

> Biau seigneur, que qu'il vos aviegne,
> de cest example vos souviegne.
> Vos qui ne creez voz amies,
> sachiez mout fetes granz folies;
> bien les deüssiez toutes croire,
> car leur diz sunt voirs conme estoire.
> S'el jurent: "Toutes somes vostres,"
> creez les conme paternostres;
> ja d'aus croire ne recreez.
> Se Reson vient, point n'an creez;

s'el vos aportoit croicefis,
n'an creez point ne quel je fis.
Se cist s'amie eüst creüe,
mout eüst sa vie creüe.

(15721–34)

(Fair lords, whatever happens to you, remember this example. You who
do not believe your sweethearts, know that you are acting very foolishly;
you should really believe them all, because what they say is as true as history. If they swear, "We are completely yours," believe them like the
Lord's Prayer; never refuse to believe them. If Reason comes, do not believe her; even if she brought you a crucifix, do not believe her any more
than I do. If this man had believed his sweetheart, his life would have
grown much longer.)

On the surface, this moral follows naturally upon its story: if Adonis had
listened to Venus, he would indeed have lived to a greater age. But what
Jean's readers hear from their mistresses are not lessons on hunting but
protestations of fidelity which may have no basis at all in fact. The Ovidian
praeceptor amoris is clearly heard here, urging his students to have sex at all
costs, and to ignore such petty concerns as whether their mistresses are
engaging in sexual intercourse with other men. And, thinking backward,
it is hard not to worry about where the *Rose* is taking its readers, if its final
exemplum ends in infidelity, incest, castration, and death.[96]

The narrator's favorable interpretation of the Pygmalion story seems
yet more peculiar when we recall that Book 10 of the *Metamorphoses*, in
which the tale is found, is the unhappy book of profane and perverse loves.
It is narrated by Orpheus, who, after Eurydice's second death, introduced
pederasty to Thrace and was stoned to death for his pains by the neglected,
indignant Thracian women.[97] And in fact, Ovid's Pygmalion is by no
means superior to his Narcissus. It would be easy for a medieval reader to
condemn Venus, Pygmalion, and Adonis (not to mention Narcissus,
Ovid, and classical myth in general) as immoral,[98] but, once again, Jean
does not put his story together in a way that offers his readers any easy
lessons, negative or positive, about art and love.[99]

The Pygmalion story, though the most dramatic, is not the only episode in which Jean urges his readers to undermine surface meanings by
using their interpretive skills. In each case in which the need for interpretation or the process is explicitly discussed (as, for example, in Jean's regu-

lar uses of such terms as *espondre* [to expound] and *gloser* [to gloss][100]),
Jean creates a complex interplay of interpretation in which his text is both
a reading of other texts and an invitation to his readers to interpret the
text themselves. Reading and writing are shown to be interdependent,
even interchangeable, activities.

One example of this procedure is found in Reson's diatribe against
Fortune, where two methods of interpretation are contrasted. Reson tells
the story of Croesus, who dreams that he will be washed by Jupiter and
dried by Phebus. Croesus's daughter, Phanie, sees the dream as an allegorical description of her father's hanging (6511–18); the king, however,
believes that such a "noble" dream can be read not allegorically but only
literally (6575–84). Now it is true this dream was meant to be allegorized:
Phanie's reading is correct, and Croesus suffers for his arrogance. But
though the tale proves Croesus wrong, it is harder for readers of the *Rose*
to know how to read this incident, for while the story itself argues against
literal interpretation, an alert reader cannot help noting that it is told by
the literal-minded Reson (her words, she says, "pris doivent estre a la letre,
/ tout proprement, sanz glose metre" [7153–54] ["should be taken literally,
in their natural sense, without a gloss"]), whose character contradicts the
principle Reson herself espouses.[101]

At other moments, too, the reader is pulled in opposite directions.
Ami, for example, in his friendly way, tells the narrator to take his lessons
at face value: "'c'est bien pleine chose / (je ne vos i metré ja glose, / ou
tiexte vos poez fier),'" (7529–31) (It's quite plain [I will never gloss it for
you: you can trust the text]). Given, however, that Ami makes this sug-
gestion shortly after giving advice on producing false tears with onion
juice, readers may justly doubt his trustworthiness.[102] Nature, too, is
wary of glosses, preferring the presumably more concrete rhetoric of the
exemplum: [103]

> Et por fere antandre la chose,
> bien an peut l'an, en leu de glose,
> a brief moz un example metre,
> por mieuz fere esclarcir la letre.
>   (16821–24)

(To make something understandable, one may, instead of a gloss, propose an example in a few words, in order better to illuminate the letter of
the text.)

Yet though *exempla* may make meanings clearer, they may also obscure
them, as we have seen with the stories of Pygmalion, Narcissus, and
Adonis. Like Andreas's fable of the disobedient wife and the poisoned
wine, each of these tales of interpretation leaves the reader bewildered.
Sometimes the surface of a text carries its message; sometimes it does not.
There is no general rule.

Ambiguity remains an essential part of the romance, rooted inextricably in its nature, as it is in the *Ars amatoria* and the *De amore*. Indeed,
just as he is about to undertake his sexual mission, the narrator pauses for
a moment to talk about the problematics of establishing meaning:

> Ainsinc va des contreres choses,
> les unes sunt des autres gloses;
> et qui l'une an veust defenir,
> de l'autre li doit souvenir,
> ou ja, par nule antancion,
> n'i metra diffinicion;
> car qui des .II. n'a connoissance,
> ja n'i connoistra differance,
> san quoi ne peut venir en place
> diffinicion que l'an face.
>
> (21543–52)

(Thus it is for contrary things: the one is the gloss of the other; and
whoever wants to define one should remember the other. Otherwise he
will never be able to make a definition, no matter what his intent; for
whoever does not know both of them will never understand difference,
without which any definition one makes will never find its place.)

Contrariety and opposition are both complementary and fundamental in
the *Rose*, as Augustine suggests they are everywhere on earth, the *regio
dissimilitudinis* (the region of difference): likeness is the domain of the
deity alone.[104] And since the romance, its subject, and its readers belong
primarily to the world, they must participate in the play of "differance"
and interpretation in the text, which can never settle down to univocity.[105]
To read R_2 in this way is not to despair of meaning but rather to recognize
that Jean's text, like Ovid's, accommodates and even creates each reader's
need to make meaning of it for him- or herself.

As we have seen, the structure of R_2, with its series of speakers and their points of view, re-creates the model of the *Ars amatoria* and the *De amore*: by burdening their readers with ambiguities and contradictions, Ovid and his disciples teach them to be responsible for the meanings they find. Luring their readers into the text by offering to teach them the art of love, the authors teach lessons about the close relationship between love and reading, between personal and artistic imagination, and between literature and experience. Like Ovid and Andreas, but more explicitly than either, Jean encourages his readers to think not only about the creativity of literary love but also about the relationship between fiction and the love they experience in their own lives. The romance's insistence on variable meaning[106] is first a lesson on reading the open-ended text and the contradictory arguments of the characters,[107] and then a lesson on reading oneself. The narrator is transformed from student to teacher,[108] and the reader follows him into the text and out the other side, perhaps having been changed by the experience.

The relationship between Jean's portion of the romance and Guillaume's provides a model for this reading. As we have noted, critics have proposed viewing R_2 as an explanatory gloss on R_1.[109] But finding out exactly what this gloss means is a more complex problem.[110] Guillaume promises to reveal the significance of his dream poem when it reaches its conclusion: at this point, he promises, "La verité, qui est coverte, / vos sera lores toute overte" (2071–72) (The truth, which is covered up, will then be completely opened up to you). The fact remains, however, that in R_1 the dream has no end;[111] its *senefiance* and *verité* therefore remain hidden[112] until each reader, of necessity appropriating the first-person rôle, becomes its "I," and, introducing his or her own desire into the text, sees him- or herself in the *Miroër* and chooses the meaning he or she will find. Readers of the *Rose* need to learn not only how to understand the text by discovering its meaning, but also to become *auctores* of their own works. Thus Jean's *Rose* does, in a way, become a mirror for lovers and teach the art of love.

Conclusion

Like his predecessors whom we considered in Chapters 2 and 3, Jean de Meun rewrites Ovid's *Ars amatoria* for a medieval audience. His text thus participates in the struggle that engaged the whole literary world of the Middle Ages—that between the classical and Christian traditions. Jean gives a voice to each side, but makes his readers responsible for resolving this conflict themselves; and in this move, he makes it clear that Ovid provides his most fundamental structural model. To Ovid Jean owes his poem's concern with secular, sexual love,[113] the links between love and poetry, the text's multivalence, and its emphasis on making the reader find the limits of the text and rely on his or her own judgment.[114] Like Andreas, Jean shows that poetry and the love it depicts pose moral problems for Christianity. Neither medieval author, however, yields completely to religion's control. Though both of them use Christianity as a tool to dissipate the illusions of love, this use is in itself an Ovidian technique which, while revealing that love is illusion, permits it to stand as a textual creation. Many medieval writers were intrigued by Ovid's secular love stories, which they imitated in their writings. Relatively few, however—Baudri of Bourgueil, Andreas Capellanus, and Jean de Meun being among the best known—found inspiration in the theoretical implications of Ovid's erotic work. For these authors, the *Ars* and *Remedia* showed that literary love could provide a key to understanding the workings of secular fiction.

As the *Ars* taught its lessons about the art of Roman amatory fiction, so R_2 provides a way of understanding how courtly love literature works. Like Ovid, Jean comes at the end of an era in which a certain kind of love and love poetry flourished, and, like Ovid's, Jean's text uses the elements and conventions of its genre to show how reader and writer collaborate on creating poetry that re-creates, transforms, and immortalizes a particular kind of love. Like Ovid, too, Jean shows that the kind of love he describes is one in which imagination and fantasy play a dominant rôle, and which is so close to love poetry that it is almost impossible to distinguish them from one another. The treatises on the art of love are thus both works of literary criticism and psychological studies,[115] within whose limits writing and sex are inextricably linked. Indeed, the text needs, seduces, and falls in love with the reader, and even reproduces itself through him or her by making the reader its maker of interpretations, meanings, and further texts. Reading and writing, from the text's point of view, are thus amatory, erotic, and even procreative experiences.[116]

Yet though it draws us further and further into the textual world, the *Miroër aus amoreus* also assaults that world's borders. The major works of R_2's literary context all isolate themselves by framing devices of one kind or another: courtly lyric, for example, is strictly conventionalized; the Breton stories of Marie de France and Chrétien de Troyes are otherworldly; and Guillaume's *Roman de la Rose* is surrounded by the strictures of garden wall and dream-vision. Jean's text, on the other hand, seems to open itself to the outside world. Still, the lessons about love R₂ offers—that literary love is only illusory, and that it should give way to an interchange not bounded by fantasy—are taught by means of a fiction. Before leaving this fiction behind, readers must work their way through Jean's massive and immensely complicated text in which Guillaume's delicate allegory finally reaches its natural erotic fulfilment—at which point the poem abruptly ends: [117]

> par grant joliveté cueilli
> la fleur du biau rosier feuilli.
> Ainsint oi la rose vermeille.
> Atant fu jorz, et je m'esveille.
> (21747–50)

(With great pleasure I plucked the flower of the beautiful, leafy rosebush. Thus I had the crimson rose. Suddenly it was day, and I awoke.)

In suggesting that there is more to love than can be contained in a book, Jean de Meun expresses a certain humility, for he thus diminishes the value of his own work, and also a certain pride, for if even his *miroër* cannot truly reflect the art of love, then Ovid and Guillaume, whom he claims to have superseded, are still greater failures in the rôle of preceptor. Yet Jean's very act of wadding his text into a ball and throwing it over his shoulder is—like so much that constitutes the *Miroër*—a gesture already prefigured by the end of the *Ars*:

> LVSVS habet finem: cycnis descendere tempus,
> duxerunt collo qui iuga nostra suo.
> ut quondam iuuenes, ita nunc, mea turba, puellae
> inscribant spoliis NASO MAGISTER ERAT.
> (*Ars amatoria* 3.809–12)

(THE GAME has reached its end. It is time to step down from the chariot which Venus's swans have pulled. As young men did before, so now, my band of girls, hang the armor of your defeated enemy as a votive offering in the temple, and inscribe it, in dedication: "OVID WAS MY TEACHER.")

Even in announcing that the art of love is only a game, and that his book is only a book, Jean is still following his Roman master. And even an iconoclastic thirteenth-century poet as sophisticated as Jean de Meun could not write about literary love in a way that had not already been modeled in the *Ars* and the *Remedia*, Ovid's treatise on the intimate relationship between illusion and disillusionment, fantasy and fiction. Whether, like Andreas, they used the *Ars* to create the beginnings of a fictional world in the face of ecclesiastical disapproval, or whether, like Jean, they sought to conquer the classical *auctores*, medieval writers, trained from childhood on the *Ars*, remained students of Ovid, the *magister amoris*, whose poems showed them how to write for their own day new works on the arts of love and fiction.[118]

Appendix. Medieval Reception and Transmission of Ovid's Amatory Works: An Overview

Classical and Late Antique Period

CITATIONS, LITERARY ATTITUDES
Ovid's works are cited by Lucan, Statius, Juvenal, Martial, Seneca.[1]

No antique commentaries on Ovid's works survive, suggesting that Ovid was less intensively studied than Vergil, Statius, Terence, Lucan, or Cicero during this period.[2]

Fifth through Eighth Centuries

CITATIONS, LITERARY ATTITUDES
The *carmina amatoria* are cited by African and Spanish authors,[3] and by the writers of the Bodensee (Lake Constance) area.[4]

Isidore of Seville (570–636) quotes from Persius, Horace, Vergil, and Ovid, including the *Remedia, Ars*, and *Amores*, though he is often highly critical of Ovid's erotic works, with which he may be familiar only from anthologies.[5]

Insular writers, including Aldhelm of Malmesbury (650–709), and Bonifatius (a missionary to Germany, ca. 680-ca. 755), cite Ovid's works on love.[6]

MANUSCRIPTS, LIBRARY CATALOGUES
The archetype of the extant manuscripts of the erotic poems may have been present in Gaul as early as the sixth or seventh century.[7]

Carolingian Renaissance (Eighth to Early Ninth Centuries)

CITATIONS, LITERARY ATTITUDES
Poetry that may imitate Ovidian forms and meters is written by Alcuin of York (ca. 735–804) and Angilbert (abbot of St. Riquier and Duke of Ponthieu, 740–814).[8]

Theodulf (b. Spain, mid-eighth century, d. 821; Bishop of Orléans, abbot of Fleury) writes a poem called "De libris quos legere solebam" (The Books I Used to Read), including a description of his seeking the truths under the "frivolities and falsehoods" of the major Roman poets (compare the discussion of *integumentum* in Chapter 2):

> Et modo Pompeium, modo te, Donate, legebam
> Et modo Virgilium, te modo, Naso loquax.
> In quorum dictis quamquam sint frivola multa,
> Plurima sub falso tegmine vera latent.[9]

(At times I would read you, Pompeius, or you, Donatus; now Virgil, now you, talkative Ovid. Though much that is frivolous is found in their writings, many truths lie hidden under a covering of falsehood.)

Modoin (bishop of Autun in 815 and friend of Theodulf) is called the "Naso" of Charlemagne's court.[10]

MANUSCRIPTS
Theodulf may bring a MS of the *carmina amatoria* to France; Tafel hypothesizes that this may be extant MS R (Parisinus latinus 7311; see below).[11]

Alcuin names Ovid as an author whose works were present in the library at York.[12]

Ninth and Tenth Centuries

CITATIONS, LITERARY ATTITUDES
Ovid, Vergil, and Fortunatus are major models for Latin verse composition in the schools.

Ovidian material is used in various Latin song and lyric collections throughout Europe (see Chapter 2).

Raban Maur (780–856, German Benedictine and student of Alcuin of York) describes Ovid as a "moral author" in his *De clericorum institutione* (*Clerical Education*).[13] Raban tells his students, "Poemata autem et libros gentilium si velimus propter florem eloquentiae legere . . . si quid in eis utile reperimus, ad nostrum dogma convertimus; si quid vero superfluum de idolis, de amore, de cura saecularium rerum, haec radamus"[14] (If we want to read the poems and books of the gentiles for the flowers of eloquence . . . if we find anything useful there, we convert it to our beliefs; if we find any superfluous material—dealing with idols, or love, or concern for things of the world—this we erase).

Florus (late eighth century-860), deacon of Lyon, felicitates his friend Modoin for having given up writing secular poetry. His epistle contains citations from the *Fasti*, the *Remedia*, the *Metamorphoses*, the *Amores*, and the *Epistulae Heroidum*, indicating either that separating Christian and secular writing was extremely difficult,[15] or that Florus was employing irony to show that he did not view secular poetry as particularly harmful.

Ovid is a favorite poet of Walafrid Strabo (ca. 808–49; student of Raban Maur; abbot of Reichenau [see mention of library catalogue, below]).[16]

Ermenrich of Ellwangen (ca. 814–74; student of Raban Maur) compares the words of the pagan poets to the foul dung that fertilizes the fields of divine study.[17]

Carolingian traditions of learning are maintained in Germany during the "Ottonian Renaissance" of Emperor Otto I (962–73).[18]

MANUSCRIPTS

Three of the most important extant MSS are copied during this period. Two are French: P (Parisinus latinus 8242; contains some of the *Heroides*, *Amores* 1.2.51–3.12.26, 14.3–15.8) and R (Parisinus latinus 7311; contains *Ars, Remedia, Amores* epigram-1.2.19, 1.2.25–50); one is Welsh: O (Oxoniensis Bodleianus Auct. F. 4. 32, the "Classbook of St. Dunstan"; contains *Ars* 1).[19]

The ninth-century catalogue of the Bodensee monastery of Reichenau lists copies of the *Ars* and the *Metamorphoses*.

The *Epistulae ex Ponto* are listed in the in ninth-century library catalogue at Murbach.[20]

The tenth-century catalogue of Bobbio contains two books of Ovid.[21]

Eleventh Century

CITATIONS, LITERARY ATTITUDES
Ovid's texts form an essential part of the curriculum of monastery schools (see Chapter 2).

Ovid comes to the forefront of classical writers (see Chapter 2).

Ovid is regularly cited by Hildebert of Lavardin, Godefroy of Reims, Guy of Amiens, Raoul de la Tourte, and Baudri of Bourgueil (see Chapter 2).

The *Carmina burana* are written.

MANUSCRIPTS
The *Fasti* are listed in the catalogue of the Montecassino library.[22]

Catalogues of German monastery libraries list Ovid's works: Benedikt-beuren,[23] Blaubeuren (including all the amatory poems), Tegernsee (*Ars, Remedia, Epistulae Heroidum*), Hamersleven (*Epistulae Heroidum, Remedia*).[24]

Ovid's works are found in French library catalogues: Beauvais (*Metamorphoses*), Toul ("quater quaterniones Ovidii de amore"), Chartres, Cluny.[25]

Twelfth Century

CITATIONS, LITERARY ATTITUDES
Conrad of Hirsau (first half of twelfth century; German Benedictine) says that any benefits to be found in secular texts are "aurum in stercore"

(gold amidst dung), but advises tolerance for the *Fasti*, the *Pontics*, and the *Nux*, among other works,[26] and says that the work of Ovid and other secular authors has merit if it is oriented toward good; the profitable parts of it can be used to educate the young and even to adorn the style and souls of Christian writers.[27]

Bernardus Silvestris (fl. ca. 1150) is an admirer of Ovid.[28]

Ovid, and love poetry in general, are extremely popular among writers, particularly in France: Chrétien de Troyes translates the *Ars* and *Remedia*; Ovid's work on love is mentioned by Marie de France in her lai *Guigemar*;[29] Ovidian influence is found in such works as the *Roman d'Eneas*, *Piramus et Tisbé*, the *Lai de Narcisse*, and the romances of Chrétien.[30]

Andreas Capellanus writes the *De amore* (1170s; see Chapter 3).

Matthew of Vendôme (ca. 1130-late twelfth century; author and literary critic) occasionally criticizes Ovid's prosody, but cites him fifty-seven times in his *Ars versificatoria* (ca. 1185).[31]

Guibert de Nogent (1053–1124), in his autobiography, laments the time he spent on the "ridiculous vanities" of Ovid and other love poetry.[32]

William of St. Thierry writes his *De natura et dignitate amoris* against Ovid (see Chapter 2); Peter of Blois (1135–1212; member of the court of Henry II and secretary to Eleanor of Aquitaine) fulminates against Ovid in his letters.[33]

Alexander Neckam (1157–1217) recommends the *Remedia amoris* as salutary, but (citing Vergil) warns the young against the dangers of the *carmina amatoria*: "Qui legitis flores o pueri fugite, hinc latet amnis [or: anguis] in herba" (O boys who pluck these flowers, run! A river [or: snake] lies hidden in the grass).[34]

MANUSCRIPTS

Ovid's amatory works (particularly *Remedia amoris*) are very well represented in the *libri manuales*, as Eva Matthews Sanford's study reveals:[35]

Century	Handbooks	Ovidian Texts	(Amatory Works)
7th–8th	1	0 (0%)	(0) (0%)
late 8th–9th	53	10 (19%)	(2) (4%)
late 9th–10th	61	3 (5%)	(3) (5%)
late 10th–11th	64	7 (11%)	(3) (5%)
late 11th–12th	*91*	*16 (18%)*	*(5) (5%)*
late 12th–13th	*107*	*34 (32%)*	*(7) (7%)*
late 13th–14th	*32*	*12 (38%)*	*(11) (34%)*
late 14th–15th	3	1 (33%)	(0) (0%)

Many of the extant MSS were produced during this period: of those listed in E. J. Kenney's Oxford edition, six copies of the *Amores* and seven each of the *Ars* and *Remedia amoris* date from the twelfth century.[36]

Nine library catalogues, including those of Rouen, Béziers, Cluny, and Durham, list Ovid's works; the amatory poems are found in the twelfth- and thirteenth-century catalogues of the Bavarian monasteries of Wessobrunn, Oberaltaich, and Benediktbeuern.[37]

Thirteenth Century

CITATIONS, LITERARY ATTITUDES
The *Ars* and *Remedia* are adapted in numerous Latin and French versions, a trend which began in the twelfth century (see Chapter 2).

Le Roman de la Rose is written by Guillaume de Lorris (1230s) and continued as *Le Miroër aus Amoreus* by Jean de Meun (1270s) (see Chapter 4).

In the 1290s, the Sorbonne library's copy of the *Metamorphoses* with *integumenta* is so popular that it has to be chained down;[38] *La Bible* (1204–9) of Guiot de Provins (monk of Clairvaux, then Cluny) cites the *Metamorphoses* frequently.[39]

The *Metamorphoses* are generally read with increasing need for commentary.

MANUSCRIPTS
Of the extant MSS, the largest number were produced during the thirteenth century: fifteen copies of the *Amores*, fourteen each of the *Ars* and *Remedia*.[40]

The erotic works are found in library catalogues: four mentions in France, including one copy of the *Amores*, two of the *Ars*, and four of the *Remedia amoris*; a complete set is found in Salzburg.[41]

The catalogue of Richard de Fournival (ca. 1250) mentions the second copy of Tibullus and the only MS of Propertius in medieval library booklists.[42]

The *Remedia amoris* are included in the *libri catoniani*, books of moral excerpts for school use, and are used at an earlier stage of the curriculum than ever before.[43]

Notes

Introduction

Unless otherwise noted, all translations of quoted passages are mine.

1. Paul Zumthor has noted that both the "I" and the lady of Old French lyric are syntactic elements of lyric discourse that have a textual and grammatical function but do not exist outside the poem. See "De La Circularité du chant (à propos des trouvères du XIIe et XIIIe siècles)," *Poétique* 1.2 (1970): 129–40, and *Essai de poétique médiévale* (Paris: Seuil, 1972), especially 205–8.

2. See Eugene Vance, *Mervelous Signals: Poetics and Sign Theory in the Middle Ages*, Regents Studies in Medieval Culture (Lincoln, NE: University of Nebraska Press, 1986), 100–105. He notes that "textuality at the expense of sexuality is not a feature of medieval lyric alone . . . but of courtly narrative as well" (105).

3. The continued success of love literature may stem from the fact that it not only evokes an emotional response already present in the reader, but actually gives shape to his or her unarticulated desires and in so doing, brings them to a sort of satisfaction. D. W. Harding writes, "What is sometimes called wish-fulfillment in novels and plays can . . . more plausibly be described as wish-formulation or the definition of desires. The cultural levels at which it works may vary widely; the process is the same. . . . It seems nearer the truth . . . to say that fictions contribute to defining the reader's or spectator's values, and perhaps stimulating his desires, than to suppose that they gratify desire by some mechanism of vicarious experience" ("Psychological Processes in the Reading of Fiction," in *Aesthetics in the Modern World*, ed. Harold Osborne [London: Thames and Hudson, 1968], 313–14, cited by Wolfgang Iser, *The Act of Reading: A Theory of Aesthetic Response* [Baltimore, MD: Johns Hopkins University Press, 1978], 158).

4. On the function of the frame in works of literary art, see Peter Travis, "Deconstructing Chaucer's Retraction," in *Reflections in the Frame: New Perspectives on the Study of Medieval Literature*, ed. Peter L. Allen and Jeff Rider, special issue of *Exemplaria* 3.1 (Spring 1991): 135–58, as well as Jonathan Culler, *On Deconstruction: Theory and Criticism after Structuralism* (Ithaca, NY: Cornell University Press, 1982), 193–99, and Jacques Derrida, "The Parergon," *October* 9 (1979): 3–40.

5. For a valuable discussion of how such frames both encourage and limit the reader's belief, see Clayton Koelb, *The Incredulous Reader: Literature and the Function of Disbelief* (Ithaca, NY: Cornell University Press, 1984).

6. Georges Poulet describes the experience of the willing reader in the following terms: "As soon as I replace my direct perception of reality by the words of a book, I deliver myself, bound hand and foot, to the omnipotence of fiction. I

say farewell to what is, in order to feign belief in what is not. I surround myself with fictitious beings; I become the prey of language. There is no escaping this takeover. Language surrounds me with its unreality. . . . Because of the strange invasion of my person in the thoughts of another, I am a self who is granted the experience of thinking thoughts foreign to him. I am the subject of thoughts other than my own. My consciousness behaves as though it were the consciousness of another" ("Criticism and the Experience of Interiority," in *Reader-Response Criticism: From Formalism to Post-Structuralism*, ed. Jane P. Tompkins [Baltimore, MD: Johns Hopkins University Press, 1980], 43–44).

7. Zumthor notes that the love lyric is completely self-referential: "De La Circularité du chant," 139 (see note 1, above).

8. See A. W. Allen, in "'Sincerity' and the Roman Elegists," *Classical Philology* 45 (1950): 146–47. On ways in which literature avoids conflicts with truth, see also Robert Guiette, "Li Conte de Bretaigne sont si vain et plaisant," *Romania* 88 (1967): 1–12, and Julia Kristeva, *Sèmeiotikè: Recherches pour une sémanalyse*, Collection Points, 96 (Paris: Les Editions du Seuil, 1969), 89.

9. Augustine defines conventional signs as follows: "Data uero signa sunt, quae sibi quaeque uiuentia inuicem dant ad demonstrandos, quantum possunt, motus animi sui uel sensa aut intellecta quaelibet" (*De doctrina christiana* 2.2.3). See B. Darrell Jackson, "The Theory of Signs in St. Augustine's *De Doctrina Christina*," in *Augustine, A Collection of Critical Essays*, ed. R. A. Markus (Garden City, NY: Doubleday, 1972), 98, and D. W. Robertson's translation of the *De doctrina: On Christian Doctrine*, Library of Liberal Arts (New York: Liberal Arts Press, 1958), 34–35. Natural signs, for Augustine, are those "which, without any desire or intention of signifying, make us aware of something beyond themselves" (2.1.2; Robertson, 34). On the rôle of the interpreter in the sign, Augustine states, "Signum est et quod se ipsum sensui, et praeter se aliquid *animo* ostendit" (emphasis added; *De dialectica* 5.9–10, quoted by Jackson in "The Theory of Signs," 95). Markus's essay in *Augustine: A Collection of Critical Essays* ("St. Augustine on Signs") contains an appendix (86–88) which notes the common points between Augustine's system of semiotics and that of Charles S. Peirce, who is famous for including the "interpretant" in his definition of the sign. See also John of Salisbury, who writes, "Signum siquidem est, quod seipsum sensui, et praeter se aliquid animo ostendit. Quaedam tamen signa sunt, quae nulli corporalium sensuum aliquid ostendunt, sed animo cuiuscumque rei specie mediante aut citra medii difficultatem uerum falsumue frequenter ingerunt. Signa etenim interdum uera, interdum falsa sunt. Quis nescit somniorum uarias esse significationes, quas et usus approbat et maiorum confirmat auctoritas?" (*Policraticus*, ed. C. J. Webb [London, 1909; rpt. Frankfurt: Minerva, 1965], 2.14, §428c).

10. Bernard E. Rollins, *Natural and Conventional Meaning: An Examination of the Distinction*, Approaches to Semiotics 45 (The Hague: Mouton, 1976), 103.

11. Paul Ricoeur notes that in writing, "the dialogical situation has been exploded. . . . With written discourse, . . . the author's intention and the meaning of the text cease to coincide" (*Interpretation Theory: Discourse and the Surplus of Meaning* [Fort Worth, TX: Texas Christian University Press, 1976], 29–30).

12. As Michael Riffaterre writes, "un mot ou groupe de mots est poétisé quand il renvoie à (et pour un groupe de mots se modèle sur) un énoncé verbal préexistant" (*Sémiotique de la poésie*, trans. Jean-Jacques Thomas [Paris: Les Editions du Seuil, 1983], 39).

13. That is, texts in which the reader, "through semiological destructurations, realizes the expansion of the work's process of semiosis" (Maria Corti, *An Introduction to Semiotics*, trans. Margherita Bogat and Allen Mandelbaum, Advances in Semiotics [Bloomington, IN: Indiana University Press, 1978], 43).

14. On the unity of reading, writing, and criticism, see Pierre Macherey, *A Theory of Literary Production* (London: Routledge and Kegan Paul, 1978), 139–40. On the viewer's rôle in producing meaning in artistic works, see Ernst Gombrich, *Art and Illusion: A Study in the Psychology of Pictorial Representation*, Bollingen Series 35.5 (Princeton, NJ: Princeton University Press, 1969), *passim*.

15. See Maureen Quilligan, *The Language of Allegory: Defining the Genre* (Ithaca, NY: Cornell University Press, 1979), 269, on the effect of the author's "you" on the reader. In this grammatical disposition, the beloved slips into the place of the "absent" third-person rôle, on which see Emile Benveniste, *Problèmes de linguistique générale*, 2 vols. (Paris; Gallimard, 1966) 1:228, 230.

16. On the effect of transferring poetic signs from one text or system to another, see Hans-Robert Jauss, *Toward an Aesthetic of Reception*, trans. Timothy Bahti, History and Theory of Literature (Minneapolis, MN: University of Minnesota Press, 1982), 106–7, and Riffaterre, *Sémiotique de la poésie*, 206 (see note 12, above). See also Vance, *Mervelous Signals*, 272 (note 2, above).

17. On the question of poetry's relationship to truth and falsehood, see Augustine *De mendacio*, in *Patrologiae cursus completus, series latina*, ed. J.-P. Migne (Paris: Garnier, 1844–64) (henceforth referred to as *PL*), 40:487–88, and John Reichert, "Do Poets Ever Mean What They Say?" *New Literary History* 13 (1981): 62; see also Koelb, *The Incredulous Reader*, 33–34 (see note 5, above); Vance, *Mervelous Signals*, 281 (note 2, above); Roman Jakobson, "Linguistics and Poetics," in *Style in Language*, ed. Thomas A. Sebeok (Cambridge, MA: MIT University Press, 1960), 371; and Wesley Trimpi, "The Quality of Fiction," *Traditio* 30 (1974): 34. On verisimilitude, see Kristeva, *Sèmeiotikè*, 51 (note 8, above). Even Augustine, who, like Plato, had little patience with poetry, does not condemn statements made without an intent to deceive, and specifically notes that jokes are not lies. For the *locus classicus* of the condemnation of poetry, see Plato, *Republic* 10; on Augustine, see Marina Brownlee, *The Status of the Reading Subject in the Libro de Buen Amor*, North Carolina Studies in the Romance Languages and Literatures, 224 (Chapel Hill, NC: University of North Carolina Press, 1985), 117–18, and Marcia Colish, *The Mirror of Language: A Study in the Medieval Theory of Knowledge*, rev. ed. (Lincoln, NE: University of Nebraska Press, 1983), 20.

18. Gombrich notes that it is impossible to watch oneself having an illusion: one always views an image from one perspective or another, never from both at once: see *Art and Illusion*, 5–6, 313, and *passim* (see note 14, above). The treatises emphasize the alternation between one understanding of love and another, pressing the contrast between the two perspectives and their incompatibility.

19. On a similar problem in nineteenth-century narrative, see Ross Chambers, *Story and Situation: Narrative Seduction and the Power of Fiction*, Theory and History of Literature, 12 (Minneapolis, MN: University of Minnesota Press, 1984).

20. On the refusal to continue reading, see Iser, *The Implied Reader: Patterns of Communication in Prose Fiction from Bunyan to Beckett* (Baltimore, MD: Johns Hopkins University Press, 1974), 275.

21. Macherey also argues that the point of breakdown is the key to a text's meaning. "This distance which separates the work from the ideology which it transforms is rediscovered in the very letter of the work: it is fissured, unmade even in its making. A new kind of necessity can be defined: by an absence, by a lack. The disorder that permeates the work is related to the disorder of ideology (which cannot be organized as a system). The work derives its form from this incompleteness which enables us to identify the active presence of a conflict at its borders. In the defect of the work is articulated a new truth: for those who seek to know this truth it establishes an original relation to the real, it establishes the revealing form of knowledge" (*A Theory of Literary Production*, 155 [see note 14, above]). John J. Winkler has proposed a related strategy of reading for another text which has traditionally been seen as bifurcated and confusing in his wide-ranging and provocative book *Auctor & Actor: A Narratological Reading of Apuleius' Golden Ass* (Berkeley and Los Angeles, CA: University of California Press, 1985). Winkler argues that reading the *Golden Ass* is a game played out between Apuleius and the reader in which only a second reading can bridge the gap between the book's main narrative and religious conclusion. See also Derrida, "The Parergon," 9 (note 4, above).

22. Iser, *The Act of Reading*, 194; see also 33 and 203 (see note 3, above). Compare also Macherey: "What begs to be explained in the work is not that false simplicity which derives from the apparent unity of its meaning, but the presence of a relation, or an opposition, between elements of the exposition or levels of the composition, those disparities which point to a conflict of meaning," *A Theory of Literary Production*, 79 (see note 14, above).

23. Thus Iser: "The reader is compelled to reduce the indeterminacies, and so to build a situational frame to encompass himself and the text," *The Act of Reading*, 66 (see note 3, above).

24. See Iser, *The Implied Reader*, 289 (see note 20, above); Koelb, *The Incredulous Reader*, 32 (see note 5, above).

25. Riffaterre, *Sémiotique*, 17, 207 (see note 12, above); emphasis original.

26. As Teun A. Van Dijk observes, "a coherent macrostructure may manifest itself in the text through discontinuous local microstructures": *Some Aspects of Text Grammars* (The Hague and Paris: Mouton, 1972), cited by Corti, *An Introduction to Semiotics*, 93 (see note 13, above).

27. Quilligan, *The Language of Allegory*, 226 (see note 15, above). On the reader's rôle in allegory, see also 67–68, 254, and 277. Brownlee describes the *Libro de Buen Amor*—a text which has many similarities to the three treatises on love discussed here—as "an allegorization of the reading process," in *The Status of the Reading Subject*, 105 (see note 17, above).

28. On crises in reading, see Koelb, *The Incredulous Reader*, 3–4 (see note 5, above); Paul De Man, *Allegories of Reading: Figural Language in Rousseau, Nietzsche, Rilke, and Proust* (New Haven, CT: Yale University Press, 1979), 57–58; and Stanley Fish, *Self-Consuming Artefacts: The Experience of Seventeenth-Century Literature* (Berkeley, CA: University of California Press, 1972), 3–4. The treatises thus explicitly perform the function Iser ascribes to aesthetic experience, which "makes us conscious of the acquisition of experience and is accompanied by continual insight into the conditions that give rise to it. This endows the aesthetic experience with a transcendental character," *The Act of Reading*, 133 (see note 22, above).

29. Zumthor, "Le Grand Chant courtois," in *Essai de poétique médiévale*, 215–16 (see note 1, above).

30. On the relationship between medieval text and theory, see, for example, D. W. Robertson, Jr., *A Preface to Chaucer: Studies in Medieval Perspectives* (Princeton, NJ: Princeton University Press, 1962), and Robertson's work on Augustine's *De doctrina christiana* generally. Rhetorical approaches may be found in Edmond Faral's *Les Arts poétiques du XIIe et XIIIe siècle* (Paris: Champion, 1924) and the numerous and useful works of James J. Murphy. See also Judson Boyce Allen's work on the *accessus* in his various books and articles, particularly *The Friar as Critic: Literary Attitudes in the Later Middle Ages* (Nashville, TN: Vanderbilt University Press, 1971); "Commentary as Criticism: Formal Cause, Discursive Form, and the Late Medieval Accessus," in *Acta Conventus Neo-Latini Lovanensis*, ed. J. IJsewijn and E. Kessler (Leuven and Munich: Wilhelm Fink, 1973): 29–48; "Commentary as Criticism: The Text, Influence, and Literary Theory of the *Fulgentius Metaphored* of John Ridewall," in *Acta Conventus Neo-Latini Amstelodamensis*, ed. P. Tuynman, G. C. Kuiper, and E. Kessler (Munich: Wilhelm Fink, 1979): 25–47; and *The Ethical Poetic of the Later Middle Ages: A Decorum of Convenient Distinction* (Toronto: University of Toronto Press, 1982). Compare also Alastair Minnis's impressive and scholarly *Medieval Theory of Authorship*, 2nd ed. (Philadelphia, PA, University of Pennsylvania Press, 1988). For further discussion of ways in which medieval text and criticism are intertwined, see Rita Copeland and Steven Melville, "Allegory and Allegoresis," and SunHee Kim Gertz, "Hab ime wîs unde wort mit mir gemeine: Perspectives in Medieval Literary Criticism," both in *Exemplaria* 3.1 (Spring 1991): 159–88, 189–220. See also Brownlee, *The Status of the Reading Subject* (see note 17, above): she presents a variety of possible readings of the *Libro de Buen Amor*, including seeing the text as *ars amatoria* and *ars poetica* (21). Compare also Vance, *Mervelous Signals*, xi (see note 2, above): "Medieval poetry built into its own performance a critical consciousness that later, with the Renaissance, would become crystallized as the autonomous discourse that we now call 'criticism.'"

31. See Roland Barthes, *Le Plaisir du texte* (Paris: Les Editions du Seuil, 1973). See also Robert Sturges, "Texts and Readers in Marie de France's *Lais*," *Romanic Review* 71 (1980): 255, as well as Lee Patterson, "Ambiguity and Interpretation: A Fifteenth-Century Reading of *Troilus and Criseyde*," *Speculum* 54 (1979): 329.

32. "La 'littérature' nous paraît aujourd'hui l'acte même qui saisit comment la langue travaille et indique ce qu'elle a le pouvoir, demain, de transformer": Kris-

teva, *Sèmeiotikè,* 9 (see note 8, above); see also Jane Tompkins, *Reader-Response Criticism from Formalism to Post-Structuralism* (Baltimore, MD: Johns Hopkins University Press, 1980), xvi.

33. We will be focusing on only part of the medieval tradition of the amatory works. The thirteenth century, in particular, witnessed a proliferation of translations and vernacular adaptations of the *Ars,* which we will not be able to examine in detail; further references can be found in Chapter 2 and the Appendix.

34. For further discussion, readers are referred to David Hult, *Self-Fulfilling Prophecies: Readership and Authority in the First "Roman de la Rose"* (New York: Cambridge University Press, 1986), and to H. M. Leicester, "Ovid Enclosed: The God of Love as *Magister Amoris* in the *Roman de la Rose* of Guillaume de Lorris," *Res Publica Litterarum* 7 (1984): 107–29.

Chapter 1

1. On seeing the *Ars* and *Remedia* as one work in four books, see N. Holzberg, "Ovids erotische Lehrgedichte und die römische Liebeselegie," *Wiener Studien,* n.F. 15 (1981), 195; Holzberg also refers to E. Pöhlmann, "Charakteristika der römischen Lehrgedichts," *Aufstieg und Niedergang der römischen Welt* 3 (1973): 813–901.

2. See Gian Biagio Conti, "Love without Elegy: The *Remedia amoris* and the Logic of a Genre," *Poetics Today* 10.3 (Fall 1989): 458.

3. I follow Leslie Cahoon in her sensible use of the term *amator* for Ovid's character—see, e.g., "Juno's Chaste Festival and Ovid's Wanton Loves: *Amores* 3.13," *Classical Antiquity* 2.1 (April 1983): 1–8.

4. See Charlton T. Lewis and Charles Short's almost panegyrical entry on *ars* in *A Latin Dictionary* (Oxford: Oxford University Press, 1969).

5. "At uos, si sapitis, uestri peccata magistri / effugite et culpae damna timete meae," 2.173–74.

6. I base my discussion of chronology on Charles Murgia's schema of dating, which suggests the following sequence: (1) first edition of the *Amores*; (2) first edition of *Ars* 1–2; (3) first edition of the *Remedia*; (4) second edition of the *Amores*; (5) publication of *Metamorphoses* 1–7; (6) second edition of *Ars* 1–2 and publication of *Ars* 3; (7) second edition of the *Remedia* ("The Date of Ovid's *Ars amatoria* 3," *American Journal of Philology* 107 [1986]: 94); see also Murgia's "Influence of Ovid's *Remedia amoris* on *Ars amatoria* 3 and *Amores* 3," *Classical Philology* 81 (1986): 203–20.

7. On self-citation as a common and noteworthy practice in classical literature, cf. Francis Cairns, "Self-Imitation Within a Generic Framework: Ovid, *Amores* 2.9 and 3.11 and the *renuntiatio amoris,*" in David H. West and T. Woodman, *Creative Imitation and Latin Literature* (Cambridge: Cambridge University Press, 1979), 121–41.

8. See R. M. Durling, "Ovid as *Praeceptor Amoris,*" *Classical Journal* 53 (1958): 164.

9. The reader's growing sophistication is foreshadowed by the opening lines of the *Ars*, cited above, and is also required by the techniques the poet employs. See Katherine Olstein's discussion of the subversiveness of *Amores* 1.3, "*Amores* 1.3 and Duplicity as a Way of Love," *Transactions of the American Philological Association* 105 (1975): 241–58. For a broader investigation of the relationship between the *doctus poeta* and the *doctus lector*, see Donald Lateiner, "Mythic and Non-Mythic Artists in Ovid's *Metamorphoses*," *Ramus* 13.1 (1984): 11.

10. Peter Green, trans., *Ovid: The Erotic Poems* (Harmondsworth: Penguin, 1982), 389. Consider also the complicated analogy the preceptor sets up at 3.439–40, where his female readers, like the Trojans, hear the prophet's true *praecepta* but, disbelieving them, are condemned to be vanquished.

11. See Molly Myerowitz, *Ovid's Games of Love* (Detroit, MI: Wayne State University Press, 1985), 177.

12. Paul Veyne notes that even in the *Amores* the poet and heroine have a *ménage à trois* with the reader: *L'Elégie érotique romaine: l'amour, la poésie, et l'occident* (Paris: Seuil, 1983), 14; cf. also Simone Viarre, *Ovide: Essai de lecture poétique*, Collection d'études latines, Série scientifique 23 (Paris: Les Belles Lettres, 1976), 19.

13. See Douglass Parker, "The Ovidian Coda," *Arion* 8 (1969): 94. Parker's insightful reading of the persona will be discussed below.

14. I use the term "reader" to include readers and audiences alike, whether ancient, medieval, or modern. Typically, of course, Romans and medieval audiences would have read, and heard, poetry aloud.

15. *Sexti Properti Carmina* (ed. E. A. Barber, 2nd ed., Oxford Classical Texts [Oxford: Clarendon Press, 1960], 1.1):

Cynthia prima suis miserum me cepit ocellis
    contractum nullis ante cupidinibus.
tum mihi constantis deiecit lumina fastus
    et caput impositis pressit Amor pedibus,
donec me docuit castas odisse puellas
    improbus, et nullo uiuere consilio.

(Cynthia made me a miserable captive with her eyes when I had never before been touched by desire. Then scornful Cupid cast down my steadfast gaze, stepped on my head, and pressed it down with his feet, shamelessly teaching me to despise chaste girls, and to live without self-awareness.)

Compare, on this subject, Warren Ginsberg, *The Cast of Character: The Representation of Personality in Ancient and Medieval Literature* (Toronto: University of Toronto Press, 1983), 29.

16. As Paul Veyne writes, "Dans les hymnes authentiques de l'ancienne Grèce, bien avant le temps de Callimaque, le 'je' était employé et ce 'je' renvoyait indifféremment au choeur, qui chantait l'hymne, au chef du choeur et aussi au poète. . . . Le moins qu'on puisse dire est que Callimaque n'en est plus là; il profite de la plurivalence apparente du 'je' hymnique pour en tirer un procédé littéraire

qui lui permettra de se mettre, comme artiste, à l'écart du reste des hommes. Il se fait ventriloque; le choeur, son chef, la foule, tout le monde parle, la réalité s'éparpille en exclamations, ordres et interrogations (nous avons vu que Properce imitera le procédé); l'absence de point de vue cohérent déréalise ce que le texte dit," *L'Elégie érotique romaine*, 31–32 (see note 12, above). See also Ginsberg, *The Cast of Character*, 36 (see note 15, above).

17. A. W. Allen has noted that sincerity in ancient criticism is primarily a rhetorical concept, not an emotional one: "*Fides* is the word which in Latin contains simultaneously the ideas contained in our word 'sincerity,' but there is an important difference. *Fides* contains simultaneously the ideas of 'sincerity' and 'persuasiveness'": "Sincerity and the Roman Elegists," *Classical Philology* 45 (1950): 146–47.

18. See the articles on "Catullus," "Clodia," "Sextus Propertius," and "Gaius Cornelius Gallus" in *The Oxford Classical Dictionary*, ed. M. Cary et al. (Oxford: Clarendon Press, 1949). The evidence for Tibullus's "Delia" and "Nemesis" is less firm. Peter Green has put forth the surprising hypothesis that Corinna was based on Ovid's first wife: see his Introduction to Ovid, *The Erotic Poems*, 23 (see note 10, above).

19. Compare L. P. Wilkinson, *Ovid Surveyed* (Cambridge: Cambridge University Press, 1962), 15–16: "And Apuleius, who can tell us confidently the real name of Lesbia, Cynthia, Delia and others, does not even mention Corinna, though he is obviously recalling every identification of a poetic pseudonym he can." Georg Luck sees Corinna as a composite of various women (*The Latin Love Elegy*, 2d ed. [London: Methuen and Co., 1969], 147), a hypothesis that is found in some of the medieval *accessus* to the *Amores* (see Chapter 2); R. O. A. M. Lyne argues that she is *not* fictional (*The Latin Love Poets from Catullus to Horace* [Oxford: Clarendon Press, 1980], 239–40), but I do not find his arguments particularly persuasive. I. M. le M. du Quesnay suggests reading Corinna as a fictional character, a solution I find the most effective: see "The *Amores*," in *Ovid*, ed. J. W. Binns (Boston, MA: Routledge and Kegan Paul, 1973), 2. Compare also Ginsberg, *The Cast of Character*, 37 (see note 15, above).

20. As Olstein reminds us in discussing 1.11 and the structure of the *Amores*, "'Corinna,' whether real or imaginary, is not truly central to the *Amores*" ("*Amores* 1.9," 300 [see note 9, above]).

21. Catullus, on the contrary, addresses his mistress by name seven times, Tibullus nine, and Propertius twenty-seven: cf. D. Donnet, "Ovide, Properce et l'élégie latine," *Les Etudes classiques* 33 (1965): 262–64. Donnet also provides statistics on the proportion of expressions of love as suffering to the number of total verses in various poets' erotic works. Once again Ovid comes up short: Lygdamus (the pseudonymous author of the poems in Tibullus's third book) has a ratio of 32:1, Tibullus 28:1, Propertius 23.9:1, and Ovid only 17.1:1 (276). Donnet also notes that Ovid's invocations to gods of love lend a lighter tone to his work. Of invocations to Venus, Amor, and Cupid, Propertius uses the latter only one time out of seventy-one instances, Tibullus only about three out of sixty, whereas Ovid speaks specifically to Cupid thirteen out of sixty-four times. "La fréquence avec laquelle Cupidon revient dans les *Amores* ne peut pas être attribuée à un recours

plus fréquent aux dieux. Elle procède d'un choix délibéré pour des représentations de l'amour, à une allure moins grave, plus frivole et superficielle" (277–78).

22. Wilfried Stroh discusses Corinna's nebulous identity in these terms: "Was ist das Gedicht dann? Wenn ich recht sehe: ein *Gedankenexperiment*" (*Die römische Liebeselegie als werbende Dichtung* [Amsterdam: Hakkert, 1971], 160). He notes also that "Corinna" was not the last fictional woman whom life imitated: "Den größten Erfolg in dieser Hinsicht will der Schlagerdichter Hans Leip gehabt haben: 250 Damen betrachteten sich als das Modell der berühmten 'Lili Marleen' (nach: *Der Spiegel* 22,1 [1.1.1968], S. 79" (157 n. 60). Stroh's chapter on Ovid is extremely insightful about all the levels of half-truth and half-fiction the poet employs; see particularly 165–70. See also Christoff Neumeister, "Mimesis und Imitatio in Ovids Elegie *Am.* 2.18," *Antike und Abenland* 28.1 (1982), 97.

23. "Quod licet, ingratum est; quod non licet, acrius urit . . . nil ego, quod nullo tempore laedat, amo" (2.19.3, 8) (What I can have, I don't want; what I can't have torments me . . . I love nothing that doesn't cause some pain); compare also 3.14.48–50.

24. Ginsberg, *The Cast of Character*, 26 (see note 15, above).

25. For another discussion of the place of readers in the Ovidian text, see Michael von Albrecht, "Ovide et ses lecteurs," *Revue des études latines* 59 (1981): 207–15. R. E. K. Pemberton notes that in his later works Ovid explicitly discusses the rôle of the audience as inspiration: "Literary Criticism in Ovid," *Classical Journal* 26 (1931): 529–30, citing particularly *Tristia* 3.14, 39f., and *Ex Ponto* IV, 2, 33–36. On the reader as accomplice in the *Amores*, see J. T. Davis, "Dramatic and Comic Devices in *Amores* 3.2," *Hermes* 107 (1979): 52.

26. "Nil non laudabile uidi, / et nudam pressi corpus ad usque meum. / cetera quis nescit? lassi requieuimus ambo" (1.5.23–25) (Nothing I saw did not merit my praise; I pressed her, naked, against my body. Who does not know what happened next? Weary, we both rested.). By not being more explicit, Ovid permits his readers to use the *Amores* as a mirror for their erotic feelings.

27. "Ingenio prostitit illa meo . . . me lenone placet, duce me perductus amator, / ianua per nostras est adaperta manus" (3.12.8, 11–12) (My art has made her a whore. . . . With me as a pimp, she's a success; lovers follow my lead, my own hands open her door).

28. Even this idea is an elegiac topos. Compare Propertius 3.24.4: "uersibus insignem te pudet esse meis."

29. Michaël Swoboda notes Ovid's assertion of poetic falsehood in "Quidnam Ovidius de poesi, poematis poetisque iudicauerit," *Symbolae Philologorum Posnaniensium* 4 (1979): 128. A more literal but less convincing reading—that the artist wants his readers to believe in illusions—is proposed by E. D. Blodgett, "The Well-Wrought Void: Reflections on the *Ars amatoria*," *Classical Journal* 68 (1973): 332. The helpful observation that myth in the Rome of Ovid's day was not a source of truth but a world of poetic images that had value precisely because of their recognized artificiality is made both by Veyne, *L'Elégie érotique romaine*, 131 (see note 12, above), and by Lyne, *Latin Love Poets*, 85–86 (see note 19, above).

30. Simone Viarre states that "Dès les *Amours*, Ovide fait entrer la théorie poétique dans le cadre de l'élégie," *Ovide: Essai de lecture poétique*, Collection

d'études latines, Série scientifique, 23 (Paris: Les Belles Lettres, 1976), 96. On reading conventional literature, compare John Barsby, *Ovid, Greece and Rome: New Surveys in the Classics* (New York: Oxford University Press, 1978), 14.

31. On a similar concept in medieval literature, see H. M. Leicester, Jr., "Ovid Enclosed: The God of Love as *Magister amoris* in the *Roman de la Rose* of Guillaume de Lorris," *Res Publica Litterarum* 2 (1984): 114, with reference to Frederick Goldin, *Lyrics of the Troubadours and Trouvères* (Garden City, New York: Anchor Books, 1973).

32. See Gerlinde Wellman-Bretzigheimer, "Ovids Ars Amatoria," in *Europäische Lehrdichtung: Festschrift für W. Naumann*, ed. Hans Gerd Rötzer and Herbert Walz (Darmstadt: Wissenschaftliche Buchgesellschaft, 1981), 4. Wellmann-Bretzigheimer notes several instances in which it is apparent that the audience is composed of both men and women, including 1.617f., 2.745f., 3.6ff.; one could also note *Remedia* 49–52. On the question of gendered reading, see Carolyn Dinshaw's excellent book, *Chaucer's Sexual Poetics* (Madison, WI: University of Wisconsin Press, 1989).

33. See 1.31–34, 3.58. If these warnings were meant to permit the *Ars* to pass through Augustus's moral censure, they were notoriously unsuccessful; Murgia notes that *Ars* 3 was published, with less than perfect timing, shortly before Augustus discovered Julia's adultery ("Date," 86 [see note 6, above]); Gordon Williams also points out that Augustus's displeasure can be inferred from the fact that the erotic works were banned from Roman public libraries after Ovid's exile: *Change and Decline: Roman Literature in the Early Empire* (Berkeley and Los Angeles, CA: University of California Press, 1978), 81, citing *Tristia* 3.1.59–82 and 3.14.5–18. More political interpretation can be found in Blodgett, "The Well-Wrought Void," 322–33 (see note 29, above), though I find Blodgett's readings overly negative.

34. Pasiphaë "tenuit laeta paelicis exta manu," notes Ovid (1.320); other details of this treatment are equally horrifying—and equally intriguing. See Blodgett, "Well-Wrought Void," 324 (note 29, above).

35. See Holzberg, "Ovids erotische Lehrgedichte und die römische Liebeselegie," 191 (note 1, above), and A. S. Hollis, "The *Ars Amatoria* and *Remedia Amoris*," in *Ovid*, ed. J. W. Binns (Boston, MA, and London: Routledge and Kegan Paul, 1973), 91.

36. See Eleanor Winsor Leach, "Georgic Imagery in the *Ars amatoria*," *Transactions of the American Philological Association* 95 (1964): 147, 149; see also Myerowitz, *Ovid's Games of Love*, 112, 124–27 (see note 11, above).

37. See Green, *Erotic Poems*, 399 (see note 10, above), and, on parallels in the *Amores*, John R. C. Martyn, "Naso: Desultor amoris (*Amores* I-III)," *Aufstieg und Niedergang der römischen Welt* 2.31.4 (1981): 2445.

38. As Myerowitz says, "On every level [the *Ars*] splits our world" (*Ovid's Games of Love*, 176 [see note 11, above]).

39. On the rhetorical nature of performance, compare Cicero, *De oratore* 2.189: "neque fieri potest ut doleat is, qui audit, ut oderit, ut inuideat, ut pertimescat aliquid, ut ad fletum misericordiamque deducatur, nisi omnes illi motus, quos orator adhibere uult iudici, in ipso oratore impressi esse atque inusti uidebuntur" (cited by Wilfried Stroh, "Rhetorik und Erotik: Eine Studie zu Ovids liebesdidak-

tischen Gedichten," *Würzburger Jahrbücher für die Altertumswissenschaft* n. F. 5 [1979]: 124). Stroh provides a detailed and useful discussion of the rhetorical tactics and situations Ovid employs in the *Ars*.

40. See Green, *Erotic Poems*, 367 (see note 10, above).

41. Compare his use of the traditional *topoi* of *militia amoris* and *seruitium amoris*—on which, see F. O. Copley, "*Seruitium amoris* in the Roman Elegists," *Transactions of the American Philological Association* 78 (1947): 285–300, and P. Murgatroyd, "*Militia amoris* and the Roman Elegists," *Latomus* 34 (1975): 59–79—and his use of *exempla* that undermine his point. Compare J. T. Davis, "Exempla and Anti-Exempla in the *Amores* of Ovid," *Latomus* 39 (1980): 412, 415, 417; see also Patricia Watson, "Mythological Exempla in Ovid's *Ars amatoria*," *Classical Philology* 78.2 (1983): 117–26. In each case, the *amator*'s use of traditional topics works against his attempts to be an effective lover. Poetry, in particular, is an unpersuasive tool in the *Amores*. (Stroh points out that poetry is similarly unpersuasive in the writings of the earlier elegists, as well, but that only Ovid admits this fact: *Die römische Liebeselegie*, 172 [see note 22, above]).

42. References and citations are from Florence Verducci, *Ovid's Toyshop of the Heart: Epistulae Heroidum* (Princeton, NJ: Princeton University Press, 1985), 30–31; Verducci paraphrases Robert Langbaum, *The Poetry of Experience* (London: Chatto and Windus, 1957), esp. 75–108.

43. On Ovid's representation and use of audiences and multiple interpretation in his poetry, see Michael von Albrecht, "Ovide et ses lecteurs," *Revue des études latines* 59 (1981): 208, 212. Durling notes the split between the "fictitious audience" of the *Ars*, those who actually accept the *praecepta*, and the "actual audience," which does not believe but admires the poetic artifice; see "Ovid as *Praeceptor Amoris*," 166 (see note 8, above); see also John Fyler, "Omnia uincit amor: Incongruity and the Limitations of Structure in Ovid's Elegiac Poetry," *Classical Journal* 66 (1971): 201.

44. As Conti states, "The genre is in fact the horizon marking the boundaries of its meaning and delimiting its real possibilities within the system of literary codification" ("Love without Elegy," 442 [see note 2, above]).

45. *Tristia* 2.355, cited by Claude Rambaux, *Trois Analyses de l'amour: Catulle, Poésies, Ovide, "Les Amours," Apulée, "Le Conte de Psyché"*, Collection d'études anciennes (Paris: Les Belles Lettres, 1985), 75. See also Swoboda, "Quidnam Ovidius de poesi," 136 (note 29, above), and Durling, "Ovid as *Praeceptor Amoris*," 166 (note 8, above).

46. See Blodgett, "The Well-Wrought Void" (note 29, above).

47. Much the same thing happens in the *Amores*, though the reversals tend to have a more comic effect. Compare the *amator*'s bombastic claims to be Love's soldier in 1.9, for example, and their deflation in 3.8, when Corinna deserts him for a real veteran. Dipsas is another dangerous rival, a more successful illusionist than the *amator*-poet himself (compare 1.8 and Green's commentary in his edition of the *Amores*, 277–78 [see note 10, above]). Poems 2.2 and 2.3 also show the *amator*'s comic inadequacy.

48. For complex and interesting developments of this pose, see *Amores* 2.19 and 3.14.

49. Translation from Green, *Erotic Poems*, 222 (see note 10, above).

50. Green, *Erotic Poems*, 388.

51. Compare Wellmann-Bretzigheimer: "Das Verhältnis zwischen Mann und Frau bahnt sich als Interessenkonflikt zwischen Käufer und Verkäuferin an, bei dem jeder auf seinen Vorteil schaut" ("Ovids *Ars amatoria*," 11 [see note 32, above]).

52. "Arma dedi Danais in Amazonas; arma supersunt, / quae tibi dem et turmae, Penthesilea, tuae," 3.1–2.

53. On the preceptor's urging belief in illusion, see Blodgett, "The Well-Wrought Void," 332 (see note 29, above).

54. *Nequitia* has a variety of meanings (Lewis and Short propose, *inter alia*, badness, idleness, levity, wantonness, and wickedness [see note 4, above]). All of them are in one way or another in conflict with traditional Roman morals, but not necessarily with Ovid's: in *Amores* 2.1.2, he describes himself as "ille ego nequitiae Naso poeta meae" (Ovid, that poet who takes his own misbehavior as his subject).

55. On disillusionment, see Egon Küppers, "Ovids Ars Amatoria und Remedia Amoris als Lehrdichtungen," *Aufstieg und Niedergang der römischen Welt* 2.31.4 (1981): 2516.

56. Fyler underlines the risks of really falling in love in this world: "A little passion, to be carefully controlled, is thus necessary. But once admitted, the rustic *barbaria* of the libido causes the pretense of the systematic strategy to collapse. It refuses to remain bound by its framework, and overwhelms the generic propriety of other categories" ("Omnia uincit amor," 201 [see note 43, above]). This representation of love's dangers is consistent with that of elegy in general: see A. S. Hollis, "The *Ars amatoria* and *Remedia amoris*," in *Ovid*, ed. J. W. Binns (Boston, MA, and London: Routledge and Kegan Paul, 1973), 94.

57. For *lusus*, Lewis and Short give the following meanings: "a playing, play, game (not in Cic.)"; "play, sport, game (that is done by way of amusement)"; "sportive dalliance" (the illustrative citation for this definition comes from the *Amores*); "jest, fun, mockery" (see note 4, above). Though Cicero did not use the term *lusus*, apparently even he did not believe that a little sexual play (he uses *ludus*, a related term) was inappropriate for a young man: "Everybody agrees in allowing youth a little fun [*ludus*]; nature itself develops a young man's desires. If these desires break out in such a way that they shatter no one's life and upturn no one's home, they are generally regarded as unproblematic: we tolerate them" (*Pro Caelio* 28, cited by Lyne, *Latin Love Poets* [see note 19, above]).

58. Compare Myerowitz, *Ovid's Games of Love*, 178 (see note 11, above).

59. On Roman games, see Green, *Erotic Poems*, 391–92 (see note 10, above).

60. For other reflections on this principle, see von Albrecht, "Ovide et ses lecteurs," 210–11 (see note 25, above); Veyne, *L'Elégie érotique romaine*, 62 (see note 16, above); Walter Nicolai, "Phantasie und Wirklichkeit bei Ovid," *Antike und Abenland* 91, 2 (1973): 110; and A. A. R. Henderson's edition of the *Remedia amoris* (Edinburgh: Scottish Academic Press, 1979), 28. See also Holzberg, "Ovids erotische Lehrgedichte," 192 (see note 1, above).

61. "Its form is façade" (Blodgett, "The Well-Wrought Void," 323 [see note 29, above]). On the classical didactic tradition, see von Albrecht, "Ovide et ses lecteurs," 208 (see note 25, above); O. A. W. Dilke, "La Tradition didactique chez

Ovide," in *Colloque présence d'Ovide*, ed. R. Chevalier, Collection Caesarodonum 17bis (Paris: Les Belles Lettres, 1982), 11; Durling, "Ovid as Praeceptor," 158 (note 8, above); and Myerowitz, *Ovid's Games of Love*, 196 n. 6 (note 11, above). On the pseudodidacticism of the *Ars*, see Hollis, "The *Ars amatoria*," 93, 110 (note 56, above); and Viarre, *Ovide*, 87 (note 30, above).

62. See Myerowitz, *Ovid's Games of Love*, 144 (note 11, above); Durling, "Ovid as *Praeceptor Amoris*," 165 (note 8, above); and Leach, "Georgic Imagery," 154 (note 36, above).

63. See Nicolai, "Phantasie und Wirklichkeit," 110 (note 60, above).

64. Holzberg, "Ovids erotische Lehrgedichte," 190 (see note 1, above), citing F. W. Lenz. Holzberg gives a fairly thorough survey of critics of the *Ars*, both positive and negative (89–90); Myerowitz does the same in *Ovid's Games of Love*, 20–23 (see note 11, above), though most of those she cites disapprove of the poem.

65. Frederick Ahl, *Metaformations: Soundplay and Wordplay in Ovid and Other Classical Poets* (Ithaca, NY: Cornell University Press, 1985), 273–74.

66. Ahl, *Metaformations*, 300.

Chapter 2

1. For a fascinating and profoundly erudite discussion of this topic, see Peter R. L. Brown, *The Body and Society: Men, Women, and Sexual Renunciation in Early Christianity* (New York, NY: Columbia University Press, 1988).

2. As Peter Dronke suggests, the classical poets offered their medieval followers not merely the "bricks" with which to build, but the "oxygen" that permitted them to live and work as writers: *Medieval Latin and the Rise of the European Love-Lyric* (Oxford: Oxford University Press, 1966), 180–81, cited by Leslie Cahoon, "The Anxieties of Influence: Ovid's Reception by the Early Troubadours," in *Ovid in Medieval Culture*, ed. Marilynn R. Desmond, spec. issue of *Mediaevalia* 13 (1989 [for 1987]): 119–56.

3. The first-century term is Varro's: compare Ralph Hexter, *Ovid and Medieval Schooling: Studies in Medieval School Commentaries on Ovid's "Ars amatoria," "Epistulae ex Ponto," and "Epistulae Heroidum,"* Münchener Beiträge zur Mediävistik und Renaissance-Forschung (Munich: Arbeo-Gesellschaft, 1986), 4–5.

4. On the conflict inherent in the educational system, particularly regarding Ovid's works, see Leo Pollmann, *Die Liebe in der hochmittelalterlichen Literatur Frankreichs: Versuch einer historischen Phänomenologie*, Analecta Romanica 18 (Frankfurt: Vittorio Klostermann, 1966), 52–53. See also Harald Hagendahl, *Latin Fathers and the Classics: A Study on the Apologists, Jerome, and Other Christian Writers*, Göteborgs Universitets Årsskrift 64, 2 (Göteborg: Elander, 1958), 311.

5. See Hagendahl, *Latin Fathers and the Classics*, 310 (note 4, above).

6. Compare Hexter's description of the textual educational system at the Tegernsee monastery in the eleventh century. There, students copied texts in a prescribed order, a progression which, "starting with elementary grammatical handbooks and moving through computistic and musical texts to treatises on dialectic

and texts and commentaries on classical *auctores*, from simpler monks' lives to Biblical exegesis, parallels the curriculum itself. The copying of texts served the monastery not only by training scribes and at the same time providing more books: it appears to have had a role in the very instruction of young religious. One did not only learn to write, one wrote to learn" *(Ovid and Medieval Schooling*, 153 [see note 3, above]). On the use of the erotic works in medieval schools, see Sigmund Tafel, *Die Überlieferungsgeschichte von Ovids Carmina amatoria* (Tübingen: Heckenhauer, 1910), 57; Franco Munari, *Ovid im Mittelalter* (Zürich and Stuttgart: Artemis, 1960), 11; and Hexter, *Ovid and Medieval Schooling*, 19 and *passim*.

7. For biographical information on medieval writers, see the *New Catholic Encyclopedia*, 18 volumes, (New York, NY: McGraw-Hill, 1967), and *Le Grand Robert des noms propres*, 5 volumes, ed. Alain Rey and Josette Rey-Debove (Paris: Robert, 1984).

8. Compare Jerome, Epistle 22, in Gerard L. Ellsperman, *The Attitude of Early Christian Writers toward Pagan Literature and Learning*, Catholic University of America Patristic Studies, vol. 82 (Washington, DC: Catholic University of America Press, 1949), 159–60, cited by James J. Murphy, "Saint Augustine and the Debate about a Christian Rhetoric," *Quarterly Journal of Speech* 46 (1960): 404.

9. Compare Deuteronomy 21:12; see Ernst Robert Curtius, *European Literature and the Latin Middle Ages*, trans. Willard R. Trask, Bollingen Series 36 (Princeton, NJ: Princeton University Press, 1953), 40, and Hagendahl, *Latin Fathers and the Classics*, 208 (see note 4, above).

10. On Jerome's relationship with classical letters, see Hagendahl, *Latin Fathers and the Classics*, 94, 111, 121, 196, 208, 231–32, 253, 323, 325 (see note 4, above).

11. Jerome, Epistle 21.13 (*PL* 22:385), cited by Pollmann, *Die Liebe*, 50 (see note 4, above).

12. Fausto Ghisalberti, "L'*Ovidius moralizatus* di Pierre Bersuire," *Società filologica romana, studi romanzi* 23 (1933): 19.

13. See the major works on this subject: Peter Dronke, *Fabula: Explorations into the Uses of Myth in Medieval Platonism*, Mittellateinische Studien und Texte, 9 (Leiden: E. J. Brill, 1974), and Paule Demats, *Fabula: Trois études de mythographie antique et médiévale*, Publications romanes et françaises, 122 (Geneva: Droz, 1973).

14. The treatments of these two handbooks were summarized by Isidore of Seville (560?-636) as follows: "Historiae sunt res verae quae facta sunt; argumenta sunt quae etsi facta non sunt, fieri tamen possunt; fabulae vero sunt quae nec facta sunt nec fieri possunt, quia contra naturam sunt" (Histories are true things which have been performed; assertions are things which, even though they have not been done, nevertheless could happen; fables, however, are things which neither have been nor could be done, since they are contrary to nature). *Etymologiae* 1.44.5, cited (with the *De inuentione* and the *Ad Herennium*) by Hennig Brinkmann, *Mittelalterliche Hermeneutik* (Tübingen: Niemayer, 1980), 163.

15. See Brinkmann, *Mittelalterliche Hermeneutik*, 223.

16. On Petronius, see Wesley Trimpi's important article, "The Quality of Fiction," *Traditio* 30 (1974): 71, n. 81, and 100 on Quintilian.

17. Demats, *Fabula*, 36 (see note 13, above); see also 33–35. Compare also Winthrop Wetherbee, "The Study of Secular Literature from Late Antiquity to the

Twelfth Century," in *The Middle Ages*, volume 2 of *The Cambridge History of Literary Criticism*, ed. Alastair Minnis (forthcoming).

18. Brinkmann, *Mittelalterliche Hermeneutik*, 386–87 (see note 14, above); Demats, *Fabula*, 19, 34 (see note 13, above); Gerald Bond, "'Iocus amoris': The Poetry of Baudri of Bourgueil and the Formation of the Ovidian Subculture," *Traditio* 62 (1986): 179ff. I am grateful to Winthrop Wetherbee for drawing my attention to this valuable study. Wetherbee notes that it was in the fifth and sixth centuries, with Macrobius and Fulgentius, that critics began to discern a gap between the "meaning" of a text and the "author's intention": see "The Study of Secular Literature" (note 17, above).

19. "Fingere namque componere dicimus; unde et compositores luti figulos uocamus" (We call poetic composition "making fictions," for which reason we call these makers "formers of clay" or "potters"): Gregory, *In Evang.*, 23.1, *PL* 76:1282, cited by Jean Leclerq, *Initiation aux auteurs monastiques: L'Amour des lettres et le désir de Dieu* (Paris: Editions du Cerf, 1957), 126.

20. On Baudri, see Bond, "'Iocus amoris'" generally (note 18, above).

21. Bond, "Composing Yourself: Ovid's *Heroides*, Baudri of Bourgueil, and the Problem of Persona," in *Ovid in Medieval Culture*, 89 (see note 2, above).

22. Baudri's works have been edited twice: *Baldricus Burgulianus Carmina*, ed. Karlheinz Hilbert, Editiones Heidelbergenses 19 (Heidelberg: Carl Winter, 1979) (the edition to which I refer), and *Les Oeuvres poétiques de Baudri de Bourgueil, 1046–1130*, ed. Phyllis Abrahams (Paris: Champion, 1926). Compare also 99.197: "Musa iocosa fuit moresque fuere pudici," and 193.107: "Musa iocosa mihi, sed uita pudica iocoso." The citation from Martial reads "lasciva est nobis pagina, vita proba" (*Epigrams* 1.4.8, cited by Bond, "'Iocus amoris,'" 184 [see note 18, above]). Ovid's defense, from *Tristia* II.353–54, reads "Crede mihi, distant mores a carmine nostro / (uita uerecunda est, musa iocosa mea)" (Believe me: my morals are separate from my writing [my life is modest, though my muse is playful]). Compare Sabine Schuelper, "Ovid aus der Sicht des Balderich von Bourgueil, dargestellt anhand des Briefwechsels Florus-Ovid," *Mittellateinisches Jahrbuch* 14 (1979) 116–17.

23. Dronke, *Fabula* 3, 4, 38, 55 (see note 13, above); Brinkmann, *Mittelalterliche Hermeneutik*, 168 (see note 14, above).

24. Conrad of Hirsau, *Dialogus super auctores*, ed. R. B. C. Huygens (Brussels: Latomus, 1955), 17.

25. Conrad of Hirsau, *Dialogus*, 17, 24, 25 (see note 24, above).

26. Roger Dragonetti, *La Vie de la lettre au Moyen Age: Le Conte du Graal* (Paris: Editions du Seuil, 1980), 77.

27. John of Salisbury, *Policraticus*, VII.12, cited by Judson Boyce Allen, *The Friar as Critic: Literary Attitudes in the Later Middle Ages* (Nashville, TN: Vanderbilt University Press, 1971), 11–12.

28. John of Garland (Giovanni di Garlandia), *Integumentum Ovidii, poemetto inedito del secolo XIII*, ed. Fausto Ghisalberti, Testi e documenti inediti o rari, 2 (Messina and Milan: Edizioni Principato, 1933), 61; *Ovide moralisé*, 15.2533–37ff., cited by Demats, *Fabula*, 174–75 (see note 13, above).

29. See Trimpi, "The Quality of Fiction," 98–99 (note 16, above); Glending

Olson, *Literature as Recreation in the Later Middle Ages* (Ithaca, NY: Cornell University Press, 1982), 130–31.

30. Jehan Bodel, *Les Saisnes*, ed. F. Menzel and E. Stengel (Marburg, 1906), v. 6–11, cited by Robert Guiette, "'Li Conte de Bretaigne sont si vain et plaisant,'" *Romania* 88 (1967): 1.

31. "The medieval thinkers were not content to create allegories, whether literary or plastic; they attempted to discover in story [or history] and fiction hidden meanings which cannot be perceived at first reading. If a hidden meaning is concealed within a true story to such a point that one reality transports the reader into another, profane reading, we must speak of allegory. If the hidden meaning is merely suggested by a fable, to the point where the reader feels himself being transported from an imaginary world into a world which is true only in a moral sense, we must speak of an integument. 'Integumentum est veritas in specie *fabulae* palliata, allegoria est veritas in versibus *historiae* palliata' (An integument is truth in the form of a fable [or fiction]; an allegory is truth in the lines of a veracious narrative)." Edgar de Bruyne, *The Esthetics of the Middle Ages*, trans. Eileen B. Hennessy (New York: Frederick Ungar, 1969), 78.

32. See Dronke, *Fabula*, 45 (see note 13, above); Leclerq, *Monks and Love in Twelfth-Century France: Psycho-Historical Essays* (Oxford: Clarendon Press, 1979), 37; Hennig Brinkmann, *Mittelalterlicher Hermeneutik*, 24 (see note 14, above). See also Wetherbee, "The *Romance of the Rose* and Medieval Allegory," in *European Writers: The Middle Ages and the Renaissance*, ed. W. T. H. Jackson (New York: Scribner's, 1983), 1:309–35. On applications to the work of Ovid, see J. B. Allen, *The Friar as Critic*, 14–15 (see note 27, above), and Fausto Ghisalberti, "L'*Ovidius moralizatus* di Pierre Bersuire," *Società filologica romana, studi romanzi* 23 (1933): 43. For discussions of multiple schemata of interpretation, especially as applied to sacred texts, see A. J. Minnis, *Medieval Theory of Authorship: Scholastic Literary Attitudes in the Later Middle Ages*, 2d ed. (Philadelphia, PA: University of Pennsylvania Press, 1988), 34; Gervais Dumiège, *Richard de Saint-Victor et l'idée chrétienne de l'amour* (Paris: Presses Universitaires de France, 1952), 24; and Conrad, *Dialogus super auctores*, 18–19 (see note 24, above).

33. De Bruyne, *Esthetics*, 162 (see note 31, above).

34. A more accommodating view was proposed by some: both Ambrose (340?–397) and William of Conches saw the human body as an *integumentum* for the soul, lacking perhaps in transcendent meaning, but necessary for life on earth. See Dronke, *Fabula* 48 n. 2, 56 n. 2 (see note 13, above). For a more extended discussion of William, see Wetherbee, "The Study of Secular Literature" (see note 17, above).

35. On the history of the *accessus*, which may date back to third-century commentaries on Aristotle, see E. A. Quain, S.J., "The Medieval *Accessus ad auctores*," *Traditio* 3 (1945), esp. 262–63; see also Ghisalberti, "Medieval Biographies of Ovid," *Journal of the Warburg and Courtauld Institutes* 9 (1946): 16.

36. Munari describes the *accessus* as a *pia fraus* which was hardly persuasive, and argues "daß man ihn [Ovid] so verstand, wie wir ihn heute verstehen" (*Ovid im Mittelalter*, 11 [see note 6, above]), a sentiment with which I agree. See also Ghisalberti, "Medieval Biographies of Ovid," 15 (see note 35, above), and Demats, *Fabula*, 109 (see note 13, above). For opposing views, see Leclerq, *Monks and*

Love, 62 (see note 32, above); J. B. Allen, "Commentary as Criticism: The Text, Influence, and Literary Theory of the 'Fulgentius Metaphored' of John Ridewall," in *Acta conuentus neo-latini amstelodamensis*, ed. P. Tuynman, G. C. Kuiper, and E. Keßler, Humanistische Bibliothek, Abhandlungen, Texte, Skripten, ser. 1, vol. 26 (Munich: Fink, 1979) 36; and Salvatore Battaglia, "La tradizione di Ovidio nel medio evo," *Filologia romanza* 6 (1959): 201 n., with references to Leclerq.

37. Brinkmann, *Mittelalterliche Hermeneutik*, 396 (see note 14, above); see also Laura Kendrick's insightful book, *The Game of Love: Troubadour Wordplay* (Berkeley and Los Angeles, CA: University of California Press, 1988), 30; Olson, *Literature as Recreation in the Later Middle Ages*, 206 (see note 29, above); and Demats, *Fabula*, 113 (see note 13, above). The famous prologue to Marie de France's *Lais* makes much the same point (Marie de France, *Lais*, ed. Jean Rychner, Classiques français du Moyen Age [Paris: Champion: 1978], 1–2).

38. Johann Huizinga, *Homo ludens: A Study of the Play Element in Culture* (1950; rpt. Boston, MA: Beacon Press, 1955), 19; see also Maria Corti, "Models and Antimodels in Medieval Culture," *New Literary History* 10 (1979): 351–52, discussing Bakhtin and the "second world" of popular festivals.

39. Sigmund Freud, "The Relation of the Poet to Day-Dreaming," in *Collected Papers* (London: Hogarth Press, 1950) 4:174. See also D. W. Winnicott, *Playing and Reality* (New York: Basic Books, 1971).

40. Huizinga, *Homo ludens*, 43, 119 (see note 38, above).

41. See Curtius, "Jest and Earnest in Medieval Literature," Excursus IV of *European Literature*, 417–36 (note 9, above).

42. Thomas Aquinas, *Summa theologica* II-II, cited by Olson, *Literature as Recreation*, 98 (see note 29, above).

43. Olson, *Literature as Recreation*, 89 (see note 29, above). Even the art of love could fit into this category, with a little manipulation. One somewhat eccentric *accessus* to the *Art d'amours* edited by Bruno Roy (*L'Art d'Amours: Traduction et commentaire de l'"Ars amatoria" d'Ovide* [Leiden: Brill, 1974], 42) creates a schema of the arts which shows how a place might be found for Ovid's teachings:

PHILOSOPHIE SUPPOSITIO (CLASSIFICATION OF THE ARTS)
1 mechanical
2 art and science combined:
   (a) liberal arts (without prohibition of justice or clergy)
   1. grammar
   2. logic, which is called the art of dialectic
   3. music
   4. medicine
   5. theology
   6. geometry
   7. arithmetic
   (b) non-liberal arts
   1. *forbidden*: poisoning, killing by treason, sorcery, death, playing
      instruments, wrestling, tournaments, etc., necromancy
   2. *neither forbidden nor permitted:* astronomy, the art of love.

Some of the classification is very strange: it is difficult to see, for example, what the playing of instruments has to do with poisoning or wrestling. But one can understand the placement of the arts of love and astronomy (not clearly distinguished from what we now call "astrology"): they are both to some degree ways of reading and attempting to modify human behavior that are subject to, and perhaps based upon, potentially flawed interpretation and mystification. (I owe this explanation to Paul Gehl.) They are pseudo-arts, designed not for education but for diversion.

44. C. Stephen Jaeger, *The Origins of Courtliness: Civilizing Trends and the Formation of Courtly Ideals, 939–1210* (Philadelphia, PA: University of Pennsylvania Press, 1985), 258; see also Olson, *Literature as Recreation*, 230 (note 29, above).

45. Paul Zumthor, *Essai de poétique médiévale* (Paris: Editions du Seuil, 1972), 214–16; Kendrick, *The Game of Love*, 170–86 (see note 37, above).

46. As Jean Frappier explains: "The courtly poets never claimed to substitute the ethics of *fine amour* for Christian morality. In reading them, one would be more likely to believe that they accepted the possibility of a tranquil coexistence of the two irreconcilable concepts. Ingenuousness or calculation? Let us not take the risk of deciding. As if by definition, courtly love placed itself ideally outside of religion (sometimes including God, if necessary, inside its sphere). The mistake which must not be made is to conclude that, just because *fine amour* was immoral in terms of Christian and feudal precepts, it did not exist" ("Sur un procès fait à l'amour courtois," in *Amour courtois et Table ronde*, Publications romanes et françaises [Geneva: Droz, 1973], 86). See also Karl D. Uitti, "Remarks on Old French Narrative: Courtly Love and Poetic Form," *Romance Philology* 26 (1972–73): 77–93, and the discussion in Roger Boase, *The Origin and Meaning of Courtly Love: A Critical Study of European Scholarship* (Manchester: Manchester University Press, 1977), 113. This love, whether we call it *fine amour* or "courtly love," is unlikely to have been a part of social praxis, but it is a major medieval literary theme. On courtly love as a literary phenomenon, see Jaeger, *The Origins of Courtliness*, 209 (see note 44, above), and E. Talbot Donaldson, "The Myth of Courtly Love," *Ventures: The Magazine of the Yale Graduate School* 5.2 (Fall 1965): 18–19. See also Edmond Faral, *Recherches sur les sources latines des contes et romans courtois du Moyen Age* (Paris: Champion, 1913), 195, cited by Jaeger, *The Origins of Courtliness*, 209; Bond, "'Iocus amoris,'" 189–93 (see note 18, above); and Leclerq, *Monks and Love*, 72–73 (see note 32, above).

47. The phrase is that of Ludwig Traube, *Vorlesungen und Abhandlungen* (Munich, 1911): see Angelo Monteverdi, "Ovidio nel medio evo," *Atti della Accademia Nazionale dei Lincei* 354 (1957), Rendiconti delle Adunanze Solenne, Adunanza solenne del 7 giugno 1957, vol. 5, fasc. 12: 697.

48. Frederick Adam Wright, *Three Roman Poets: Plautus, Catullus, Ovid* (London, 1938), 246, cited by Dorothy A. Robathan, "Ovid in the Middle Ages," in *Ovid*, ed. J. W. Binns (Boston, MA: Routledge and Kegan Paul, 1973), 198.

49. See Ovid, *The Erotic Poems*, trans. Peter Green (Harmondsworth: Penguin, 1982), 43–49.

50. See M. Cary et al., eds., *The Oxford Classical Dictionary* (Oxford: Clarendon Press, 1949), s.v. Ovid, p. 631. For one recent, if not always persuasive view

of the poet's life, see Green's introduction to *Ovid: The Erotic Poems*, esp. 44–48 (note 49, above); see also Ghisalberti, "Medieval Biographies of Ovid," 16 (note 35, above).

51. Walther Kraus, "Ovidius Naso," *Paulys Real-Encyclopädie der classischen Altertumswissenschaft*, 2d ed. (Munich: K. Mittelhaus, 1943), vol. 18, 2, cols. 1978–79.

52. See Aldo Scaglione, "The Classics in Medieval Education," in *The Classics in the Middle Ages*, ed. Aldo S. Bernardo and Saul Levin, special issue of *Medieval and Renaissance Texts and Studies* 69 (1990): 343–44; but compare Wetherbee, "The Study of Secular Literature" (see note 17, above).

53. See Wetherbee, "The Study of Secular Literature" (see note 17, above).

54. Tafel, *Überlieferungsgeschichte*, 69 (see note 6, above); F. J. E. Raby, *A History of Secular Latin Poetry in the Middle Ages*, 2 volumes, 2d edition (Oxford: 1957), 1.203–4.

55. Tafel, *Überlieferungsgeschichte*, 71 (see note 6, above).

56. Raby, *A History of Secular Latin Poetry*, 1.247, 303, 305 (see note 54, above); Pollmann, *Die Liebe*, 59 (see note 4, above).

57. See in particular Hexter, *Ovid and Medieval Schooling* 13 (note 3, above), on the Benedictine monastery of Tegernsee as an early center of Ovidian studies; Hexter cites in this connection Peter Dronke, "A Note on *Pamphilus*," *Journal of the Warburg and Courtauld Institutes* 42 (1979): 230.

58. Raby, *Secular Latin Poetry*, 1.319 (see note 54, above).

59. Joseph de Ghellink, S.J., *Littérature latine au Moyen Age*, Bibliothèque Catholique des Sciences Religieuses (n.p.: Bloud and Gay, 1939), 2 vols., 1.111–12. See also Munari, *Ovid im Mittelalter*, 9–10 (note 6, above), and Wetherbee, "The Study of Secular Literature" (note 17, above).

60. See Bond, "Composing Yourself," 85 (note 2, above), on the dramatic impact of the "New Ovid" (the amatory works) in eleventh-century France.

61. Hexter, *Ovid and Medieval Schooling*, 17 (see note 3, above).

62. Georges Duby, *The Knight, the Lady, and the Priest: The Making of Modern Marriage in Medieval France*, trans. Barbara Bray (New York: Pantheon Books, 1983), 117. The Frankish church, in its struggle with Germanic practices, had prohibited married men from keeping concubines as early as 829 (*The Knight, the Lady, and the Priest*, 27–30).

63. Bishop Yvo of Chartres expressed some of these concerns in the 1090s, writing that as "it was the wife who was the instigator of lewdness in a marriage, so she must be strictly held in check": Yvo of Chartres, *PL* 161, *Decretum* VIII, 42, cited by Duby, *The Knight, the Lady, and the Priest*, 164 (see note 62, above); see also 99, 106. Yvo also ordained that men should not trouble themselves unduly with their appearance. As we noted in the *Ars*, and will see again in the *De amore* and the *Roman de la Rose*, efforts to manipulate and control women reinforce gender boundaries in ways that limit men as well.

64. As Georges Duby reminds us: "The terms which mark membership in the group—*miles, chevalier*—have no feminine" (*Histoire de la France*, ed. Duby [Paris: Larousse, 1970], 138).

65. Unpublished sermons of Jacques de Vitry, cited by Duby, *The Knight, the Lady, and the Priest*, 212 (see note 62, above); on *L'Art d'Amours*, see Leclerq, *Monks*

and Love, 74–75 (see note 32, above). For a fuller treatment of the subject, see R. Howard Bloch's article and book: "Medieval Misogyny," *Representations* 20 (Fall 1987): 1–24, and *Medieval Misogyny and the Invention of Western Romantic Love* (Chicago, IL: University of Chicago Press, 1991).

66. The *Decretum* of Bourchard of Worms (1007–12) prescribed its heaviest allotment of days of penance for adultery, along with bestiality, abduction, and sexual involvement with nuns; civil laws assigned punishments for adultery that ranged from public humiliation to death. See Duby, *The Knight, the Lady, and the Priest*, 67 (note 62, above); John F. Benton, "Clio and Venus: An Historical View of Medieval Love," in *The Meaning of Courtly Love*, ed. F. X. Newman (Albany, NY: SUNY Press, 1968), 24–25. See also Bloch, *Etymologies and Genealogies: A Literary Anthropology of the French Middle Ages* (Chicago, IL: University of Chicago Press, 1983), esp. chapter 2.

67. Benton, "Clio and Venus," 27 (see note 66, above).

68. The *locus classicus* of the latter point of view is D. W. Robertson, *A Preface to Chaucer: Studies in Medieval Perspectives* (Princeton, NJ: Princeton University Press, 1962); see further the essays in Newman, ed., *The Meaning of Courtly Love* (note 66, above), and, for a more balanced view, Donaldson, "The Myth of Courtly Love" (note 46, above).

69. Raby, *Secular Latin Poetry*, 1.315, 320, 359; 2.23 (see note 54, above).

70. See Raby, *Secular Latin Poetry*, 1.335 (see note 54, above).

71. Pollmann, *Die Liebe*, 65 (see note 4, above).

72. Jean Leclerq also sees Baudri as primarily secular and therefore distinct from his contemporaries, in whom, Leclerq argues, the reading of Ovid generally provoked guilty consciences (*Monks and Love*, 66 [see note 32, above]). To me, on the other hand, Baudri seems to be proceeding in the same direction as his fellow poets, and if he went further than they did, it was along the path later to be taken by the major French writers on love of the twelfth and thirteenth centuries. On *amor* and its problematic place in Baudri's eleventh-century culture, compare Bond, "Composing Yourself," 97 (see note 21, above). Baudri's definition of the word *clericus* is one example of this cross-fertilization: though normally the word meant "a member of the clergy," for Baudri a *clericus* was someone who was "witty, light-hearted, playful (or: poetry-loving), amicable," with a character shaped by classical literature (130.1–3) (citation from Bond, "'Iocus amoris,'" 190 [see note 18, above]; Bond's translation).

73. Compare Bond, "'Iocus amoris,'" 162–63, 165 (see note 18, above). The term "specialis amicus" also occurs in 99.131; in the next line Baudri asks Godefroy, to whom the poem is addressed, to be his "alter ego." See particularly 97.45–54; compare "'Iocus amoris,'" 169; Raby, *Secular Latin Poetry*, 1.345–46 (see note 54, above); and Monteverdi, "Ovidio nel medio evo," 702 n. 24 (see note 47, above). See further, on Baudri, John Boswell, *Christianity, Social Tolerance, and Homosexuality: Gay People in Western Europe from the Beginning of the Christian Era to the Fourteenth Century* (Chicago, IL: University of Chicago Press, 1980), 237, 244–47.

74. Poem III, "Ad eum qui Ovidium ab eo extorsit," suggests that Baudri owned a copy of the text; cf. Bond, "'Iocus amoris,'" 146 n. 7 (see note 18, above). See *Baldricus Burgulianus Carmina*, ed. Karlheinz Hilbert, Editiones Heidelber-

genses 19 (Heidelberg: Carl Winter, 1979), and *Les Oeuvres poétiques de Baudri de Bourgueil, 1046–1130*, ed. Phyllis Abrahams (Paris: Champion, 1926). Both editions are necessary for a thorough study of the poet's works, since Hilbert provides the better text but only Abrahams offers notes. On Baudri's literary relationships, see Raby, *Secular Latin Poetry* 1.337–38 (see note 54, above), and Max Manitius, *Geschichte der lateinischen Literatur des Mittelalters* (Munich: Beck, 1931), 3 volumes, 3.895. Another link with Ovid is Baudri's repeated use of the term "Naso nouus" for poets or friends he wished to compliment: see 39.3–4, 85.15, 90.22; and Raby, *Secular Latin Poetry*, 1.316.

75. Compare poem 193, for example (see note 74, above). Elsewhere, when Baudri asks Godefroy to be his *specialis amicus*, he speaks of love in one line, in the next of his pen (99.133–34), and the epistolary exchange with Constantia (poems 200–201) plays suggestively on the relationship between sex and writing, attributing to each activity the qualities of the other. Bond believes that these two poems "present a theory and practice of the sublimation of *amor* into *littera*" ("'Iocus amoris,'" 168 [see note 18, above]). But rather than sublimating love, Baudri may also be sexualizing writing—he is adding risk to a presumably "safe" activity rather than removing it from a dangerous one. For further consideration of this exchange, compare Stephen G. Nichols, "Medieval Women Writers: *Aisthesis* and the Powers of Marginality," *Yale French Studies* 75 (1988): 86–88, and "Rewriting Marriage in the Middle Ages," *Romanic Review* 79 (1988): 54–56.

76. Bond, "'Iocus amoris,'" 186; see also 167, 185 (note 18, above).

77. Bond explains that in the Middle Ages even personal letters were commonly read by messengers and others as they were carried to their addressees, and so private messages had to be couched in public language: "Speaking to a double audience—to the known and private, 'cui proprie legatur epistola' (5/XL.23) (by whom the letter was properly read), and to the unknown and public—forces the author to resort to double systems of meaning. As a slightly later letter-writer expressed it: 'Ad alios uerba, ad te intencionem dirigo' (I direct my words to others, my intention to you)" ("'Iocus amoris,'" 161, citing *Epistolae duorum amantium: Briefe Abaelards und Heloises?*, ed. Ewald Könsgen [Leiden and Cologne: E. J. Brill, 1974], 11).

78. See Bond, "'Iocus amoris,'" 176, 183–84 (on 99/CLXI.183–99) (see note 18, above), as well as Pollmann, *Die Liebe* (see note 4, above), 66 (on CXLVII, CCXXXVIII, CCXXXIX). Compare also poem 12, entitled "LUDENDO DE TABULIS SUIS" (Playing with His Tablets), and 1.33–34: "Crede michi, numquam nocuerunt uerba iocosa; / Me semper munit pectoris integritas" (Believe me, playful words never hurt anyone; integrity of the soul always protects me).

79. Bond notes, accurately, that the personae in which Baudri wrote are so varied that they cannot all be attributed to an eleventh-century abbot; see "Composing Yourself," *passim* (note 21, above), and "'Iocus amoris,'" 178 (see note 18, above).

80. Charles Homer Haskins, *The Renaissance of the Twelfth Century* (Cambridge, MA: Harvard University Press, 1928), 7–8.

81. See Dumiège, *Richard de Saint-Victor*, 1–3 (see note 32, above); see also Haskins's *The Renaissance of the Twelfth Century*, 158–59 (see note 80, above).

82. Curtius, *European Literature*, 387 (see note 9, above).

83. Jaeger, *The Origins of Courtliness*, 114, 174–75 (see note 44, above); see also 9.

84. See Jaeger, *The Origins of Courtliness*, 224–26 (see note 44, above); de Ghellinck, *Littérature latine*, 190 (see note 59, above).

85. Leclerq, *Monks and Love*, 9–14 (see note 32, above).

86. Pollmann, *Die Liebe*, 252 (see note 4, above). I am grateful to Peter Dahlström and Magnus Rosander for assistance with this passage.

87. Compare also the famous poem about the (fictional) Council of Remiremont: P. Lehmann, *Die Parodie im Mittelalter* (Munich, 1922), 159, cited by Munari, *Ovid im Mittelalter*, 20–21 (see note 6, above): "Intromissis omnibus   virginum agminibus / lecta sunt in medium   quasi evangelium / precepta Ovidii   doctoris egregii." Raby dates the poem to the mid-twelfth century: *Secular Latin Poetry*, 2.294 (see note 54, above).

88. Leclerq, *Monks and Love*, 27–29, 81, 129 (see note 32, above).

89. On Richard and Gérard, see Dronke, *Medieval Latin*, 1.62–63 (note 2, above); see also Aelred of Rievaulx, *L'Amitié spirituelle*, ed., trans. J. Dubois, Bibliothèque de Spiritualité Médiévale (Bruges and Paris: Editions Charles Beyaent, 1948).

90. Ghisalberti, "L'*Ovidius moralizatus*," 13 (citing Alain's *De arte predicatoria* I, *PL* 210:114), 19 (see note 12, above).

91. Curtius, *European Literature*, 53 (see note 9, above).

92. Dumiège, *Richard de Saint-Victor*, 27 (see note 32, above), citing Alain's *De fide catholica*, L. I, c. 30, *PL* 210:333.

93. Abelard, *Sic et non*: "By doubting we come to inquiry, and by inquiry we perceive truth," cited by Haskins, *The Renaissance of the Twelfth Century* (see note 80, above): "Inerrancy he grants only to the Scriptures, apparent contradictions in which must be explained as due to scribal mistakes or defective understanding; subsequent authorities may err for other reasons, and when they disagree he claims the right of going into the reasonableness of the doctrine itself, of proving all things in order to hold fast that which is good" (354–55).

94. Hexter claims that instruction in the medieval classroom was "value-free" (*Ovid and Medieval Schooling*, 25 [see note 3, above]); see also D. H. Alton and D. E. W. Wormwell, "Ovid in the Medieval Schoolroom," *Hermathena* 94 (1960): 27–31. Scaglione, "The Classics in Medieval Education" (see note 52, above) takes a more orthodox view (344, 351).

95. See Birger Munk-Olsen, "Les Classiques latins dans les florilèges médiévaux antérieurs au 13ᵉ siècle," *Revue d'histoire des textes* 9 (1979): 54–56. See also Raby, *Secular Latin Poetry*, 2.67–69 (note 54, above).

96. See Eva Matthews Sanford, "The Use of Classical Latin Authors in the *Libri Manuales*," *Transactions of the American Philological Association* 55 (1924): 190–248.

97. Louise Vinge, *The Narcissus Theme in Western European Literature up to the Early Nineteenth Century*, trans. Robert Dewsnap et al. (Lund: Gleerups, 1967), 55.

98. *Carmina Burana*, eds. Alfons Hilka, Otto Schumann, and Bernhard Bischoff (Heidelberg: Carl Winter, 1930–).

99. *Pamphilus*, ed. Stefano Pittaluga, and *Geta*, ed. Ferruccio Bertini, in Fer-

ruccio Bertini, ed., *Commedia Latina del XII° e XIII° secolo*, 4 vols., Pubblicazioni dell' Istituto classica e medievale, (Genoa: Istituto di filologia classica e medievale, 1986), 3.13–137 and 141–241. See also Maurice Wilmotte, *Origines du roman en France: L'Evolution des sentiments romanesques jusqu'en 1240*, Académie Royale de Langue et de Littérature françaises de Belgique, Mémoires 15 (Brussels and Liége: Palais des Académies, 1941), 176; see also Monteverdi, "Ovidio nel medio evo," 703–4 (note 47, above), and Paul Lehmann, *Pseudo-antike Literatur des Mittelalters*, Studien der Bibliothek Warburg, 13 (Leipzig and Berlin: Teubner, 1927).

100. In the famous preface to *Cligés*, Chrétien described himself as an author who "les comandemanz d'Ovide / Et l'art d'amors an romans mist" (put the commandments of Ovid and the art of love into the French language) (*Cligés*, ed. Alexandre Micha, Classiques français du Moyen Age [Paris: Champion, 1978], vv. 2–3). On Chrétien's relationship with Ovid, see, most usefully, Roy, ed., *L'Art d'Amours*, 34 (note 43, above); see also John of Garland, *Integumentum Ovidii*, Introduction, 14 (note 28, above); somewhat less usefully, Reginald Hyatte, "'Ovidius, doctor amoris': The Changing Attitudes towards Ovid's Eroticism in the Middle Ages as Seen in the Three Old French Adaptations of the *Remedia amoris*," *Florilegium* 4 (1982): 125, and Foster E. Guyer, "The Influence of Ovid on Crestien de Troyes," *Romanic Review* 12.2 (1921): 219.

101. One Ovidian piece probably contemporary with Chrétien's works is a short Latin poem containing a good deal of amatory advice, Aurigena's *Facetus*. Dronke dates this work to the 1170s at the latest, noting that it provides evidence of a context within which Andreas Capellanus wrote his *De amore*. See A. Morel-Fatio, ed., "Facetus," *Romania* 15 (1886): 224–35, and Peter Dronke, "Pseudo-Ovid, *Facetus* and the Arts of Love," *Mittellateinisches Jahrbuch* 11 (1976): 126–27, 130.

102. Munari, *Ovid im Mittelalter*, 22 (see note 36, above). On Ovid as an ethical writer, see particularly Demats, *Fabula*, 116–31 (see note 13, above).

103. On Abelard, see generally *Abélard et Héloïse, Correspondance*, trans. Paul Zumthor, Bibliothèque du Moyen Age (Paris: Union Générale des Editions, 1979), as well as Dronke, *Fabula*, 64 (note 13, above); Munari, *Ovid im Mittelalter*, 19–20 (note 36, above); Hexter, *Ovid and Medieval Schooling*, 17 (note 3, above). On Ovid as a resource on lovesickness, see Robathan, "Ovid in the Middle Ages," 200–201 (note 48, above), and, more generally, Mary Frances Wack, *Lovesickness in the Middle Ages: The Viaticum and Its Commentaries* (Philadelphia, PA: University of Pennsylvania Press, 1990).

104. William of St. Thierry, *De natura et dignitate amoris*, cited by Leclerq, *Monks and Love*, 66–67 (see note 32, above); see Minnis, *Medieval Theory of Authorship*, 51 (note 32, above).

105. Demats, *Fabula*, 132 (see note 13, above).

106. Conrad of Hirsau, *Dialogus*, 15, 51 (see note 24, above).

107. See Curtius, *European Literature*, 466, citing 64, 1ff. (note 9, above), as well as Leclerq, *Monks and Love*, 41–43 (note 32, above) and *Initiation aux auteurs monastiques*, 114–15 (note 19, above).

108. Elisabeth Pellegrin, "Les *Remedia amoris* d'Ovide, texte scolaire médiévale," *Bibliothèque de l'Ecole des Chartes* 115 (1957): 172–73; see also Hexter, *Ovid and Medieval Schooling*, 18–19 (note 3, above).

109. R. B. C. Huygens, ed., *Accessus ad auctores*, Collection Latomus 15 (Ber-

chem and Brussels: Latomus, 1954), 25 (Accessus Ovidii epistolarum II). Huygens's *accessus* are drawn from three manuscripts: the twelfth-century Tegernsee MS CLM (Codex Latinus Monacensis: Munich Bavarian Library) 19475; the late twelfth- or early thirteenth-century Tegernsee MS CLM 19474, and Vatican Palatinus lat. 242, s. xii/xiii (5–6). See also Minnis, *Medieval Theory of Authorship*, 55–56 (note 32, above) and "The Influence of Academic Prologues on the Prologues and Literary Attitudes of Late-Medieval English Writers," *Medieval Studies* 43 (1981): 347–48; and Raby, *Secular Latin Poetry*, 2.214 (note 54, above). Another extremely common formulation of this kind of position is frequently found in medieval textual commentaries, which instruct their readers that "this book is classified under ethics [*ethice subponitur*] because it deals with behavior" (translation by J. B. Allen, *The Friar as Critic*, 41 [see note 32, above]). With this approach, one could argue, as some commentators did, that "omnes fere auctores ad ethicam tendunt" (almost all authors are ethically inclined): Demats, *Fabula*, 119 (see note 13, above), citing MS CLM 4610; Conrad, *Dialogus super auctores*, 23 (see note 24, above).

110. Biographical interest in Ovid continues, both in classical scholarship and, lately, in an excellent work of fiction, Christoph Ransmayr's *The Last World* (1988), trans. John E. Woods (New York: Grove Weidenfeld, 1990).

111. Huygens, ed., *Accessus ad auctores*, "Accessus Ouidii sine titulo" (II) 32 (emphasis added) (see note 109, above).

112. Thus his *nomen*, Ovidius (fancifully derived from *ovum dividens*), indicated his philosophical ability to distinguish among the parts of the "egg" of the cosmos (a representation of the heavens [the shell], the air [the membrane], the water [the white], and the earth [the yolk]). His *cognomen*, Naso, came either from "the moral sagacity which enabled him to smell out the difference between virtue and vice" or from the putative prominence of his nose, which was thought to betoken his impressive genital endowment. The former explanations are cited by Ghisalberti, "Medieval Biographies of Ovid," 27–28 (see note 35, above); the latter is to be found in Kendrick, *The Game of Love*, 104 (see note 45, above).

113. Fausto Ghisalberti relates an amusing anecdote from MS. Paris (B.N. lat.) 8255: "In discussing Ovid's supposed intrigue with the empress, the commentator says that the poet climbed to her window on a bronze ladder. Virgil took some of the rungs out of this ladder whilst Ovid was with the empress, so that when the latter descended, he fell and broke his leg. For this, among other reasons, Ovid hated Virgil" (Ghisalberti, "Medieval Biographies of Ovid," 14 [see note 35, above]; the other explanations are found on p. 32).

114. See Leclercq, *Initiation*, 113–14 (note 19, above), as well as Alton and Wormwell, "Ovid in the Medieval Schoolroom," 69 (note 94, above). Vergil had been similarly Christianized on the basis of his fourth eclogue; the same fate had befallen Statius: see Dante, *Purgatorio* 21, 22. The *De vetula* was often recognized as spurious, even by medieval readers (see Demats, *Fabula*, 124–25), and belief in Ovid as a Christian could not be reconciled with the poet's other writings: Ghisalberti, "Medieval Biographies of Ovid," 17 (see note 35, above); see also Hexter, *Ovid and Medieval Schooling*, 131–32 (note 3, above), Munari, *Ovid im Mittelalter*, 26 (note 6, above). The other side of the argument is presented, though not persuasively in my view, by Leclercq, *Initiation*, 115–16, 141 (see note 19, above), and by Robathan, "Ovid in the Middle Ages," 202 (see note 48, above).

115. "Sunt autem Pathmos et Thomos insule contigue," the manuscript explains: "The islands of Patmos [the Aegean island, used as a penal colony by the Romans, on which John experienced the vision recorded in Revelation 1:9] and Tomis [the port on the Black Sea—now Costança, in Romania—to which Ovid was relegated] are next to one another": see Bernhard Bischoff, "Eine mittelalterliche Ovid-Legende," *Historisches Jahrbuch* 71 (1952): 268–73.

116. As the manuscripts' varied and imaginative explanations for the lack of an official name for the *Amores* (often called the "Liber sine titulo") show. Several *accessus* explain this lack by turning to the opening of poem 1.1. They explain that Ovid wanted to write a military poem—perhaps about Augustus' war against Antony and Cleopatra—and that the book was to be called the "liber armorum" (The Book of Arms). Cupid's attack made the title "liber amorum" (The Book of Loves) more appropriate, and the confusion between the two names left the work without any title at all. Another explanation cites the poet's concern not to offend Augustus any more than he had already done by writing the (supposedly anterior) *Ars*; Huygens, ed., *Accessus ad auctores*, "Accessus Ouidii sine titulo (I), (II), 31–33 (see note 109, above).

117. Ghisalberti, "Medieval Biographies of Ovid," 46 (see note 35, above).

118. Alton and Wormwell, "Ovid in the Medieval Schoolroom," 73 (see note 94, above), citing the "Versus Bursarii Ovidii" (Berol. Lat. 4 219; Leyden Lat. Lips. 39).

119. Huygens, *Accessus ad auctores*, "Accessus Ouidii de remedio amoris," 29–30 (see note 109, above). Compare also Ghisalberti, "Medieval Biographies of Ovid," 45 (see note 35, above), Appendix D (Cod. Paris. 11318): "Ovidius autem quadam mollicie depravatus et nimia prosperitate gavisus, . . . telumque Cupidinis sepissime lacessitus, effeminate lascivie sue relaxens, librum de Arte Amatoria composuit in quo quam plurimos contraxit in errorem per amoris varia documenta. . . . [But his readers suffered by taking his advice on love too seriously:] quidam ad suspendium, quidam ad incendium, ceterique ad ceterorum genera mortis presonpcione amoris intollerancia cogebantur. Hac de causa compulsus, Ovidius ad eorum remedia hoc opus suscipere destinavit." The *Fasti* were also considered to have been written as penitence for the *Ars*: see Huygens, *Accessus ad auctores*, 33 (note 109, above).

120. Huygens, *Accessus ad auctores*, 26–27 (see note 109, above).

121. On the relationship between text and society, see Kendrick, *The Game of Love*, 7–8, 47 (note 45, above); Benton, "Clio and Venus," esp. 31 (note 66, above); and Lee Patterson, "Ambiguity and Interpretation: A Fifteenth-Century Reading of *Troilus and Criseyde*," *Speculum* 54 (1979): 297–330, including a discussion of Benton's "Clio and Venus" (319). (This article forms part of Patterson's thought-provoking book, *Negotiating the Past: The Historical Understanding of Medieval Literature* [Madison, WI: University of Wisconsin Press, 1987]). See further my essay, "A Frame for the Text? History, Literary Theory, Subjectivity, and the Study of Medieval Literature," in Peter L. Allen and Jeff Rider, eds., *Reflections in the Frame: New Perspectives in the Study of Medieval Literature*, spec. issue of *Exemplaria: A Journal of Theory in Medieval and Renaissance Literature* 3.1 (1991): 1–25. Compare also J. B. Allen, *The Friar as Critic*, 92 (see note 27, above).

122. See Charles Muscatine, *Chaucer and the French Tradition* (Berkeley, CA:

University of California Press, 1956), 76; see also Wetherbee, *Platonism and Poetry in the Twelfth Century: The Literary Influence of the School of Chartres* (Princeton, NJ: Princeton University Press, 1972), 256–57.

123. On the general subject of translation, see F. Douglas Kelly, "Translatio studii: Translation, Adaptation, and Allegory in Medieval French Literature," *Philological Quarterly* 57 (1978): 287–310, as well as Michelle A. Freeman, *The Poetics of 'translatio studii' and 'conjointure': Chrétien de Troyes' 'Cligés'*, French Forum Monographs 12 (Lexington, KY: French Forum, 1979).

124. Edward Kennard Rand, discussing these increases, writes, "Perhaps we may liken Ovid's career in the schools to that of Aristotle in the universities—first ostracized, then tolerated, then prescribed" ("The Classics in the Thirteenth Century," *Speculum* 4 [1929]: 260).

125. Demats, *Fabula*, 136 (see note 13, above).

126. *Le Grand Robert des noms* (see note 7, above), s.v. Brunetto Latini; see also Concetto Marchesi, "Volgarizzamenti dell'*Ars amatoria* nei secoli XIII e XIV," *Memorie del Reale Istituto Lombardo di Science e Lettere*, Classe di lettere, scienze morali e storiche, vols. 23–24, ser. 3 (Milan, 1917): 321.

127. Munari, *Ovid im Mittelalter*, 29–30 (see note 6, above).

128. E. J. Thiel, "Mittellateinisches Nachdichtungen in Ovid—*Ars. Am.* und *Rem. Am.*," *Mittellateinisches Jahrbuch* 5 (1968): 124, 168–80.

129. Roy, ed., *L'Art d'Amours*, 4–5, 9 (see note 43, above); see also Robert H. Lucas, "Medieval French Translations of the Latin Classics to 1500," *Speculum* 45 (1970): 242.

130. This "répugnance qu'éprouvaient les auteurs didactiques à s'adresser directement aux femmes" follows earlier practices. For example, an eleventh-century manuscript of the *Ars*, MS. London B. M. Add. 14086 (ca. 1100), contains commentary only on Books 1 and 2 (Roy, ed., *L'Art d'Amours* 5, 14–16 [see note 43, above]); compare Leclerq, *Monks and Love*, 77–78 (see note 32, above). Roy's text contains a third book, but he believes it is a later addition: see pp. 14–15.

131. Roy, ed., *L'Art d'Amours*, 7 (see note 43, above).

132. Hyatte, "Ovidius, doctor amoris," 124 (see note 100, above).

133. As Roy notes: "Aucun auteur n'avoue, à notre connaissance, avoir connu Ovide à travers une version française" (*L'Art d'Amours*, 57 [see note 43, above]).

134. Jaeger, *Origins of Courtliness*, 256–57 (see note 44, above).

135. John Boswell summarizes the social changes in the late thirteenth and early fourteenth centuries as follows: "The Jews were expelled from England and France; the order of the Templars dissolved on charges of sorcery and deviant sexuality; Edward II of England [1284–1327], the last openly gay medieval monarch, deposed and murdered; lending at interest equated with heresy and those who supported it subjected to the Inquisition; and lepers all over France imprisoned and prosecuted on charges of poisoning wells and being in league with Jews and witches" (*Christianity, Social Tolerance, and Homosexuality*, 272; see also 293 [note 73, above]).

136. Boswell, *Christianity*, 14–15, 270–71, 293 (see note 73, above).

137. See Daniel Poirion, *Résurgences: Mythe et Littérature à l'âge du symbole (XIIe siècle)*, Ecriture (Paris: Presses Universitaires de France, 1986), 217.

138. Max Manitius, *Philologisches aus alten Bibliothekskatalogen (bis 1300)*, Ergänzungsheft zum *Rheinisches Museum* 47 (1892): 33.

139. Pellegrin, "Les *Remedia amoris* d'Ovide, texte scolaire médiéval," *Bibliothèque de l'école des chartes* 15 (1957): 179.

140. See Minnis, "The Influence of Academic Prologues on the Prologues and Literary Attitudes of Late-Medieval English Writers," *Mediaeval Studies* 43 (1981): 381; see also his "Literary Theory in Discussions of *Formae Tractandi* by Medieval Theologians," *New Literary History* 11 (1979): 140–41. Compare J. B. Allen, *The Friar as Critic*, 83–87 (see note 27, above).

141. See Peter F. Dembowski, "Learned Latin Treatises in French: Inspiration, Plagiarism, and Translation," *Viator* 17 (1986): 268.

142. See Ghisalberti, "*L'Ovidius moralizatus*," 26–31 (note 32, above).

143. Hexter, *Ovid and Medieval Schooling*, 214 (see note 3, above); see also Ghisalberti, "*L'Ovidius moralizatus*," 5 (see note 32, above).

144. As Alain de Lille put it, "Omnis mundi creatura / quasi liber et scriptura / nobis est et speculum" ("De incarnatione Christi," *PL* 210:579A).

145. Battaglia, "La tradizione di Ovidio," 188 (see note 36, above).

146. Battaglia, "La tradizione di Ovidio," 186 (see note 36, above).

Chapter 3

1. *De amore* §1.6, p. 40; 2.1, p. 224. (P. G. Walsh largely adopts Trojel's 1892 Latin text, but his translation is more accurate and his notes much more comprehensive than Parry's [*The Art of Courtly Love*, tr. John Jay Parry (New York: Columbia University Press, 1941)]. I will cite Walsh's text and translation.)

2. On the text's reception, see Alfred Karnein, *De amore in volkssprachlicher Literatur: Untersuchungen zur Andreas-Capellanus-Rezeption im Mittelalter und Renaissance, Germanisch-romanische Monatsschrift*, Beiheft 4 (Heidelberg: Carl Winter, 1985), 26–27, and Bruno Roy, "A la Recherche des lecteurs médiévaux du 'De amore' d'André le Chapelain," *Revue de l'université d'Ottawa* 55.1 (1985): 45–73; see also Walsh, "Introduction," 4–5 (see note 1, above). For a feminist reading of the text, see Toril Moi, "Desire in Language: Andreas Capellanus and the Controversy of Courtly Love," in David Aers, ed., *Medieval Literature: Criticism, Ideology, and History* (New York: St. Martin's Press, 1986), 11–33.

3. One example is Etienne Tempier, a thirteenth-century bishop of Paris. See Alexander Denomy, S.J., "The *De amore* of Andreas Capellanus and the Condemnation of 1277," *Medieval Studies* 8 (1946): 107–49. The text of Tempier's condemnation is to be found in *Chartularium universitatis parisiensis*, ed. Henri Denifle and Emile Chatelain, 4 vols. (Paris: Delalain, 1889–97), 1:543–58.

4. On the Church's interest in governing interpretation of medieval literature and art, see Laura Kendrick, *The Game of Love: Troubadour Wordplay* (Berkeley and Los Angeles, CA: University of California Press, 1988), esp. pp. 7–9 (Kendrick's emphasis is on the resistance to ecclesiastical univocity); and, more broadly, Stephen G. Nichols, Jr., *Romanesque Signs: Early Medieval Narrative and Iconography* (New Haven, CT: Yale University Press, 1983). For Augustine, see *On Chris-*

tian Doctrine, tr. Durant W. Robertson, Jr., Library of Liberal Arts 80 (New York: Liberal Arts Press, 1958), with applications in Robertson's "The Doctrine of Charity in Medieval Literary Gardens: A Topical Approach through Symbolism and Allegory," *Speculum* 26 (1951): 24–49, and *A Preface to Chaucer* (Princeton, NJ: Princeton University Press, 1962), of which pp. 391–448 are devoted to Andreas. On Andreas's use of imagery deriving from medical models of lovesickness, see Mary F. Wack, "Imagination, Medicine, and Rhetoric in Andreas Capellanus' *De amore*," in *Studies in Honor of Robert Earl Kaske*, ed. Arthur Gross et al. (New York: Fordham University Press, 1986), 101–15.

5. Walsh's introduction to his edition of the text contains the most comprehensive survey of the *De amore*'s literary context I have found (see note 1, above); see also Karnein, *De amore in volkssprachlicher Literatur* (note 2, above).

6. For a brief introduction to these genres, see Pierre Bec, ed., *Anthologie des troubadours*, Bibliothèque médiévale (Paris: 10/18, 1979), 42–51. Wesley Trimpi suggests another possible origin for this structure, seeing it as that of a scholastic debate: "The Quality of Fiction," *Traditio* 30 (1974): 81. On Andreas's reading (and misreading) of troubadour love poetry in general, see Paolo Cherchi, "New Uses of Andreas' *De amore*," *Mittelalterbilder aus neuer Perspektive: Kolloquium Würzburg 1984* (Munich: W. Fink, 1985): 22–30.

7. For a long time critics have taken the references to Marie de Champagne and to her court as indications that Marie was likely to have been Andreas's patron. See Walsh's introduction, pp. 2–3 (note 1, above), for a summary of this point of view; a dissenting voice is John Benton's: "The Evidence for Andreas Capellanus Re-examined Again," *Studies in Philology* 59 (1962): 471–78. Most recently Karnein has proposed, on evidence from several manuscripts and other documentation, that Andreas was more likely to have been a chaplain at the royal court in Paris than at Troyes: *De amore in volkssprachliche Literatur*, 23–24 (see note 2, above); see also Pascale Bourgain, "Aliénor d'Aquitaine et Marie de Champagne mises en cause par André le Chapelain," *Cahiers de civilisation médiévale* 29 (1986): 29–36. Karnein's hypothesis on the identities of Andreas and Gualterius are plausible, though I am unable to accept his more-or-less Robertsonian reading of the *De amore* as a whole. See Don A. Monson's salutary article, "Andreas Capellanus and the Problem of Irony," *Speculum* 63.3 (July 1988): 539–72, esp. 551–52.

8. Compare Monson: "The identification of Andreas as 'chaplain of the king of France' rests on only three manuscripts out of forty-one. Ursula Liebertz-Grün has recently advanced a very plausible explanation of these rubrics as a late amplification of a passage within the treatise where Andreas refers to himself as 'chaplain of the king,' which passage Liebertz-Grün interprets as a reference to the King of Love" ("Andreas Capellanus" 551 [see note 7, above]).

9. "Et quamvis multum credamur *in amoris arte* periti et *amoris praedocti remedia*, vix tamen eius novimus pestiferos laqueos evitare et sine carnis <nos> contagione removere," (1.8.5, p. 212 [emphasis added]; compare Walsh, note 206 [see note 1, above]). See also *Praefatio* 1 and Gualterius's request to Andreas, "docere qualiter inter amantes illaesus possit amoris status conservari, pariterve qui non amantur quibus modis sibi cordi affixa valeant Veneris iacula declinare." Compare Pietro Palumbo, "La questione della Reprobatio Amoris nel trattato di An-

drea Cappellano," in *Saggi e richerche in memoria di Ettore Li Gotti*, Centro di Studi Filologici e Linguistici Siciliani, Bollettino 7 (Palermo: Sige, 1962): 2.437.

10. Like Andreas, Gualterius may have had a historical identity. Karnein identifies him with Gautier le Jeune, son of Gautier de Villebéon, chamberlain of Louis VII and Philippe-Auguste, and uses this link to date the text to the early 1180s, *De amore in volkssprachliche Literatur*, 30–32 (see note 2, above). Karnein is careful to note, however, that this identification is a hypothesis, and he allows also for the possibility of a fictive Gualterius (32 n. 25). On the question of whether Marie could have been Andreas's patron, see (in favor of this idea) Walsh, Introduction, 6 (note 1, above), citing Moshé Lazar, *Amour courtois et "fin'amors" dans la littérature du XIIe siècle* (Paris: Klincksieck, 1964), 268, and (against it) John Benton, "The Court of Champagne as a Literary Center," *Speculum* 36 (1961): 586, and Karnein, *De amore*, 26–27.

11. Again in 2.5.23, p. 245, Andreas refers to Gualterius as a "diligens indagator amoris."

12. Lay men and women are also divided explicitly by class in the dialogues of Book 1. Little scholarship with which I am familiar discusses this question; one exception is Moi, "Desire in Language" (see note 2, above).

13. See Robertson, *A Preface to Chaucer*, 403 (note 4, above), and John F. Benton, "Clio and Venus: An Historical View of Medieval Love," in *The Meaning of Courtly Love*, ed. F. X. Newman (Albany, NY: SUNY Press, 1968), 30.

14. Roy, "A la Recherche," 53, 65; compare note 2, above.

15. On this episode, see Betsy Bowden, "The Art of Courtly Copulation," *Medievalia et Humanistica* n.s. 9 (1979): 67–85, (and a cautionary evaluation by Monson, "Andreas Capellanus" (note 7, above); see also Walsh, "Introduction," 18 (note 1, above), with references to E. M. Grimes, "Le Lai du Trot," *Romanic Review* (1935): 313ff., and W. A. Neilson, "The Purgatory of Cruel Beauties," *Romania* (1900): 85ff.

16. Such charges fly in both directions, of course: women may accuse men of fraud too, as in 1.6.130–31, p. 76.

17. Compare Achille Luchaire, *Social France at the Time of Philip Augustus*, trans. Edward B. Krehbiel (1909; rpt. New York: Harper and Row, 1967), 179, and chapters 6 and 7 generally.

18. See R. Howard Bloch, "Medieval Misogyny," *Representations* 20 (Fall 1987): 19.

19. As Moi has noted: "It is interesting to observe that in the modern debate over the 'true' meaning of the *De amore*, the critics accurately enact the problematics of the text: like hermeneutically distraught lovers, they untiringly try to decipher the sibylline utterances of the lady, who now, in a final twist of the plot, turns out to be Andreas himself" ("Desire in Language," 29 ([see note 2, above]). See, on the same topic, Joan M. Ferrante, "Male Fantasy and Female Reality in Courtly Literature," *Women's Studies* 11 (1984): 67–68.

20. Best known among these is the "Altercatio Phyllidis et Florae" (The Argument of Phyllis and Flora), in *Die Liebeslieder*, ed. Otto Schumann, vol. 1.2 of the *Carmina Burana*, ed. Alfons Hilka, Otto Schumann, and Bernhard Bischoff (Heidelberg: Carl Winter, 1930–).

21. "Et hoc est quod evangelica clamat auctoritas; videns enim Dominus suos clericos iuxta humanae naturae infirmitatem in varios lapsuros excessus, ait in evangelio: 'Super cathedram Moisi sederunt scribae et pharisaei; omnia quaecunque dixerint vobis servate et facite, secundum autem opera illorum nolite facere', quasi dicat: 'Credendum est dictis clericorum quasi legatorum Dei, sed quia carnis tentationi sicut homines ceteri supponuntur, eorum non inspiciatis opera, si eos contigerit in aliquo deviare.' Sufficit ergo mihi, si altari assistens meae plebi Dei studeam verbum annuntiare" (1.6.486–87, p. 184, with allusion to Matthew 23.2ff [Walsh n. 174; see note 1, above]) (This is what the authority of the gospel proclaims. The Lord saw that His clerics, by reason of the weakness of human nature, would fall into various excesses, and so He says in the gospel: "The scribes and pharisees are seated on the chair of Moses. Maintain and do all that they bid you do; do not do as they themselves do." He is really saying "You must believe the words of clerics because they are God's ambassadors, but because they are subject to the temptations of the flesh like other men, do not eye their deeds in case they happen to go astray in some respect." So it is enough for me if I stand at the altar and can announce the word of God to my people).

22. On the question of priests, love, and poetry, see particularly Leo Pollmann, *Die Liebe in der hochmittelalterlichen Literatur Frankreichs: Versuch einer historischen Phänomenologie*, Analecta Romanica 18 (Frankfurt: Vittorio Klostermann, 1966), esp. pp. 50–59, 65–66, and 252.

23. See 1.6.367–68, p. 146. In Book 2, it is Countess Ermengarde of Narbonne who makes this pronouncement; on Ermengarde, see R. R. Bezzola, *Les Origines et la formation de la littérature courtoise en occident* (Paris, 1963), III.2, 334, cited by Walsh 257 n. 34 (see note 1, above). On adultery, see John Benton, "Clio and Venus: An Historical View of Medieval Love," in *The Meaning of Courtly Love*, ed. Newman, 19–42 (see note 13, above). Benton's argument is historically cogent, but his paper, like most of the others in the volume, goes too far in denying that what is commonly referred to as "courtly love" (a useful if much-maligned term) existed even within literature.

24. On Drouart's translation, see Barbara Nelson Sargent, "A Medieval Commentary on Andreas Capellanus," *Romania* 94 (1973): 536–37, as well as Peter F. Dembowski, "Two Old French Recastings/Translations of Andreas Capellanus' *De amore*," in *Medieval Translators and Their Craft*, ed. Jeanette Beer, Medieval Institute Publications (Kalamazoo, MI: Western Michigan University, 1988), 1–28. See also Salvatore Battaglia's edition of two fourteenth-century Italian translations: Andrea Capellano, *Trattato d'amore: Testo latino del sec. xii con due traduzioni toscane inedite del sec. xiv*, (Rome: Perrella, [1947]).

25. Roy, "A la Recherche," 50 (see note 2, above).

26. Roy, "A la Recherche," 46.

27. See, for example, Paul Zumthor, "Notes en marge du traité de l'amour d'André le Chapelain," *Zeitschrift für romanische Philologie* 63 (1943): 181; Paolo Cherchi, "Andreas' *De amore*: Its Unity and Polemical Origin," in his *Andrea Cappellano, i trovatori, e altri temi romanzi*, Biblioteca di cultura, 128 (Rome: Bulzoni, 1979): 109–11; Moshé Lazar, *Amour courtois* 148 (see note 10, above); Douglas Kelly, "Courtly Love in Perspective: The Hierarchy of Love in Andreas Capel-

lanus," *Traditio* 24 (1968): 119–20; W. T. H. Jackson, "The *De amore* of Andreas Capellanus and the Practice of Love at Court," *Romanic Review* 49 (1958): 247; Trimpi, "The Quality of Fiction," 84–85 (see note 6, above); and Michael D. Cherniss, "The Literary Comedy of Andreas Capellanus," *Modern Philology* 72 (1975): 237.

28. Scholars who have argued for courtly love as a historical twelfth-century phenomenon include Paul Zumthor, "Notes en marge," 189 (see note 27, above) and Jackson, "*De amore*," 243–51 (see note 27, above). See also Benton, "Clio and Venus," 24–27 (see note 13, above). E. Talbot Donaldson notes that whether the poets of courtly love had sexual relations with their ladies is not the business of literary criticism: "The Myth of Courtly Love," *Ventures* 5.2 (Fall 1965): 18–19. Larry Benson notes that "By the fourteenth century, courtly love becomes a real social entity, whatever it may have been earlier" ("Courtly Love in the Chivalric Class in the Late Middle Ages," in Robert Yeager, ed., *Fifteenth-Century Studies: Recent Essays* [Hamden, CT: Archon Books, 1984], 247–58), but such practice seems to have been part of the fourteenth century's revival and literalization of aspects of life described in twelfth-century literature, rather than a continuation of twelfth-century practice.

29. See Zumthor, "Notes en marge," 181 (note 27, above); Karnein, *De amore*, 44, 107 (note 2, above); and Cherchi, "Andreas' *De amore*," 96–97 (note 27, above).

30. Various scholars have approached this view, though without interpreting Andreas's text in quite this way. See Moshé Lazar, "Cupid, the Lady, and the Poet: Modes of Love at Eleanor of Aquitaine's Court," in William W. Kibler, ed., *Eleanor of Aquitaine: Patron and Politician*, Symposia in the Arts and Humanities, 3 (Austin, TX: University of Texas Press, 1976), 37; Michael D. Cherniss, "Literary Comedy," 224–25 (note 27, above); Karnein, *De amore*, 262 (note 2, above); and C. S. Lewis, *The Allegory of Love: A Study in Medieval Tradition* (London: Oxford University Press, 1936), 40.

31. On the ideological implications of choosing a context for interpretation, see Lee Patterson, "Ambiguity and Interpretation: A Fifteenth-Century Reading of *Troilus and Criseyde*," *Speculum* 54 (1979): 327–28, and his noteworthy book *Negotiating the Past: The Historical Understanding of Medieval Literature* (Madison, WI: University of Wisconsin Press, 1987).

32. For the links with secular contexts, see Walsh, "Introduction," 3–11 (note 1, above); see also Gustavo Vinay, "Il 'De amore' di Andrea Cappellano nel quadro della letteratura amorosa e della rinascità del secolo XII," *Studi medievali* 17 (1951): 268. Cherchi explicitly places Andreas in the Christian, anti-courtly love tradition ("Andreas' *De amore*," 88 [see note 27, above]), but Walsh argues that Andreas does *not* follow in the important twelfth-century tradition of treatises on spiritual love of Hugh of St. Victor, William of St. Thierry, Bernard of Clairvaux, Aelred of Rievaulx, and Peter of Blois (Introduction, pp. 10–11), a judgment with which I am inclined to agree. Felix Schlösser says that Andreas's system of courtly love is not anti-Christian but un-Christian: *Andreas Capellanus: Seine Minnelehre und das christliche Weltbild um 1200* (Bonn: H. Bouvier und Co., 1960), 383. A balance is found in Karnein, "La Réception du *De amore* d'André le Chapelain au XIIIe siècle," *Romania* 102 (1981): 502.

33. This table must be considered only an approximate guide to citations, since Andreas, like most medieval authors, usually quotes allusively, without mentioning the name of his authorities. For the sake of convenience and consistency, these calculations are based on the citations identified by Walsh's footnotes and index (pp. 326–29).

34. William Allan Neilson, *The Origins and Sources of the "Court of Love,"* Studies and Notes in Philology and Literature 6 (1899) 176. See also Pollmann, *Die Liebe*, 321–22 (note 22, above); Walsh, Introduction, 12–15 (note 1, above); Karl-heinz Hilbert, "Amor und amor in der Liebeslehre bei Ovid und Andreas Capellanus," *Der altsprachliche Unterricht* 21.1 (1978): 28; Jackson, "The *De amore*," 245–46 (note 27, above); and Karnein, *De amore*, 98 (note 2, above).

35. On overall structural parallels between the *De amore* and the *Ars*, compare Neilson, "Origins," 177 (see note 15, above).

36. Compare Pollmann, who notes that Andreas's inclusion of a *reprobatio amoris* does not (*pace* Robertson and Palumbo) negate his books 1 and 2, but simply follows in the Ovidian and medieval tradition (*Die Liebe*, 321 n. 157 [see note 22, above]).

37. On palinodes and their ambiguity, see the preface of Eleanor Jane Winsor (Leach), "A Study in the Sources and Rhetoric of Chaucer's *Legend of Good Women* and Ovid's *Heroides*," Ph.D. dissertation, Yale University, 1963; as well as Peter W. Travis, "Deconstructing Chaucer's Retraction," *Exemplaria* 3.1 (Spring, 1991): 135–58.

38. Augustine, *De mendacio*, PL 40:514–15 (c. 19); *Lying*, trans. Sr. Mary Sarah Muldowney, in Augustine, *Treatises on Various Subjects*, The Fathers of the Church (Washington, DC: Catholic University of America Press 1952, rpt. 1965), 105; see also 78, 86–88.

39. Petrus Cantor, *Summa de sacramentis* (Munich: Staatsbibliothek, CLM 5426, fol. 163ʳ), cited by Benton, "Clio and Venus," 30–31 (see note 13, above); see also Trimpi, "The Quality of Fiction," 115 (note 6, above). For more on Peter (d. 1197), see Schlösser, *Andreas Capellanus*, esp. p. 370 (note 32, above), on Peter's warning that "Sunt quidem fatui sacerdotes tantum nomine, qui credunt simplicem fornicationem esse veniale peccatum."

40. Robert Guiette, "Symbolisme et 'senefiance' au Moyen Age," in *Questions de littérature, Romanica Gandensia* 8: 46–47.

41. Kendrick has come to much the same conclusion about the "opaque lines and phrases" of Provençal song (*The Game of Love*, 30 [see note 4, above]), and Marina Brownlee's reading of the *Libro de Buen Amor* also focuses on the text's challenge to the reader, though I cannot agree that the *Libro* is precisely innovative in this regard (*The Status of the Reading Subject in the Libro de Buen Amor*, North Carolina Studies in the Romance Languages and Literatures, 224 [Chapel Hill, NC: University of North Carolina Department of Romance Languages, 1985], 105). See also the much-quoted beginning of the Prologue to Marie de France's *Lais*, which makes a remarkably similar point: *Lais*, ed. Jean Rychner, Classiques français du Moyen Age 93 (Paris: Champion, 1978), vv. 1–27. In rhetorical terms, the text may be seen as an *enigma*, an allegory that retains a certain amount of obscurity. On *enigma* and its rhetorical background in Quintilian, Isidore, Bede,

and William of Conches, see Peter Dronke, *Fabula: Explorations into the Uses of Myth in Medieval Platonism*, Mittellateinische Studien und Texte, 9 (Leiden and Cologne: E. J. Brill, 1974), 45.

42. Jehan Bodel, *Les Saisnes*, cited by Guiette, "Li Conte de Bretaigne sont si vain et plaisant," *Romania* 88 (1967): 4 n.

43. On the attitudes of twelfth-century Platonists toward literary uses of the imagination, see Dronke, *Fabula*, 4, 38 (note 41, above).

44. For a broad sampling of authors who take this position, compare Kendrick, *The Game of Love*, 170–86 (see note 4, above); Lazar, "Cupid," 57, n. 42 (see note 10, above), citing Charles S. Singleton, "Dante: Within Courtly Love and Beyond," in *The Meaning of Courtly Love*, ed. Newman, 43–54 (see note 13, above); Douglas R. Butturff, "The Comedy of Coquetry in Andreas' *De amore*," *Classical Folia* 28 (1974): 181–90; Bowden, "The Art of Courtly Copulation" (see note 15, above); Trimpi, "The Quality of Fiction," 84 n. 97 (also citing Singleton; see note 6, above); Donaldson, "The Myth of Courtly Love," 20 (see note 28, above); Joan Ferrante, "The Conflict of Lyric Conventions and Romance Form," in *In Pursuit of Perfection*, ed. Joan Ferrante and George D. Economou (Port Washington, NY: Kennikat Press, 1975), 136; and Dragonetti, "Trois motifs de la lyrique courtoise confrontés avec les *Arts d'aimer*," *Romanica Gandensia* 7 (1959): 7.

45. Salvatore Battaglia, Introduction, Andrea Capellano, *Trattato d'amore*, xxvii (see note 24, above).

46. On play and love in Andreas, compare Abbé Norbert de Paepe, "*Amor* und *verus amor* bei Andreas Capellanus. Versuch einer Lösung des reprobatio-Problems," *Mélanges offerts à René Crozet*, ed. Pierre Gallais and Yves-Jean Riou (Poitiers: Société des Etudes médiévales, 1966) II: 921–27.

47. See, for example, Zara Patricia Zaddy, "'Le Chevalier de la Charrette' and the 'De Amore' of Andreas Capellanus," in *Studies in Medieval Literature and Languages in Memory of Frederick Whitehead*, ed. W. Rothwell et al. (Manchester: Manchester University Press, 1973), 396–97; Zaddy includes references to Gaston Paris and other earlier critics; compare Walsh, "Introduction," 8 (see note 1, above). Dragonetti ("Trois motifs") and Dronke (*Medieval Latin and the Rise of European Love-Lyric* [Oxford: Clarendon Press, 1965] 1, 85) insist on the divergence between Andreas's views on love and those of other medieval poets; Douglas Kelly rebuts this view in "Courtly Love in Perspective: The Hierarchy of Love in Andreas Capellanus," *Traditio* 24 (1968): 143–44.

48. Karnein reaches similar conclusions: he sees twelfth-century literary criticism in literary texts themselves, and sees the poetry of "Minnedidaxis" as an "Insider-Kommentar zu fiktionalen Texten" (*De amore*, 17, 139 [see note 2, above]). On a similar function of the *Libro de Buen Amor*, see Marina Brownlee, *The Status of the Reading Subject*, 21–22 (note 41, above). Peter F. Dembowski makes a related point about late medieval vernacularizations of serious Latin texts, arguing that they become works of hermeneutics: see his article "Learned Latin Treatises in French: Inspiration, Plagiarism, and Translation," *Viator* 17 (1986): 268.

49. An early version of this chapter was presented at a panel arranged by the Division on Comparative Studies in Medieval Literature at the 1988 Convention of the Modern Language Association of America.

Chapter 4

1. See David Hult, "1277, 7 March: Jean de Meun's *Roman de la Rose*," in *A New History of French Literature*, ed. Denis Hollier (Cambridge, MA: Harvard University Press, 1989), 97–102; see also Per Nykrog, *L'Amour et la Rose: Le Grand Dessein de Jean de Meun*, Harvard Studies in Romance Languages 41 (Lexington, KY: French Forum, 1986), 82–85, and A. J. Denomy, "The *De amore* of Andreas Capellanus and the Condemnation of 1277," *Mediaeval Studies* 8 (1947): 107–49.

2. Guillaume names his work *Li Romanz de la Rose* (v. 37); Jean calls his *Li Miroër aus Amoreus* (v. 10621): see Guillaume de Lorris and Jean de Meun, *Le Roman de la Rose*, ed. Félix Lecoy, 3 vols., Classiques Français du Moyen Age (Paris: Champion, 1973–85), from which edition all citations will be taken. The best English translation is that of Charles Dahlberg: *The Romance of the Rose* (Hanover, NH: University Press of New England, 1983). Dahlberg follows the line numbering of Ernest Langlois's edition (5 vols., Société des anciens textes français, Paris: Didot [Vols. 1–2], Champion [Vols. 3–5], 1914–24), but provides as an appendix (p. 427) a table of concordance between Langlois and Lecoy.

3. On this project in the first *Roman de la Rose*, see H. Marshall Leicester, "Ovid Enclosed: The God of Love as *Magister Amoris* in the *Roman de la Rose* of Guillaume de Lorris," *Res Publica Litterarum* 2 (1984): 107–29. On the *Rose*'s links with Ovid, see Alan M. F. Gunn, *The Mirror of Love* (Lubbock, TX: Texas Tech Press, 1952), 33; Sylvia Huot, "From *Roman de la Rose* to *Roman de la Poire*: The Ovidian Tradition and the Poetics of Courtly Literature," *Medievalia et Humanistica*, n.s., 13 (1985): 95–111; Kevin Brownlee, "Reflections in the *Miroër aus Amoreus*: The Inscribed Reader in Jean de Meung's *Roman de la Rose*," in *Mimesis: From Mirror to Method, Augustine to Descartes*, ed. John D. Lyons and Stephen G. Nichols, Jr. (Hanover, NH: University Press of New England, 1982), 62; Leslie Cahoon, "Juno's Chaste Festival and Ovid's Wanton Loves: *Amores* 3.13," *Classical Antiquity* 2.1 (April 1983): 2.

4. On the reader's responsibilities in the *Rose*, see Hult, "1277, 7 March," 103 (see note 1, above). In regard to the changing epistemology of the thirteenth century, see Daniel Poirion, "De la signification selon Jean de Meun," in Lucie Brind'Amour and Eugene Vance, eds., *Archéologie du signe*, Papers in Medieval Studies, 3 (Toronto: Pontifical Institute of Medieval Studies, 1983): 165–85.

5. Nykrog also notes that by passing through Narcissus's mirror and into the world of love, the narrator parallels Alice's trip through the looking glass (*L'Amour et la Rose*, 16 [see note 1, above]). See, for interesting speculations on the looking glass world, Martin Gardner, ed., *The Annotated Alice* (New York: Bramhall House, 1960), 180–84.

6. Or, as Roger Dragonetti claims, *pretends* to continue (in which case the question of *auctoritas* would become even more complex): compare Dragonetti, "Pygmalion, ou les pièges de la fiction dans le *Roman de la Rose*," in *Orbis mediaevalis: Mélanges de langue et de littérature médiévales offerts à Reto Raduolf Bezzola à l'occasion de son quatre-vingtième anniversaire*, ed. George Güntert, Marc-René Jung, and Kurt Ringger (Bern: Francke, 1978), 90.

7. There are also fifty-three passages directly translated from authorial texts. See Nancy Freeman Regalado, "'Des Contraires Choses': La Fonction poétique de

la citation et des *exempla* dans le 'Roman de la Rose' de Jean de Meun," *Littérature* 41 (February 1981): 64.

8. On Alain, compare Winthrop Wetherbee, "The Function of Poetry in the *De planctu naturae* of Alain de Lille," *Traditio* 25 (1969): 87–125. Daniel Poirion maintains that "il est impossible d'établir une filiation théologique avec l'oeuvre de Jean de Meun" ("Alain de Lille et Jean de Meun," in *Alain de Lille, Gautier de Châtillon et leur temps: Actes du Colloque de Lille, Octobre 1978*, ed. Henri Roussel and F. Suard, *Bulletin du Centre d'Etudes médiévales et dialectales de l'Université de Lille* 3 [1980]: 135). This may be true in the very strictest sense, but the connections between the two works are nevertheless patent. See also Marc M. Pelen, *Latin Poetic Irony in the "Roman de la Rose*," Vinaver Studies in French 4 (Liverpool: Cairns, 1987), 133.

9. Ernest Langlois, *Origines et sources du Roman de la Rose* (Paris: Ernest Thorin, 1891), 119–27.

10. Langlois, *Origines et sources*, 95, 102 (see note 9, above).

11. Compare Edward Kennard Rand, "The Metamorphosis of Ovid in *Le Roman de la Rose*," *Studies in the History of Culture*, ed. Percy W. Long (Menasha, WI, 1942; rpt. Freeport, NY: Books for Libraries, 1969), 103–4.

12. Jean catalogues these works in his dedicatory preface to the Boethius translation: Venceslas L. Dedeck-Héry, ed., "Boethius' *De consolatione* by Jean de Meun," *Medieval Studies* 14 (1952): 168, cited by Peter F. Dembowski, "Learned Latin Treatises in French: Inspiration, Plagiarism, and Translation," *Viator* 17 (1986): 260 n. 14. John Fleming sees both Boethius and Aelred as links between Jean, Augustine, and Cicero, and sees the *Confessions* as the background text most basic to R$_2$: *Reason and the Lover* (Princeton, NJ: Princeton University Press, 1984), 83, 186. See also Gunn, *The Mirror of Love*, 445, 449 (note 3, above).

13. Langlois, *Origines et sources*, 170 (see note 9, above). See also Patricia J. Eberle, "The Lovers' Glass: Nature's Discourse on Optics and the Optical Design of the *Romance of the Rose*," *University of Toronto Quarterly* 46 (1976–77): 250.

14. See Paul Zumthor, "Récit et anti-récit: *Le Roman de la Rose*," *Medioevo romanzo* 1 (1974): 5–24.

15. The citations follow:

(1)   Ausint le doivent cil savoir
       qui d'amors veulent joie avoir,
       car povres n'a don s'amor pesse,
       si con Ovides le confesse.

                   (7953–56)

(Thus those who want to have joy of their love should know this, since a poor man has nothing with which to feed his love, as Ovid confesses).

(2)   "D'amer povre home ne li chaille,
       qu'il n'est riens que povre home vaille;
       se c'iert Ovides ou Homers,
       ne vaudroit il pas .II. gomers."

                   (La Vielle, 13587–90)

("Let her [the female student of love] not care to love a poor man, for a poor man is worth nothing; even if he were Ovid or Homer, he would not be worth a couple of drinking glasses.")

> (3)   "Ainsinc sunt arz avant venues,
>   car toutes choses sunt vaincues
>   par travaill, par povreté dure,
>   par quoi les genz sunt en grant cure;
>   car li mal les angins esmeuvent
>   par les angoisses qu'il i trevent.
>   Ausinc le dit Ovides, qui
>   ot assez, tant con il vesqui,
>   de bien, de mal, d'anneur, de honte,
>   si comme il meïsmes raconte."
>   (Genius, 20145–54)

("Thus the arts came into the world, because all things are conquered by labor and by harsh poverty, because of which people are in great unhappiness. For bad things call forth ingenuity because of the sufferings people find. This is what Ovid says: while he lived, he had plenty of good, bad, honor, and shame, as he tells us himself.")

16. See, on the significance of this passage, Karl D. Uitti, "From *Clerc* to *Poète*: The Relevance of the *Romance of the Rose* to Machaut's World," in *Machaut's World: Science and Art in the Fourteenth Century*, ed. Madeleine Pelner Cosman and Bruce Chandler, *Annals of the New-York Academy of Sciences* 314 (1978): 209–16.

17. See Paul Zumthor, "Narrative and Anti-Narrative: *Le Roman de la Rose*" [translation of "Récit et anti-récit"], *Yale French Studies* 41 (1974): 195. Guillaume describes his poem as "li *Romanz de la Rose*, / ou l'art d'Amors est tote enclose" (37–38) (the *Romance of the Rose*, in which the art of love is completely enclosed). Gunn notes (*The Mirror for Lovers*, 31 [see note 3, above]) that at least eighty manuscripts have colophons that echo this passage in approximately the following words: "Explicit li Roumanz de la Rose / Ou l'Art d'Amors est tote enclose." Compare Ernest Langlois, *Les Manuscrits du "Roman de la Rose": Description et classement* (Lille: Tallandier; Paris: Champion, 1910).

18. This passage closely echoes *Amores* 3.9. Compare lines 5–10:

> ille tui uates operis, tua fama, Tibullus
>   ardet in exstructo corpus inane rogo.
> ecce puer Veneris fert euersamque pharetram
>   et fractos arcus et sine luce facem;
> aspice, demissis ut eat miserabilis alis
>   pectoraque infesta tundat aperta manu.

It is interesting to note that, except for this allusion, Tibullus was virtually unknown in the thirteenth century (see Appendix); Amor's frame of reference is thoroughly Ovidian, even when he is trying to put Ovid out of the picture.

19. On the death of Guillaume in Amor's discourse, compare lines 10531–72, as well as Hult, *Self-Fulfilling Prophecies: Readership and Authority in the First "Roman de la Rose,"* (New York: Cambridge University Press, 1986), 259–60, and Martin Thut, "Narcisse versus Pygmalion: Une Lecture du *Roman de la Rose,*" *Vox romanica* 61 (1982): 131; see also Roger Dragonetti, "Pygmalion, ou les pièges de la fiction dans le *Roman de la Rose,*" in *Orbis mediaevalis,* 99 (note 6, above).

20. Like Tibullus, Catullus and Gallus could not have been more than names to Jean de Meun. Only a single line of Gallus's poetry survives; as for Catullus, his texts were virtually unknown until the end of the thirteenth century: see *Catullus: A Commentary,* ed. C. J. Fordyce (Oxford: Oxford University Press, 1961), xxii–xxviii.

21. On Jean's relationship with Guillaume, see particularly Hult, "Closed Quotations: The Speaking Voice in the *Roman de la Rose,*" *Yale French Studies* 67 (1984): 267, and Zumthor, "Narrative and Anti-Narrative," 203 (note 17, above), and his *Essai de poétique médiévale* (Paris: Seuil, 1972), 373–75. See also Eberle, "The Lovers' Glass," 245–46 (note 13, above).

22. See Zumthor, "Narrative and Anti-Narrative," 199 (note 17, above). Winthrop Wetherbee sees Jean's self-canonization as a "largely satirical" gesture, though he believes that it is a step toward a medieval continuation of the classical tradition (*Chaucer and the Poets: An Essay on Troilus and Criseyde* [Ithaca, NY: Cornell University Press, 1984], 62).

23. Thut, "Narcisse," 106 (see note 19, above), citing Karl August Ott. Dragonetti has made the provocative assertion that "Guillaume de Lorris" is only a literary fiction invented by Jean de Meun, "Pygmalion," 90 (see note 6, above); see also Hult, *Self-Fulfilling Prophecies,* 19 (note 19, above). Hult also notes that Guillaume never names himself, and that his name was probably not associated with R_1 before Jean de Meun: "'Guillaume de Lorris,'" therefore, "refers both to a person and a text" (20, 101). See also Thut, "Narcisse," 105 (note 19, above).

24. Compare lines 21–30:

> El vintieme an de mon aage,
> el point qu'Amors prent le paage
> des jones genz, couchier m'aloie
> une nuit, si con je souloie,
> et me dormoie mout forment,
> et vi un songe en mon dormant
> qui mout fu biaus et mout me plot;
> mes en ce songe onques riens n'ot
> qui tretot avenu ne soit
> si con li songes recensoit.

(In my twentieth year, at the point when Love takes a toll from young people, I went to bed one night, as usual, and, while sleeping, had a dream which was very beautiful, and which I liked very much; but there was nothing in this dream which did not happen very soon just as the dream recounted.)

25. Evelyn Birge Vitz, "The *I* of the *Roman de la Rose,*" *Genre* 6 (1963): 52–54; see also Vitz's "Inside/Outside: First-Person Narrative in Guillaume de Lorris' *Ro-*

man de la Rose," Yale French Studies 58 (1979): 148–64, and Michelle A. Freeman, "Problems in Romance Composition: Ovid, Chrétien de Troyes, and the *Romance of the Rose," Romance Philology* 30 (1976): 164. Paul Strohm suggests that the dream "represents a kind of ideal biography which happens to touch on the narrator's own experience at several points" ("Guillaume as Narrator and Lover in the *Roman de la Rose," Romanic Review* 59 [1968]: 8).

26. Charles Dahlberg, "First Person and Personification in the *Roman de la Rose*: Amant and Dangier," *Mediaevalia* 3 (1977): 412; Thut, "Narcisse versus Pygmalion," 131 (see note 19, above). See also Leo Spitzer, "Note on the Poetic and Empirical 'I' in Medieval Authors," in *Romanische Literaturstudien: 1936–1956* (Tübingen: Niemeyer, 1959), 100–12; Paul Zumthor, "Autobiography in the Middle Ages?," *Genre* 6.1 (1963): 35, 43 (translation of "Autobiographie au Moyen Age?," in *Langue, texte, énigme* [Paris: Editions du Seuil, 1975]: 165–80); Vitz, "Inside/Outside," 151 and "The 'I,'" 51 (note 25, above); and Dahlberg, "First Person," 38.

27. See Zumthor, "Récit et anti-récit," 16 (note 17, above).

28. Hult suggests that R₁ seduces the reader and the lady together: *Self-Fulfilling Prophecies,* 8 (see note 19, above).

29. See Gunn, *The Mirror of Love,* 321 (note 3, above).

30. In order to keep as close to the original text as possible, I cite the names of the allegorical personae in Old French: Reson, Atenance Contrainte, La Vielle, etc. In each case I follow Lecoy's Table des Noms, 3:196–98. Other personages (Croesus, Heloise) are given their standard English names, as is the Jealous Husband, who is not mentioned by name in the text.

31. Lesbianism, almost alone among human relationships, is ignored, perhaps because it was not a common topic in classical and medieval literature. On medieval attitudes toward homosexuality generally, see John Boswell, *Christianity, Social Tolerance, and Homosexuality: Gay People in Western Europe from the Beginning of the Christian Era to the Fourteenth Century* (Chicago, IL: University of Chicago Press, 1980).

32. The conflict between Love and Reason, as we have seen, is well attested in the classical period; in Old French literature, it is found in many places, among them Chrétien de Troyes' *Chevalier de la Charrete* (ed. Mario Roques, Classiques Français du Moyen Age 86 [Paris: Champion, 1970]), for example, lines 370–74.

33. Compare Andreas, *De amore* 1.1, p. 32: "Amor est passio quaedam innata procedens ex visione et immoderata cogitatione formae alterius sexus, ob quam aliquis super omnia cupit alterius potiri amplexibus et omnia de utriusque voluntate in ipsius amplexu amoris praecepta compleri" (Love is an inborn suffering which results from the sight of, and uncontrolled thinking about, the beauty of the other sex. This feeling makes a man desire before all else the embraces of the other sex, and to achieve the utter fulfilment of the commands of love in the other's embrace by their common desire).

34. Venus also warns the narrator against Reson: 15730, 20745ff.

35. Wetherbee, "The *Romance of the Rose* and Medieval Allegory," in *European Writers: The Middle Ages and the Renaissance,* ed. W. T. H. Jackson (New York: Scribners, 1983), 1:329. See also Wetherbee, *Platonism and Poetry in the Twelfth*

Century: The Literary Influence of the School of Chartres (Princeton, NJ: Princeton University Press, 1972), 258–59.

36. On Reson's place in R₁, see Pelen, *Latin Poetic Irony*, 109 (note 8, above); for R₂, see Stephen G. Nichols, Jr., "The Rhetoric of Sincerity in the *Roman de la Rose*," in *Romance Studies in Memory of Edward Billings Ham*, ed. Urban T. Holmes (Hayward, CA: California State College, 1967), 124–25.

37. Gunn, *The Mirror of Love*, 169, 343 (see note 3, above).

38. See Thomas D. Hill, "Narcissus, Pygmalion, and the Castration of Saturn: Two Mythological Themes in the *Roman de la Rose*," *Studies in Philology* 71 (1974): 421. See also George D. Economou, "The Two Venuses and Courtly Love," in *In Pursuit of Perfection: Courtly Love in Medieval Literature*, ed. Joan M. Ferrante (Port Washington, NY: Kennikat Press, 1975), 29–30. Such a point of view, shared by the present writer, among others, is opposed to that of John Fleming: see *Reason and the Lover*, 3–4 (note 12, above).

39. Compare Fleming: "The love of which he (Ami) speaks so knowingly is at best sordid stuff, shoddy goods connived for and bought with gifts; such love is the pleasure of the rich, and no poor man can aspire to it. Amis has the manners of a *doctor amoris*, to be sure, but the mind of a pimp," *The "Roman de la Rose": A Study in Allegory and Iconography* (Princeton, NJ: Princeton University Press, 1969) 143.

40. "La *fine amour* apparaît bien ici comme un masque du simple désir sexuel," notes Jean Batany (*Approches du "Roman de la Rose"* [Paris: Bordas, 1973], 102).

41. Gérard Paré notes that, for Ami, marriage is *contra naturam: Les Idées et les lettres au XIII* siècle: Le Roman de la Rose*, Bibliothèque de Philosophie (1941; rpt. Montreal: Université de Montréal, 1947), 151.

42. About "barat," Batany writes, "le mot désigne un certain art de tourner les choses (par la parole ou l'action) de façon à servir ses propres intérêts; *Barat* n'est pas proprement la duplicité, mais, en acceptant de vivre dans le monde de la culture où il règne, l'amoureux se laisse entraîner à suivre les conseils d'Ami, qui lui prescrit cette duplicité vis-à-vis Malebouche (7357–60)" (*Approches*, 102 [see note 40, above]).

43. Compare also 7765–70, 7789–96.

44. For the fifteenth-century "Querelle de la *Rose*," see Eric Hicks, ed., *Le Débat sur le "Roman de la Rose"* (Paris: Champion, 1977).

45. It derives principally from the anti-feminist treatises of Saint Jerome (via John of Salisbury's *Policraticus*), Walter Map, and Juvenal: compare Lecoy's notes at 8531–8802.

46. Sylvia Huot, in an illuminating letter, has explained to me that some *Rose* manuscripts do attribute the Jaloux's discourse to him as a character (as do the participants in the *Querelle*), but that his speech is not rubricated as consistently as those of the other named speakers. See also Lionel J. Friedman, "'Jean de Meung,' Antifeminism, and 'Bourgeois Realism,'" *Modern Philology* 57 (1959): 13–23; Friedman's major point is that the Jealous Husband's sentiments cannot be attributed to Jean de Meun himself.

47. This is not to imply that the Vielle is not an important figure in the *Rose*:

compare Rosemond Tuve, *Allegorical Imagery: Some Medieval Books and Their Posterity* (Princeton, NJ: Princeton University Press, 1966), 243; Lee Patterson, "'For the Wyves Love of Bathe': Feminine Rhetoric and Poetic Resolution in the *Roman de la Rose* and the *Canterbury Tales*," *Speculum* 58.3 (July 1983): 659.

48. Alan Gunn hints at the Vielle's transvestite rôle in noting that she is the figure in which Jean parodies himself (*The Mirror of Love*, 386 [see note 3, above]).

49. Some characters and readers respond to the Vielle with sympathy: compare Bel Acueil's response to her monologue, 14517–28, and L. Beltrán, "La Vielle's Past," *Romanische Forschungen* 84 (1972): 77–96. Armand Strubel argues, on the other hand, that her discourse is essentially only "un art de séduire" (*Le Roman de la Rose*, Etudes Littéraires [Paris: Presses Universitaires de France, 1984], 79).

50. On Genius and the good (and bad) he represents, see Wetherbee, "The Literal and the Allegorical: Jean de Meun and the *De planctu naturae*," *Medieval Studies* 33 (1971): 284, 287.

51. The close association between Nature and sex may be foreshadowed by Greek usage: "*Natura* and *physis* in the language of folk medicine are regular terms for male or female genitals. Apuleius uses the word *natura* rather than another of the many words for the same thing in order to underline the point that in becoming an ass, Lucius has become the phallic animal *par excellence*," explains John J. Winkler in *Auctor & Actor: A Narratological Reading of Apuleius's "Golden Ass"* (Berkeley and Los Angeles, CA: University of California Press, 1985), 174.

52. Huot notes that some medieval rubricators of the *Rose* announced Genius's discourse as "'la déclaration du songe'" ("The Medusa Interpolation in the *Romance of the Rose*: Mythographic Program and Ovidian Intertext," *Speculum* 62.4 [October 1987]: 877). Poirion sees Genius "couronnant la progression et formulant, sans doute, la pensée dernière de l'auteur" ("De la signification," 182 [see note 4, above]). Zumthor sees Nature as being above the other gods ("Narrative and Anti-Narrative," 190 [see note 17, above]); Michael Cherniss, in Robertsonian idiom, suggests that Genius ironically directs the reader to the true meaning of love, the opposite of the sexuality he suggests: "Irony and Authority: The Ending of the *Roman de la Rose*," *Modern Language Quarterly* 36 (1975): 238.

53. Compare Wetherbee: "Nature and Genius interest themselves in [the narrator's] situation, and play a major role in his final sexual conquest, but they evoke no perceptible moral awakening" (*Platonism and Poetry*, 257 [see note 35, above]; on Nature and her relation to her predecessor in Alain, see also 188–97); see also Richard Kenneth Emmerson and Ronald B. Herzman, "The Apocalyptic Age of Hypocrisy: Faus Semblant and Amant in the *Roman de la Rose*," *Speculum* 62 (1987): 631–32. Rosemond Tuve sees Nature as incomplete and her view inadequate (*Allegorical Imagery*, 273 [see note 47, above]); Eberle points out that Jean de Meun's Nature, unlike Alain's, is concerned only with the sublunary realm ("The Lovers' Glass," 250 [see note 47, above]).

54. Paré explains that the doctrine of love expounded in the *Rose* comes from thirteenth-century Aristotelianism, which saw love as a simple physiological function. "Le plus étonnant est que cet amour et cette morale sont supposés conduire à la vision béatifique surnaturelle, telle que les théologiens scolastiques la conçoivent. Le Roman de Jean de Meun se présente ainsi comme l'illustration d'une théorie de l'amour qui est la négation radicale de l'amour courtois. C'est

dans cette perspective, que ses grossièretés de langage, sa misogynie, son hétéro-
doxie même trouvent leur principale raison d'être et leur explication" (*Les Idées et
les lettres*, 341 [see note 41, above]). I would suggest that this doctrine is clearly the
one expounded by Nature and Genius, but not necessarily the lesson of the entire
romance.

55. Thut, "Narcisse versus Pygmalion," 122 (see note 19, above). A parallel
may be found in *Amores* 3.1, where Elegy embarrasses Tragedy by pointing out that
the latter is speaking in Elegy's own meter.

56. One ambiguous passage in the text may give further support to this reading. As we have seen, both Nature and Genius are deeply concerned with writing.
Like the Vielle, Nature wants very much to establish her female doctrine as au-
thoritative; Genius, as a male cleric (see, for example, 19393–403), is more interested in ensuring the propagation of interpretive orthodoxy. But their emphasis
on sex takes the narrator beyond the stage of literary fantasy, inverting Genius's
metaphor of sex as writing. By means of a *double entendre* that seems to link many
of the major themes of the poem (love, sex, writing, and money), the narrator, as
he readies himself for the assault on the rose, makes himself ready to transcend
textuality by means of his sexual organs.

> Mout me fist grant honeur Nature
> quant m'arma de ceste armeüre
> et m'an ansaigna si l'usage
> que m'an fist bon ouvrier et sage.
> Ele meïsmes le bourdon
> m'avoit apparaillié por don,
> et vost au doler la main metre
> ainz que je fusse mis a letre;
> mes du ferrer ne li chalut,
> n'onques por ce mains n'an valut.
> Et puis que je l'oi receü,
> pres de moi l'oi tourjorz eü
> si que nou perdi onques puis,
> ne nou perdré pas, se je puis,
> car n'an voudroie estre delivres
> pour .V.C. foiz .C. mile livres.
> (21347–62)

While the more expected meaning of *livres* in this context would clearly be
"pounds" (in the monetary sense), the fact that the narrator has learned to use his
staff (penis) before learning to read supports the *interpretatio difficilior* of *livres* as
"books" in this context. That anyone—character or author—in the courtly tradition should value anything over reading and writing is extraordinary; yet even
admitting the medieval penchant for hyperbole, the lover's valuation of his penis
over 50,000,000 books must be taken seriously. Nichols, along these lines, suggests
that the lover "becomes the physical act, or the organ of it, on which he has concentrated for so long" ("The Rhetoric of Sincerity," 128 [see note 36, above]).

57. On obsessive male imitation of the "feminine" vice of garrulousness, see

Carolyn Dinshaw, *Chaucer's Sexual Poetics* (Madison, WI: University of Wisconsin Press, 1989), 6.

58. On this point and others, see Leslie Cahoon, "Raping the Rose: Jean de Meun's Reading of Ovid's *Amores*," *Classical and Modern Literature* 6.4 (1986): 261–85.

59. Huot notes that Pierre Col (fifteenth century) claimed "to know a young man who was cured of his addiction to 'fol amour' by a reading of the *Rose*" ("Medieval Readers of the *Roman de la Rose*: The Evidence of Marginal Notes," *Romance Philology* 43 [1990]: 408 n. 10, citing Eric Hicks, *Le Débat sur le "Roman de la Rose*," 106 [see note 44, above]).

60. "In the thirteenth century the symbolic, anagogical vision of nature which had coexisted with and gradually displaced the rationalist view of the Chartrians came into contact with a materialist view in which the beauty and fertility of nature were accepted with increasing frankness as goods in themselves, gifts which God had intended for man's enjoyment," writes Wetherbee (*Platonism and Poetry*, 256 [see note 35, above]). Compare Gunn, *The Mirror of Love*, 494 (see note 3, above); see also Jean-Charles Payen, "Amour, mariage, et transgression dans *Le Roman de la Rose*," in *Amour, mariage, et transgressions au Moyen Age: Actes du colloque des 24–27 mars 1983, Université de Picardie, Centre d'études médiévales*, ed. Danielle Buschinger and André Crépin, Göppinger Arbeiten zur Germanistik 420 (Göppingen: Kümmerle, 1984), 335–37, and Poirion, *Le Roman de la Rose*, Connaissance des lettres (Paris: Hatier, 1973): "La thèse du livre est . . . qu'il faut assumer notre vie charnelle" (175). See further Payen, *La Rose et l'utopie: révolution sexuelle et communisme nostalgique chez Jean de Meun* (Paris: Editions Sociales, 1976), 201.

61. Eberle, "The Lovers' Glass," 244–45 (see note 13, above).

62. Fleming notes this ambiguity: "Part of the wit of *Le Roman de la Rose* is that it advances simultaneous and unresolved claims to be both a *somnium* and an *insomnium*, a work requiring allegorical explanation and a work unworthy of it" (*Reason and the Lover* 161 [see note 12, above]). Poirion is mistaken, I believe, in stating that in R_2 "la fiction du songe est oubliée" (introduction to his edition of the *Rose*, 14 [see note 60, above]): Jean may suppress the dream, but he maintains its structure, as his closing shows.

63. See particularly Paul Verhuyck, "Guillaume de Lorris ou la multiplication des cadres," *Neophilologus* 58 (1974): 283–93.

64. William Calin argues that because he speaks so freely about dishonesty, Faus Semblant is the most honest character in R_2: *A Muse for Heroes: Nine Centuries of the Epic in France* (Toronto: University of Toronto Press, 1983), 127. See also Strubel, *Le Roman de la Rose*, 91 (note 49, above).

65. See Eberle, "The Lovers' Glass," 252, on the rôle of the earthly atmosphere in mediating between God's foreknowledge and human free will (note 13, above).

66. Eberle, "The Lovers' Glass" 253–54 (see note 13, above).

67. One of Jean's sources on optics, Seneca's *Naturales quaestiones*, recounts the story of Hostius Quadra, who used mirrors to magnify the sexual parts of both men and women to increase his lust (Seneca, *Naturales quaestiones*, Loeb ed., vol. 1, 16.2–4, cited by Eberle, "The Lovers' Glass," 258 [see note 13, above]).

68. See Poirion, "Narcisse et Pygmalion dans le *Roman de la Rose*," in *Essays in Honor of Louis Francis Solano*, ed. Raymond J. Cormier and Urban T. Holmes, Studies in the Romance Languages and Literatures 92 (Chapel Hill, NC: University of North Carolina Press, 1970), 154.

69. "Nusquam corpus erat, croceum pro corpore florem / inueniunt foliis medium cingentibus albis," *Metamorphoses* 3.509–10, ed. D. E. Bosselaar and B. A. van Proosdij, Griekse en latijnse Schrijvers met Aantekeningen 22, 23 (Leiden: E. J. Brill, 1975). Louise Vinge notes, however, that medieval readers often read the flower negatively: "The flower is beautiful and useless, it withers after a short life, the narcissus flower is late, is sterile, has a soporific perfume, is poisonous, bends over water or grows by it, is visually attractive and isolated" (*The Narcissus Theme in Western European Literature up to the Early 19th Century*, trans. Robert Deswsnap et al. [Lund: Gleerups, 1967], 18).

70. See Huot, "From *Roman de la Rose*," 101 (note 3, above); Poirion, "Narcisse et Pygmalion," 154 (note 68, above); Thut, "Narcisse versus Pygmalion," 111 (note 19, above); Huot, *From Song to Book: The Poetics of Writing in Old French Lyric and Lyrical Narrative Poetry* (Ithaca, NY: Cornell University Press, 1987), 87; and Joan Kessler, "La Quête amoureuse et poétique: La Fontaine de Narcisse dans *Le Roman de la Rose*," *Romanic Review* 73.2 (March 1982): 136. Dragonetti suggests a possible instance of word play that would reinforce this interpretation:

> C'est li miroërs perilleus,
> ou Narcisus, li orgueilleus,
> mira sa face et ses ieuz vers,
> *dont il jut puis morz toz envers* [that is, *en vers*].
> (1569–72, emphasis added)

(This is the perilous mirror, in which the proud Narcissus admired his face and his green eyes; and because of it *he then lay on his back, completely dead* [or: *He then lay dead totally in poetic verse*]).

(Dragonetti, "Pygmalion," 110 [see note 6, above]; compare Hult, *Self-Fulfilling Prophecies*, 297–98 [see note 19, above]).

71. On the allegory of the crystals (1535–68), see, among other studies, Erich Köhler, "Narcisse, la fontaine d'Amour et Guillaume de Lorris," *Journal des Savants* (1963): 86–103; also in *L'Humanisme médiéval dans les littératures romanes du XIIe au XIVe siècles*, ed. Anthime Fourrier (Paris: Klincksieck, 1964); Jean Rychner, "Le Mythe de la fontaine de Narcisse dans le *Roman de la Rose* de Guillaume de Lorris," in *Le Lieu et la formule: Hommage à Marc Eigeldinger* (Neuchâtel: Baconnière, 1978), 33–46; Hult, *Self-Fulfilling Prophecies*, 277–79 (note 19, above); Hult, "The Allegorical Fountain: Narcissus in the *Roman de la Rose*," *Romanic Review* 72 (1981): 125–48. Of the readings that seek a meaning for the crystals, I prefer that of Huot, who suggests that "the crystals in the Fountain are the tangible presence, in Guillaume's Garden, of previous texts: not only Chrétien's *Cligés*, but also Ovid's *Metamorphoses* and the Old French *Narcissus*, to name a few" ("From *Roman de la Rose*," 100 [see note 3, above]). Another approach, however, is to recognize, with

Poirion, that "Le texte est un peu incertain" ("Narcisse et Pygmalion," 161 n. 8 [see note 68, above]), and to accept the presence of a certain obscurity. As Larry H. Hillman writes, "Guillaume is not known as a poet of obscure or hidden meaning, and it is the nature of allegory to identify the critical elements which compose the drama. If the poet had ascribed a greater significance to the crystals, he would undoubtedly have made his intentions crystal clear" ("Another Look into the Mirror Perilous: The Role of the Crystals in the *Roman de la Rose*," *Romania* 101 [1980]: 238).

72. On the general question of Narcissism, see the following: John B. Friedman, "L'Iconographie de Vénus et de son miroir à la fin du moyen âge," in *L'Erotisme au moyen âge*, ed. Bruno Roy (Montreal: L'Aurore, 1977), 73 (with reference to Augustine, *Soliloquia*); Marta Powell Harley, "Narcissus, Hermaphroditus, and Attis: Ovidian Love and the Fontaine d'Amors in Guillaume de Lorris's *Roman de la Rose*," *PMLA* 101 (1986): 335; Verhuyck, "Guillaume de Lorris," 292 n. 35 (see note 63, above); Thut, "Narcisse," 114 n. 41 (see note 19, above); Wetherbee, "The Theme of Imagination in Medieval Poetry and the Allegorical Figure 'Genius,'" *Medievalia et Humanistica* 7 (1976): 56; Zumthor, "Narrative and Anti-Narrative," 187 (see note 17, above).

73. See Köhler, "Narcisse," 101 (note 71, above); Poirion, "Narcisse et Pygmalion," 161 (note 68, above); Rand, "The Metamorphosis of Ovid," 117 (note 11, above); and Strubel, *Le Roman de la Rose*, 66 (note 11, above). Poirion notes Alain de Lille's reading of Narcissus: "Ars magicae Veneris hermaphroditat eum" (*PL* 210–431.1) ("Alain de Lille et Jean de Meun," 146 [see note 8, above]).

74. See Harley, "Narcissus," 324–37 (note 72, above). Harley notes that at a later meeting the rose is full of seed (*Rose* 3351–52); like a phallus, it gains importance in this passage by increasing in size (3339–42). Harley remarks that "the autoerotic and homoerotic nuances of the Ovidian myths further the notion of the insubstantiality of the Lady" (335).

75. Rupert T. Pickens, "'Somnium' and Interpretation in Guillaume de Lorris," *Symposium* 28 (1974): 183. Ann Tukey Harrison (incorrectly, in my opinion) accepts the narrator's gloss as a lesson to readers: "Echo and Her Medieval Sisters," *The Centennial Review* 26.4 (October 1982): 339–40.

76. For a more standard medieval interpretation, compare Arnulf of Orléans's twelfth-century reading (here translated into French by Eric Hicks): "Il est dit de Narcisse qu'il aima son ombre parce qu'il aima par-dessus tout sa propre supériorité. C'est ainsi que, trompé par l'erreur, il dépérit comme une chose sans importance. Voilà pourquoi il fut changé en fleur, autant dire en une chose inutile. Et il n'a guère vécu en effet, à l'instar des fleurs qui se fanent" (in Hicks, "La Mise en roman des formes allégoriques: hypostase et récit chez Guillaume de Lorris," in *Etudes sur le Roman de la Rose de Guillaume de Lorris*, ed. Jean Dufournet, Collection Unichamp 4 [Paris: Champion, 1984], 58). Hicks argues that Guillaume could not have been unaware of this tradition. See also Poirion, "Narcisse et Pygmalion," 157–58 (note 68, above); Hill, "Narcissus," 413 (note 38, above); and Vinge, *The Narcissus Theme*, 76 (note 69, above). Interpretations of the Narcissus story proliferate; compare Hult, "Vers la société de l'écriture," *Poétique* 12 (1982): 172, *Self-Fulfilling Prophecies*, 263–65 and 285 (see note 19, above), and "The Alle-

gorical Fountain," 146 (see note 71, above). See also Zumthor, "Narrative and Anti-Narrative," 187 (note 17, above); and Harley, "Narcissus," 331 (note 74, above).

77. See Hult, "The Allegorical Fountain," 144–46 (note 71, above).

78. Rosemond Tuve is shocked by "the ludicrous assumption by Nature's priest Genius that entrance into the Heavenly Jerusalem is *his* gift": *Allegorical Imagery*, 275 (see note 47, above). She discusses (277) an illumination of Genius's fountain in which its water issues from what appear to be the breasts and a penis of a figure carved in stone (Bodl. MS Douce 195, f. 146r, conveniently reproduced as plate 43 in Dahlberg's translation of the *Rose*). Tuve views this representation as a deliberate misportrayal that illustrates Genius's unlikely conception of how to enter "'heaven'." See also Poirion, "Alain de Lille et Jean de Meun," 146 (note 8, above).

79. For some further critical views on the *Rose* as mirror, see Strubel, *Le Roman de la Rose*, 68 (note 49, above); Hult, "The Allegorical Fountain," 145 (note 71, above); Gunn, *The Mirror of Love*, 269 (note 3, above); Friedman, "L'Iconographie du miroir," *passim* (note 72, above); Batany, *Approches*, 53 (note 40, above); and Eberle, "The Lovers' Glass," 259 (note 13, above).

80. Gunn, *The Mirror of Love*, 492 (see note 3, above).

81. Eberle, "The Lovers' Glass," 254–55 (see note 13, above).

82. Compare Eberle, "The Lovers' Glass," 248, 260 (see note 13, above); Hult, *Self-Fulfilling Prophecies*, 287 (see note 19, above); Huot, *From Song to Book*, 98–99 (see note 70, above).

83. Kevin Brownlee, "Reflections," 60 (see note 3, above).

84. On the question of R₂'s structural completeness and independence, see Hult, *Self-Fulfilling Prophecies*, 101 and *passim* (see note 19, above).

85. See on this subject Guillaume de Lorris and Jean de Meun, *The Romance of the Rose*, trans. Charles Dahlberg (Hanover, NH, and London: University Press of New England, 1983), 395–96.

86. Sex as a remedy for love was, of course, recommended by Ovid in the *Remedia amoris*, but it is also found in a variety of texts that were fundamental to medical science in the Middle Ages, including the writings of Rufus of Ephesus, the *Divisiones* of Rhazes (al-Rāzī) (b. 865), Constantine's *De coitu* (late eleventh century), and Gerard of Berry's *Notule super Viaticum* (ca. 1200). See Mary Frances Wack, *Lovesickness in the Middle Ages: The* Viaticum *and Its Commentaries* (Philadelphia, PA: University of Pennsylvania Press, 1990), 11, 41, 200.

87. Regalado notes that while more than half of Jean's classical *exempla* have less than twelve lines, the Pygmalion story is nearly 400 lines long, expanded from only fifty-four verses in Ovid (*Metamorphoses* 10.243–97), "'Des Contraires Choses,'" 67 (see note 7, above). On the function of *exempla* in general, see Kenneth J. Knoespel, "Fable and the Epistemology of Expanding Narrative: An Example from the *Roman de la Rose*," *University of Hartford Studies in Literature* 17.2 (1985): 35.

88. On the question of gender-switching, see Vinge, *The Narcissus Theme*, 87 (note 69, above).

89. For a selection of views, see Strubel, *Le Roman de la Rose*, 98–99 (note 49, above); Poirion, "Narcisse et Pygmalion" (note 69, above), 153–56, 159 ("Après

Narcisse, l'homme du regard, Pygmalion, l'homme de la main"), and *passim*; Huot, *From Song to Book*, 98, 146 (note 70, above); Kevin Brownlee, "Orpheus' Song Re-Sung: Jean de Meun's Reworking of *Metamorphoses*, X," *Romance Philology* 36 (1982): 204–5; and Knoespel, "Fable," 31 (note 87, above); compare also Calin, *A Muse for Heroes*, 139 (see note 64, above).

90. Wetherbee, "The *Romance of the Rose* and Medieval Allegory," 332 (see note 35, above).

91. Hill, "Narcissus, Pygmalion," 408 (see note 38, above); compare Tuve, *Allegorical Imagery*, 278 (see note 47, above).

92. Cahoon, "Raping the Rose," 265 (see note 58, above).

93. Thut, "Narcisse versus Pygmalion," 126 (see note 19, above); compare Emmerson and Herzman, "The Apocalyptic Age of Hypocrisy," 630 (see note 53, above).

94. It is worth noting that Jean's misogyny here ("touz bons eürs eüst eüz / s'il n'eüst esté deceüz / par Mirra, sa fille, la blonde, / que la vielle, que Dex confonde, / qui de pechié doutance n'a, / par nuit en son lit li mena" [21159–64]) is not to be found in Ovid's version.

95. Kevin Brownlee, "Orpheus' Song Re-Sung," 203 (see note 89, above).

96. On the troubling links between Pygmalion and Adonis in the *Rose*, see Thut, "Narcisse versus Pygmalion," 128–29 (note 19, above), and Strubel, *Le Roman de la Rose*, 99–100 (note 49, above). Hill notes that Adonis "is consistently glossed *in bono* in mythographical treatises ("Narcissus, Pygmalion," 409 [see note 38, above]), but it is difficult to know how to apply this information to Jean's treatment of the story.

97. On the complex narrative implications even in Jean's source, see my article, "The Structure of Orpheus' Song: *Metamorphoses* X," *Papers on Language and Literature* 17 (1981): 23–32. On Jean's use of other works by Ovid at this point, see, on the *Ars*, Poirion, "Narcisse et Pygmalion," 156–57 (note 69, above), and, on the *Amores*, Cahoon, "Raping the Rose," 283 (note 58, above).

98. As does Pelen, *Latin Poetic Irony*, 165–66 (see note 8, above).

99. It may be, as Regalado suggests, that Jean's narrative and the stories he uses to illustrate it are ultimately irreconcileable, that "the alterity of the *exemplum* remains, in the *Roman de la Rose*, irreversible" ("'Des Contraires Choses,'" 71 [see note 7, above]). Compare also Walter Nicolai, "Phantasie und Wirklichkeit bei Ovid," *Antike und Abenland* 19.2 (1973): 116, discussing Pygmalion: "Wo die Phantasie quasi als Magd der Befriedigung menschlichen Wünsche und Bedürfnisse dient, ist sie fragwürdig und unvollkommen wie alles menschliche Tun; wenn dagegen der Künstler, ohne auf die Realität zu schielen, seine Phantasie als autonomes Gebilde in eine vollendete Form bringt, ist sie selig in sich selbst."

100. References: 6332, 6511, 6517, 6576, 6583–84, 7052, 7162, 7166, 7174, 11576–77, 11807 (Strubel, *Le Roman de la Rose*, 72–74 [see note 49, above]). Huot argues that when Ami and la Vielle use such words as "texte" and "glose," they are parodying learned discourse: "Medieval Readers," 404 (see note 59, above).

101. How a narrator governs his or her tale is a subject discussed in other well-known contexts, particularly by means of the famous Aesopean question, recalled in the fables of Marie de France, "Who painted the lion?" Knoespel notes

that the very nature of fable, like that of allegory, incites its readers to look for meaning beyond the text ("Fable," 42 [see note 87, above]).

102. On this passage, compare Strubel, *Le Roman de la Rose*, 94–95 (see note 49, above). One is tempted to think about glosses as the literary counterpart to cosmetics, adding a beauty of meaning to the text which may not, in fact, be present in it.

103. Dragonetti notes that, in medieval rhetoric, the *exemplum* was the metaphorical equivalent of the *speculum* ("Le 'Singe de Nature' dans le *Roman de la Rose, Travaux de linguistique et de littérature* 16 [1978]: 152).

104. Augustine, *Confessions* 7.10; compare Dahlberg, "First Person and Personification," 39 (see note 26, above).

105. On this passage, see Poirion, "De la signification," 181–82 (note 4, above); Strubel, *Le Roman de la Rose*, 80 (note 49, above) (though I disagree with his reading, which states that "à travers la glose, la vérité se manifeste sous ses multiples facettes"); and Regalado, "'Des Contraires Choses,'" in which she argues that "les 'contraires choses,' les *exempla*, fournissent à Jean de Meun le vocabulaire nécessaire pour parler littéralement de la partie de l'expérience humaine qui échappe au langage, l'expérience érotique" (77 [note 7, above]). Claire Nouvet suggests that "in opening itself up to such an interpretive act, the courtly discourse of the *Romance of the Rose* opens it up to its own reversal, calls forth its own subversion" ("Les Inter-dictions courtoises: Le Jeu des deux bouches," *Romanic Review* 76.3 [May 1985]: 243).

106. Compare Uitti, "From *Clerc* to *Poète*," 213 (see note 16, above). On reading the *Rose*, see also Huot, *From Song to Book*, 2 (note 70, above); Kessler, "La Quête amoureuse," 146 (note 70, above); Pelen, *Latin Poetic Irony*, 129 (note 8, above); Vitz, "The *I*," 56–57 (note 25, above); Thut, "Narcisse versus Pygmalion," 129 (note 19, above); Strubel, *Le Roman de la Rose*, 60 (note 49, above); and Fleming, *Reason and the Lover*, 66, 176 (note 12, above).

107. See Knoespel, "Fable," 30 (note 87, above); Gunn, *The Mirror of Love*, 201, 448 (note 3, above); Cherniss, "Irony and Authority," 230 (note 52, above); Leicester, "Ovid Enclosed," 5–6 (note 3, above); Nichols, "The Rhetoric of Sincerity," 120 (note 36, above); Calin, *A Muse for Heroes*, 133–34 (note 64, above); and Maureen Quilligan ("The readers' method of reading becomes the subject of the poem"), *The Language of Allegory: Defining the Genre* (Ithaca, NY: Cornell University Press, 1979), 242. See also Huot, "Medieval Readers," 414–15 (note 59, above).

108. Cherniss, "Irony and Authority," 237 (see note 52, above).

109. Compare Strubel, *Le Roman de la Rose*, 104, 109; Nichols, "The Rhetoric of Sincerity," 119 (see note 36, above); Poirion, "De la signification," 181 (see note 4, above).

110. Hult, *Self-Fulfilling Prophecies*, 120 (see note 19, above); for related sentiments, see Hicks, "La Mise en roman," 54 (note 76, above); Wetherbee, "The *Romance of the Rose*, 325–26 (note 35, above); and Strubel, *Le Roman de la Rose*, 34–35 (note 49, above).

111. Douglas Kelly, working from this passage and several others, predicts that the end of Guillaume's poem would have entailed the taking of the castle: "'Li

Chastiax . . . qu'Amors prist puis par ses esforz': The Conclusion of Guillaume de Lorris' *Rose*," in *A Medieval French Miscellany*, ed. Norris J. Lacy (Lawrence, KS: University of Kansas Press, 1973), 61–78. Note Hult's argument in *Self-Fulfilling Prophecies* that R_1 is complete as it stands (see note 19, above).

112. Nouvet, "Les Inter-dictions courtoises," 248 (see note 105, above); compare also Strubel, *Le Roman de la Rose*, 31–33 (see note 49, above), as well as Poirion's insightful discussion of *l'arbitraire du signe* ("De la signification," 175 [see note 4, above]).

113. On the Ovidian, secular nature of the *Rose*, compare, among others, Gunn, *The Mirror of Love* 65 (see note 3, above), on Ovid and Boethius in the *Rose*; Batany, *Approches*, 20 (see note 40, above), on the *romans d'antiquité* and their avoidance of Christian morality; Payen, *La Rose et l'utopie*, 11 (see note 60, above): "Dieu prend le parti de ceux qui aiment"; Hill, "Narcissus," 426 (see note 38, above): love in R_2 is morally ambivalent; Hult, *Self-Fulfilling Prophecies*, 267–68, noting that both *paradis* and *Dieu* in R_1 have secular meanings—the garden and the God of Love (see note 19, above); Poirion, *Le Roman de la Rose*, 64, on reading the poem as humorous rather than ironic (see note 60, above); and Quilligan, "Words and Sex: The Language of Allegory in the *De planctu naturae*, the *Roman de la Rose*, and Book III of *The Faerie Queene*," *Allegorica* 2 (1977): 214 n. 17, citing Tuve, *Allegorical Imagery*, 265–84, on the inappropriateness of Christian allegorical readings of R_2 (see note 47, above).

114. Compare Carolynn Van Dyke, *The Fiction of Truth: Structures of Meaning in Narrative and Dramatic Allegory* (Ithaca, NY: Cornell University Press, 1985), 84.

115. See Dragonetti, *La Vie de la lettre au moyen âge (Le Conte du Graal)*, Connexions du champ freudien (Paris: Editions du Seuil, 1980), 166–67; Quilligan, *The Language of Allegory*, 244 (note 106, above); Strubel, *Le Roman de la Rose*, 59 (note 49, above); Jean R. Scheidegger, "La Peinture à l'or du *Roman de la Rose*," in *L'Or au moyen âge: monnaie, métal, objets, symbole*, Senefiance 12 (Aix-en-Provence: Publications du CUER-MA, 1983), 403; Cesare Segre, "Ars amandi classica e medievale," in *La Littérature didactique, allégorique, et satirique*, ed. Hans-Robert Jauss, Grundriß der romanischen Literaturen des Mittelalters, ed. Hans-Robert Jauss and E. Köhler (Heidelberg: C. Winter, 1968), 6.1, III n. 110. See also Huot, *From Song to Book*, 103, and Patterson, "'For the Wyves Love of Bathe,'" 668 (note 47, above). It is worth noting that even the William of St. Thierry, a great enemy of Ovid, started his anti-*Ars* by stating that "the art of arts is the art of love" (*The Nature and Dignity of Love*, trans. Thomas X. Davis, Cistercian Fathers Series, 30 [Kalamazoo, MI: Cistercian Publications, 1981], 47 [prologue, sect. 1]).

116. See Huot, "The Medusa Interpolation," 868 (note 52, above).

117. On the ending of the *Rose* and the way in which it effaces the text, see Dragonetti, "Le 'Singe de Nature,'" 159 (note 103, above).

118. A version of this chapter was presented at the 1989 conference of the Modern Language Association of America. I would like to thank for their help in my work the Pomona College and Claremont Graduate School students in my Spring 1990 seminar on courtly love.

Appendix

1. Walther Kraus, "Ovidius Naso," *Paulys Real-Encyclopädie der classischen Altertumswissenschaft*, 2d ed. (Munich: K. Mittelhaus, 1943), vol. 18, 2, cols. 1978–79.

2. Ralph J. Hexter, *Ovid and Medieval Schooling: Studies in Medieval School Commentaries on Ovid's* Ars amatoria, Epistulae ex Ponto, *and* Epistulae Heroidum, Münchener Beiträge zur Mediävistik und Renaissance-Forschung (Munich: Arbeo-Gesellschaft, 1986), 7. Sigmund Tafel's still useful Munich dissertation records the relatively few poets in the fourth through sixth centuries who borrowed from Ovid: *Die Überlieferungsgeschichte von Ovids Carmina amatoria, verfolgt bis zum XI Jahrhundert* (Tübingen: Heckenhauer, 1910), 64–65.

3. Tafel, *Überlieferungsgeschichte*, 72 (see note 2, above).

4. Hexter, *Ovid and Medieval Schooling, passim* (see note 2, above).

5. Tafel, *Überlieferungsgeschichte*, 55, 65 (see note 2, above), as modified by Winthrop Wetherbee, "The Study of Secular Literature from Late Antiquity to the Twelfth Century," in *The Middle Ages*, volume 2 of *The Cambridge History of Literary Criticism* (forthcoming).

6. Tafel, *Überlieferungsgeschichte*, 66, 72 (see note 2, above); Kraus, "Ovidius Naso" 1979 (see note 1, above); Ernst Robert Curtius, *European Literature in the Latin Middle Ages*, trans. Willard R. Trask, Bollingen Series 36 (Princeton, NJ: Princeton University Press, 1953), 449; but see Wetherbee, "The Study of Secular Literature" (note 5, above).

7. Tafel, *Überlieferungsgeschichte*, 33 (see note 2, above), citing Luc. Müller, *De re metrica*.

8. F. J. E. Raby, *A History of Secular Latin Poetry in the Middle Ages*, 2d ed. (Oxford: Clarendon Press, 1957), 2 vols., 1.184, 201–2.

9. Theodulf, "De libris quos legere solebam" (*Poet.* I, 543, V.9ff.), cited by Tafel, *Überlieferungsgeschichte*, 53 (see note 2, above); see also Raby, *Secular Latin Poetry* 1.187 (note 8, above).

10. Tafel, *Überlieferungsgeschichte*, 69 (see note 2, above); Raby, *Secular Latin Poetry* 1.203–4 (see note 8, above).

11. See Tafel, *Überlieferungsgeschichte*, 67–69 (note 2, above); Angelo Monteverdi, "Ovidio nel medio evo," *Atti della Accademia Nazionale dei Lincei* 354 (1957), Rendiconti delle Adunanze solenne, Adunanza solenne del 7 giugno 1957, vol. 5, fasc. 12, 698; P. Ovidi Nasonis, *Amores, Medicamina faciei femineae, Ars amatoria, Remedia amoris*, ed. E. J. Kenney (Oxford: Clarendon Press, 1961), v–xii, 111, 203.

12. Wetherbee, "The Study of Secular Literature" (see note 5, above).

13. Fausto Ghisalberti, "L'*Ovidius moralizatus di Pierre Bersuire*," *Società filologica romanza, Studi romanzi* 23 (1933): 9.

14. Raban Maur (Hrabanus Maurus), *De institutione clericorum* III, c. 18, "De arte grammatica et speciebus eius," cited by Tafel, *Überlieferungsgeschichte*, 54 (see note 2, above); compare Raby, *Secular Latin Poetry*, I.225 (see note 8, above).

15. Raby, *Secular Latin Poetry*, 1.234 (see note 8, above).

16. Tafel, *Überlieferungsgeschichte*, 60 (see note 2, above).

17. Raby, *Secular Latin Poetry*, 1.239 (see note 8, above).

18. Charles Homer Haskins, *The Renaissance of the Twelfth Century* (Cambridge, MA: Harvard University Press, 1928), 19. For a study of the social and educational conditions of the Ottonian period, see C. Stephen Jaeger, *The Origins of Courtliness: Civilizing Trends and the Formation of Courtly Ideals, 939–1210* (Philadelphia, PA: University of Pennsylvania Press, 1985).

19. See Hexter, *Ovid and Medieval Schooling*, 26–41 (see note 2, above).

20. Tafel, *Überlieferungsgeschichte*, 70 (see note 2, above). Interestingly, the earliest catalogue mention of Tibullus in the Middle Ages and the only one before about 1250 is also found in the ninth century, in France: see Max Manitius, *Philologisches aus alten Bibliothekskatalogen (bis 1300)*, Ergänzungsheft zum *Rheinisches Museum* 47 (1892): 31.

21. Tafel, *Überlieferungsgeschichte*, 50 (see note 2, above).

22. See Tafel, *Überlieferungsgeschichte*, 56 (note 2, above), and Raby, *Secular Latin Poetry*, 1.383–87 (note 8, above).

23. J. B. Allen, *The Friar as Critic: Literary Attitudes in the Later Middle Ages* (Nashville, TN: Vanderbilt University Press, 1971), 36.

24. Tafel, *Überlieferungsgeschichte*, 51, 61 (see note 2, above).

25. Manitius, *Philologisches*, 31 (see note 20, above); Raby, *Secular Latin Poetry*, 1.309, 2.52 (see note 8, above); Tafel, *Überlieferungsgeschichte*, 51 (see note 2, above).

26. Conrad of Hirsau, *Dialogus super auctores*, ed. R. B. C. Huygens (Brussels: Latomus, 1955), 15, 51.

27. See Curtius, *European Literature*, 466 (note 6, above), citing Conrad, *Dialogus* 64,1ff. (see note 26, above); Jean Leclerq, *Monks and Love in Twelfth-Century France: Psycho-Historical Essays* (Oxford: Clarendon Press, 1979), 41–43; Leclerq, *Initiation aux auteurs monastiques du moyen âge: L'Amour des lettres et le désir de Dieu* (Paris: Editions du Cerf, 1957), 114–15.

28. Leclerq, *Monks and Love*, 68 (see note 27, above); Raby, *Secular Latin Poetry*, 2.12–13 (see note 8, above).

29. In *Guigemar*, Venus is shown casting Ovid's book into the fire; scholars debate whether it is the *Remedia* (which seems to me more likely) or the *Ars*. Compare Monteverdi, "Ovidio nel medio evo," 703–4 (see note 11, above), and Edmond Faral, *Recherches sur les sources latines des contes et romans courtois du Moyen Age* (Paris: Champion, 1939), esp. 3–157.

30. Compare Dorothy A. Robathan, "Ovid in the Middle Ages," in *Ovid*, ed. J. W. Binns (Boston, MA: Routledge and Kegan Paul, 1973), 199; and Jaeger, *The Origins of Courtliness*, 233 (see note 18, above).

31. Raby, *Secular Latin Poetry*, 2.32 (see note 8, above); Monteverdi, "Ovidio nel medio evo," 701–2 (see note 11, above); Franco Munari, *Ovid im Mittelalter* (Zürich and Stuttgart: Artemis, 1960), 23; Robathan, "Ovid in the Middle Ages," 194 (see note 28, above).

32. Maurice Wilmotte, *Origines du roman en France: L'Evolution du sentiment romanesque jusqu'en 1240*, Académie Royale de Langue et de Littérature Françaises de Belgique: Mémoires, Tome 15 (Brussels and Liége: Palais des Académies, 1941), 178, citing Guibert de Nogent, *De vita sua* (Paris, 1823): 424. Guibert's text has been translated as *Self and Society in Medieval France: The Memoirs of Abbot Guibert*

de Nogent, ed., tr. John F. Benton, Medieval Academy Reprints for Teaching (Toronto: University of Toronto Press, 1984); see 17, 87.

33. Leo Pollmann, *Die Liebe in der hochmittelalterlichen Frankreichs: Versuch einer historischen Phänomenologie*, Analecta Romana 18 (Frankfurt: Vittorio Klostermann, 1966), 52, citing Peter of Blois' Epistle 76, *PL* 207.233.

34. Elisabeth Pellegrin, "Les *Remedia amoris* d'Ovide, texte scolaire médiévale," *Bibliothèque de l'Ecole des Chartes* 115 (1956): 172–73; the citation is from Vergil's *Bucolics*, 3.92–93. See also Edward Kennard Rand, "The Classics in the Thirteenth Century," *Speculum* 4 (1929): 259.

35. Eva Matthews Sanford, "The Use of Classical Latin Authors in the *Libri Manuales*," *Transactions of the American Philological Association* 55 (1924): 25–46.

36. Ovid, ed. Kenney, 3, III, 203 (see note 11, above). Compare also Peter Dronke, *Medieval Latin and the Rise of European Love Lyric*, 2 vols. (Oxford: Clarendon Press, 1965), 1.180.

37. Charles H. Haskins notes that those libraries founded in the twelfth century concentrated almost exclusively on patristic writings, but that the Tegernsee monasteries continued to lend classical texts: *The Renaissance of the Twelfth Century* (Cambridge, MA: Harvard University Press, 1927), 41.

38. Ghisalberti, introduction to John of Garland (Giovanni di Garlandia), *Integumenta Ovidii: Poemetto inedito del secolo XIII*, ed. Fausto Ghisalberti, Testi e documenti inediti o rari (Messina and Milan: Edizioni Principato, 1933), 1–2.

39. Ghisalberti, "L'*Ovidius moralizatus*," 11 (see note 13, above).

40. Ovid, *Amores*, etc., ed. Kenney, 3, III, 203 (see note 11, above).

41. Tafel, *Überlieferungsgeschichte*, 61 (see note 2, above).

42. Manitius, "Philologisches," 31 (see note 20, above).

43. On the *libri catoniani* see Pellegrin, "Les *Remedia amoris*," 173–74 (note 34, above); and Rand, "The Classics in the Thirteenth Century," 261 (note 34, above).

Index

University of Pennsylvania Press
MIDDLE AGES SERIES
Edward Peters, General Editor

F. R. P. Akehurst, trans. *The* Coutumes de Beauvaisis *of Philippe de Beaumanoir.* 1992

Peter L. Allen. *The Art of Love: Amatory Fiction from Ovid to the* Romance of the Rose. 1992

David Anderson. *Before the Knight's Tale: Imitation of Classical Epic in Boccaccio's* Teseida. 1988

Benjamin Arnold. *Count and Bishop in Medieval Germany: A Study of Regional Power, 1100–1350.* 1991

Mark C. Bartusis. *The Late Byzantine Army: Arms and Society, 1204–1453.* 1992

J. M. W. Bean. *From Lord to Patron: Lordship in Late Medieval England.* 1990

Uta-Renate Blumenthal. *The Investiture Controversy: Church and Monarchy from the Ninth to the Twelfth Century.* 1988

Daniel Bornstein, trans. *Dino Compagni's* Chronicle *of Florence.* 1986

Betsy Bowden. *Chaucer Aloud: The Varieties of Textual Interpretation.* 1987

James William Brodman. *Ransoming Captives in Crusader Spain: The Order of Merced on the Christian-Islamic Frontier.* 1986

Kevin Brownlee and Sylvia Huot. *Rethinking the* Romance of the Rose*: Text, Image, Reception.* 1992

Otto Brunner (Howard Kaminsky and James Van Horn Melton, eds. and trans.). Land *and Lordship: Structures of Governance in Medieval Austria.* 1992

Robert I. Burns, S.J., ed. *Emperor of Culture: Alfonso X the Learned of Castile and His Thirteenth-Century Renaissance.* 1990

David Burr. *Olivi and Franciscan Poverty: The Origins of the* Usus Pauper *Controversy.* 1989

Thomas Cable. *The English Alliterative Tradition.* 1991

Anthony K. Cassell and Victoria Kirkham, eds. and trans. *Diana's Hunt/Caccia di Diana: Boccaccio's First Fiction.* 1991

Brigitte Cazelles. *The Lady as Saint: A Collection of French Hagiographic Romances of the Thirteenth Century.* 1991

Anne L. Clark. *Elisabeth of Schönau: A Twelfth-Century Visionary.* 1992

Willene B. Clark and Meradith T. McMunn, eds. *Beasts and Birds of the Middle Ages: The Bestiary and Its Legacy.* 1989

Richard C. Dales. *The Scientific Achievement of the Middle Ages.* 1973

Charles T. Davis. *Dante's Italy and Other Essays.* 1984

Katherine Fischer Drew, trans. *The Burgundian Code.* 1972

Katherine Fischer Drew, trans. *The Laws of the Salian Franks.* 1991

Katherine Fischer Drew, trans. *The Lombard Laws.* 1973

Nancy Edwards. *The Archaeology of Early Medieval Ireland.* 1990

Margaret J. Ehrhart. *The Judgment of the Trojan Prince Paris in Medieval Literature.* 1987

Richard K. Emmerson and Ronald B. Herzman. *The Apocalyptic Imagination in Medieval Literature.* 1992

Felipe Fernández-Armesto. *Before Columbus: Exploration and Colonization from the Mediterranean to the Atlantic, 1229–1492.* 1987

Robert D. Fulk. *A History of Old English Meter.* 1992

Patrick J. Geary. *Aristocracy in Provence: The Rhône Basin at the Dawn of the Carolingian Age.* 1985

Peter Heath. *Allegory and Philosophy in Avicenna (Ibn Sînâ), with a Translation of the Book of the Prophet Muḥammad's Ascent to Heaven.* 1992

J. N. Hillgarth, ed. *Christianity and Paganism, 350–750: The Conversion of Western Europe.* 1986

Richard C. Hoffmann. *Land, Liberties, and Lordship in a Late Medieval Countryside: Agrarian Structures and Change in the Duchy of Wrocław.* 1990

Robert Hollander. *Boccaccio's Last Fiction: Il Corbaccio.* 1988

Edward B. Irving, Jr. *Rereading* Beowulf. 1989

C. Stephen Jaeger. *The Origins of Courtliness: Civilizing Trends and the Formation of Courtly Ideals, 939–1210.* 1985

William Chester Jordan. *The French Monarchy and the Jews: From Philip Augustus to the Last Capetians.* 1989

William Chester Jordan. *From Servitude to Freedom: Manumission in the Sénonais in the Thirteenth Century.* 1986

Ellen E. Kittell. *From* Ad Hoc *to Routine: A Case Study in Medieval Bureaucracy.* 1991

Alan C. Kors and Edward Peters, eds. *Witchcraft in Europe, 1100–1700: A Documentary History.* 1972

Barbara M. Kreutz. *Before the Normans: Southern Italy in the Ninth and Tenth Centuries.* 1992

E. Ann Matter. *The Voice of My Beloved: The Song of Songs in Western Medieval Christianity.* 1990

María Rosa Menocal. *The Arabic Role in Medieval Literary History.* 1987

A. J. Minnis. *Medieval Theory of Authorship.* 1988

Lawrence Nees. *A Tainted Mantle: Hercules and the Classical Tradition at the Carolingian Court.* 1991

Lynn H. Nelson, trans. *The Chronicle of San Juan de la Peña: A Fourteenth-Century Official History of the Crown of Aragon.* 1991

Charlotte A. Newman. *The Anglo-Norman Nobility in the Reign of Henry I: The Second Generation.* 1988

Joseph F. O'Callaghan. *The Cortes of Castile-León, 1188–1350.* 1989

William D. Paden, ed. *The Voice of the Trobairitz: Perspectives on the Women Troubadours.* 1989

Edward Peters. *The Magician, the Witch, and the Law.* 1982

Edward Peters, ed. *Christian Society and the Crusades, 1198–1229*: Sources in Translation, including The Capture of Damietta by Oliver of Paderborn. 1971

Edward Peters, ed. *The First Crusade*: The Chronicle of Fulcher of Chartres *and Other Source Materials*. 1971

Edward Peters, ed. *Heresy and Authority in Medieval Europe*. 1980

James M. Powell. *Albertanus of Brescia: The Pursuit of Happiness in the Early Thirteenth Century*. 1992

James M. Powell. *Anatomy of a Crusade, 1213–1221*. 1986

Michael Resler, trans. Erec *by Hartmann von Aue*. 1987

Pierre Riché (Michael Idomir Allen, trans.). *The Carolingians: A Family Who Forged Europe*. 1993

Pierre Riché (Jo Ann McNamara, trans.). *Daily Life in the World of Charlemagne*. 1978

Jonathan Riley-Smith. *The First Crusade and the Idea of Crusading*. 1986

Joel T. Rosenthal. *Patriarchy and Families of Privilege in Fifteenth-Century England*. 1991

Steven D. Sargent, ed. and trans. *On the Threshold of Exact Science: Selected Writings of Anneliese Maier on Late Medieval Natural Philosophy*. 1982

Sarah Stanbury. *Seeing the* Gawain-*Poet: Description and the Act of Perception*. 1992

Thomas C. Stillinger. *The Song of Troilus: Lyric Authority in the Medieval Book*. 1992

Susan Mosher Stuard. *A State of Deference: Ragusa/Dubrovnik in the Medieval Centuries*. 1992

Susan Mosher Stuard, ed. *Women in Medieval History and Historiography*. 1987

Susan Mosher Stuard, ed. *Women in Medieval Society*. 1976

Jonathan Sumption. *The Hundred Years War: Trial by Battle*. 1992

Ronald E. Surtz. *The Guitar of God: Gender, Power, and Authority in the Visionary World of Mother Juana de la Cruz (1481–1534)*. 1990

Patricia Terry, trans. *Poems of the Elder Edda*. 1990

Frank Tobin. *Meister Eckhart: Thought and Language*. 1986

Ralph V. Turner. *Men Raised from the Dust: Administrative Service and Upward Mobility in Angevin England*. 1988

Harry Turtledove, trans. *The* Chronicle *of Theophanes: An English Translation of* Anni Mundi *6095–6305 (A.D. 602–813)*. 1982

Mary F. Wack. *Lovesickness in the Middle Ages: The* Viaticum *and Its Commentaries*. 1990

Benedicta Ward. *Miracles and the Medieval Mind: Theory, Record, and Event, 1000–1215*. 1982

Suzanne Fonay Wemple. *Women in Frankish Society: Marriage and the Cloister, 500–900*. 1981

This book has been set in Linotron Galliard. Galliard was designed for Mergenthaler in 1978 by Matthew Carter. Galliard retains many of the features of a sixteenth-century typeface cut by Robert Granjon but has some modifications that give it a more contemporary look.

Printed on acid-free paper.